SHOCKING VIOLENCE

Author proceeds from the sale of this book will be donated to the
New Jersey Psychological Association Youth Anti-Violence Projects Fund.

SHOCKING VIOLENCE

Youth Perpetrators and Victims–
A Multidisciplinary Perspective

Edited by

ROSEMARIE SCOLARO MOSER, Ph.D., ABPN

RSM Psychology Center, LLC

and

CORINNE E. FRANTZ, Ph.D.

*Graduate School of Applied
and Professional Psychology
Rutgers University*

With a Foreword by

Rush Holt

*United States Representative
Member of Congress*

Charles C Thomas
P U B L I S H E R • L T D.
SPRINGFIELD • ILLINOIS • U.S.A.

Published and Distributed Throughout the World by

CHARLES C THOMAS • PUBLISHER, LTD.
2600 South First Street
Springfield, Illinois 62704

©2000 by CHARLES C THOMAS • PUBLISHER, LTD.

ISBN 0-398-07120-9 (hard)
ISBN 0-398-07121-7 (paper)

Library of Congress Catalog Card Number: 00-057736

Printed in the United States of America

CR-R-3

Library of Congress Cataloging-in-Publication Data

Shocking violence : youth perpetrators & victims--a multidiscipli-
nary perspective / edited by Rosemarie Scolaro Moser and
Corinne E. Frantz ; with a foreword by Rush Holt.
    p. cm.
Includes bibliographical references and index.
ISBN 0-398-07120-9 -- ISBN 0-398-07121-7 (pbk.)
    1. Juvenile delinquency--United States. 2. Violence--United
States.
    I. Moser, Rosemarie Scolaro. II. Frantz, Corinne E.

HV9104 .S447 2000
364.36'0973--dc21
                                                              00-057736

To the safety, protection, and care of our children,
our most precious gifts, and our hope for the future.

ABOUT THE CO-EDITORS

Rosemarie Scolaro Moser, Ph.D., ABPN is a licensed psychologist, certified school psychologist, and director of the RSM Psychology Center, LLC, in Lawrenceville, New Jersey, where she provides psychotherapy and neuropsychological services to the school-age through older adult populations. She received her Bachelor of Arts in psychology and her Ph.D. degree in professional psychology from the University of Pennsylvania. She completed postdoctoral training at the University of Maryland at Baltimore. Her publications have covered the topics of personality, violence, parenting techniques, brain disorder, learning disability, and psychophysiological illness. Dr. Moser is a diplomate of the American Board of Professional Neuropsychology, the American Board of Medical Psychotherapists, and the American Academy of Experts in Traumatic Stress. She is a National Board Certified Clinical Hypnotherapist and is certified by the APA College of Professional Psychology in Alcohol and Substance Use Disorders. Dr. Moser is also Past President of the New Jersey Neuropsychological Society, serves on the Executive Board of the New Jersey Psychological Association, and is a former faculty member of the University of Pennsylvania.

Corinne E. Frantz, Ph.D., is a licensed psychologist who practices clinical psychology and neuropsychology with children and adults in Springfield, New Jersey. She received her Bachelor of Science degree in psychology from Tulane University, and her Ph.D. degree in Clinical Psychology from the University of Florida with a minor specialization in neuroscience. She took her postdoctoral training in psychoanalysis and psychotherapy at Adelphi University in the Institute for Advanced Psychological Studies. She is on the Contributing Faculty of the Graduate School of Applied and Professional Psychology, Rutgers University, and is a Clinical Associate of the American Projective Drawing Institute, New York City. Her publications have been in the areas of projective assessment, neuropsychological disorders, and correlates of early childhood trauma. She is Past President of the New Jersey Neuropsychological Society and a member of the Executive Board of the New Jersey Psychological Association.

ABOUT THE CONTRIBUTORS

Christopher R. Barbrack, Ph.D., Esq,. is a licensed psychologist in New Jersey who graduated with a law degree from the University of Pennsylvania and is engaged in the full-time practice of law. A past tenured associate professor at the Graduate School of Applied and Professional Psychology of Rutgers University, he is a member of the subcommittee on Regulations of the New Jersey Board of Psychological Examiners and a lecturer before the New Jersey Institute for Continuing Education (ICLE).

Maria Luisa Briones received her Bachelor's Degree in music from the University of the Phillippines and theological training with the Dominican Roman Catholic Congregation. Her professional experience includes serving as a high school teacher in the Phillippines and as a music and Spanish teacher in Illinois. She is presently the School Liturgist, Organist, and Children's Choir Director at Saints Peter and Paul Church in Naperville, Illinois.

Celene E. Domitrovich, Ph.D., is Assistant Director of the Penn State Prevention Research Center. She received her degree in child clinical psychology from the Pennsylvania State University. Dr. Domitrovich is currently working on designing and evaluating preventive interventions for preschool children at risk for developing mental health problems.

Karen Dunne-Maxim, RN, MS, is an internationally recognized expert on issues related to survivors of suicide and co-editor of the book, *Suicide and Its Aftermath.* She is currently the co-coordinator for the Suicide Prevention Project at the University of Medicine and Dentistry of New Jersey–University Behavioral HealthCare.

Michael B. Greene, Ph.D., is Executive Director of the Violence Institute of New Jersey at the University of Medicine and Dentistry of New Jersey where he has been responsible for the development of a multitiered, comprehensive database of violence incidents, prevention services, and resources.

Lt. Colonel Dave Grossman, U.S. Army (Ret.), is an internationally recognized scholar, soldier, speaker, and expert in the field of human aggression and violent crime. A past West Point Psychology professor, he was a lead trainer of mental health professionals in the Jonesboro, Arkansas, school shooting incident, is author of *On Teaching Our Kids to Kill: How Violence in TV, Movies, and Video Games Cause Violent Crime*, and has received a Pulitzer Prize nomination for his book, *On Killing*.

Daniel E. McNeill, Ph.D., is a licensed clinical psychologist and neuropsychologist at the RSM Psychology Center in Lawrenceville, New Jersey. His research and publications have covered the areas of brain trauma, neuropsychology, rehabilitation, families, childrens' play therapy, and patient rights. He is a diplomate of the American Academy of Experts in the Treatment of Posttraumatic Stress and a Fellow of the American Board of Disability Analysts.

Louis B. Schlesinger, Ph.D., is a forensic psychologist on the faculty of John Jay College of Criminal Justice, City University of New York who also practices privately in Maplewood, New Jersey. A past president of the New Jersey Psychological Association, he has published six books on murder, sexual homicide, and criminal psychopathology. His newest book is titled *Serial Offenders*.

Nathanya Simon, Esq., is a partner in Schwartz, Simon, Edelstein, Celso, & Kessler, LLP, in Florham Park, New Jersey, specializing in the representation of Boards of Education in all legal and labor matters, with a concentration in special education litigation. She also served as in-house Counsel to the New Jersey School Boards Association.

Maureen M. Underwood, MSW, LCSW, has been working for the past twenty years in crisis services for children. She is the coordinator of the New Jersey Adolescent Suicide Prevention Project and a trauma specialist at the University of Medicine and Dentistry of New Jersey University Behavioral Health Care.

Reverend J. William Wauters, Jr., MDiv., is chaplain of The Lawrenceville School in Lawrenceville, New Jersey. He is a past Secondary School Fellow of the United States Institute of Peace. From work with Cesar Chavez to youth gangs, his interests include international, urban programs to reduce violence.

Janet A. Welsh, Ph.D., is a developmental psychologist who received her degree from the Pennsylvania State University. She is currently a research associate on the FAST Track project, a multisite project for the prevention of conduct problems.

Book cover art by Princeton Display Group, Inc. Lawrenceville, New Jersey.

FOREWORD

Youth. Violence. These are two words that have unfortunately been paired all too often over the past few years. Times have changed so that what once would have been a fistfight in a schoolyard can become a bullet-ridden bloodbath.

We know that over the past twenty years, there has been a clear rise in the episodes of youth violence. Gangs are no longer limited to the inner city; they have found their way into the midst of mainstream suburban life. Furthermore, violent episodes are no longer associated only with gangs. Of late, the media has unveiled the reality of the isolated, withdrawn teen as the perpetrator of violence.

The events at Littleton, Paducha, Jonesboro, and other sites have raised questions about every aspect of our children's world—our parenting, policing, teaching, school administrating, counseling, the prevalence of violence in our media, the availability of guns, and many more things.

As adults, parents, professionals, and citizens, we are now challenged more than ever by this pressing phenomenon of youth violence. We must be able to provide safe schools, homes, and communities in which our children can thrive and feel comfortable—where they do not have to feel bullied, harassed, or alienated. We have learned that those who are the victims of such bullying, harassment, and alienation may be predisposed to become the future perpetrators.

We must educate not only the adults who interact with youth but youth themselves. All of us must learn the warning signs, address the harassment, heal the victimized, and help those at risk from resorting to violence as a response. We must stop denial and encourage openness and communication regarding the reality of violence in our society. To this end, I helped initiate a program titled Voices on Violence, which began with a gathering of hundreds of students in Washington, D.C. and is continuing in many regions around the country, including in my own district in central New Jersey.

In my many visits to schools, it has become apparent to me that we must listen more closely to the students. They have important, perceptive things to say and far too many tell me that they have no one who listens. Listening is part of the diagnosis of the problem, and, I believe, part of the cure.

Voices on Violence is but one of many anti-youth violence initiatives which are beginning to appear across the country. It is up to us as citizens to encourage our legislators on the state and national levels to continue to support programs and efforts to address the needs of our youth and to help keep our schools, homes, and communities safe.

Likewise, please join me in supporting efforts such as this book, *Shocking Violence*, that can provide current, invaluable knowledge to all of us. Knowledge is the first step on the road to problem solving. I think that as you read *Shocking Violence* you will appreciate its multidisciplinary focus. We can all learn from the perspectives of psychologist, teacher, attorney, parent, social worker, educator, clergy, and others; then we must put our heads together, integrate our approaches, and coordinate our knowledge in the best interests of our youth.

Rush Holt
United States Representative
Member of Congress

A MESSAGE FROM THE COMMISSIONER OF THE STATE OF NEW JERSEY DEPARTMENT OF HEALTH AND SENIOR SERVICES–YEAR 2000

These chapters sample our current understanding about youth violence from experts in the fields of mental health, law, religion, and education. The issues discussed–morality, cultural influence, physiology, and psychology– demonstrate that everyone has a part to play in the prevention of youth violence and in fostering the growth of our children.

I am gratified that New Jersey professionals assembled this material because their efforts are a reflection of our state's commitment to addressing this critical issue of youth violence that is affecting our communities, schools, and families. As part of this commitment, Governor Christine Todd Whitman, with the strong support of the general public, has launched a V-Free initiative that encourages youth to take responsibility and action toward reducing youth violence. V-Free stands for violence-free, victimization-free, and vandalism-free. This initiative empowers youth, giving them the resources they need to protect themselves and others.

Just as the editors and authors of this book have committed themselves to spreading the word, so too should we encourage our youth to spread the word against youth violence. The V-Free program begins with a pledge "to respect myself and all people; to respect my school and property that does not belong to me; to assume responsibility for my own behavior and to think about the consequences of my actions; and to promote an environment free of violence, vandalism, and victimization." By supporting our youth with grants to students for creative ideas on how to make their neighborhoods and schools safer, and with a confidential tip line that connects teens with law enforcement counselors, we are empowering our youth to join the adult community, their teachers, parents, neighbors, clergy, and others in preventing youth violence.

Many of the issues presented in *Shocking Violence* will enable us to better understand youth violence and help us all to walk down the V-Free path. I commend the editors and authors for donating their time to prepare this valuable book. It is my sincere hope that *Shocking Violence* stays off the book-

shelf and remains in the hands of parents, teachers, mental health professionals, and people who have faith in our youth.

> Christine Grant
> Commissioner
> State of New Jersey
> Department of Health and
> Senior Services

PREFACE

Although we are co-editors of this book, we are also psychologists, educators, but most importantly, mothers. And so it was that after a Saturday morning meeting of the New Jersey Psychological Association (NJPA) Committee on Neuropsychology, of which we are co-chairs, our discussion about youth violence began. Over decaffeinated coffee, we shared our own experiences as mothers of children who had viewed or experienced the aggressive behaviors of other children. To each other, we described detailed stories of preschool bullies and middle school sexual molestation. We discussed the issue of denial we had observed not only in the school officials but in the students and in the parents of students. We initiated our mission and solidified our commitment to the endeavor of educating both professionals and our communities about the problem of youth violence.

This was back in 1997, before the more horrific episodes of Jonesboro, Columbine, and others. We set forth to convince the New Jersey Psychological Association to include as one of its initiatives a comprehensive educational experience regarding youth violence. We believed that this experience should cater not only to psychologists, but be a statewide effort to include a multitude of organizations. With a core committee, and the invaluable support of NJPA, we created a landmark conference, the goals of which included: 1) to provide a forum where various groups that interface with youth violence can coordinate knowledge and expertise, rather than continue to proceed in isolation, often replicating efforts or lacking protocols; 2) to provide cutting edge information regarding the prevention of youth violence, the identification of at-risk youth, treatments and interventions with youth, and responses to acts of violence; and 3) to integrate scientific research, practical approaches, and the needs of those who interact on a regular basis with youth.

This conference was both impressive and alarming in its success. The Honorable Christine Todd Whitman presided as Honorary Co-chair and our major sponsors included Toys 'R Us, the American Psychological Association, and the New Jersey State Department of Health and Senior Services. Other organizations and individuals joined on as Advisory

Committee members: Assemblywoman Barbara Wright, Catholic Charities, Diocese of Camden, International Critical Incident Stress Foundation, Mercer County Medical Society, N.J. Association of Mental Health Agencies, N.J. Association of School Psychologists, N.J. Association of School Social Workers, N.J. Counseling Association, N.J. Department of Education, N.J. Education Association, N.J. Institute for Continuing Legal Education, N.J. Principals and Supervisors Association, N.J. School Counselors Association, N.J. School Nurses Association, N.J. State Association of Chiefs of Police, N.J. State Nurses Association, Probation Association of New Jersey, Spring Lake Heights Police Department, Temple Emanu-el of West Essex, and the Violence Institute of New Jersey. An exhaustive list!

We desired to produce a product that would capture the spirit of this conference so that others could benefit from this unique endeavor. Thus, the idea for this book came about. Many but not all of the chapter authors were involved in the conference. However, each author presents a diverse point of view on the problem of youth violence. We have attempted to include a variety of perspectives: developmental psychologist, neuropsychologist, forensic psychologist, teacher, parent, military officer, attorney, clergy, trauma responder, and public health expert. We also wanted to address the issues of both the perpetrators and the victims. As we did so, it became increasingly apparent to all that these two roles overlapped and blurred. An individual whose name was withheld by request poignantly illustrated this paradox in a letter to the editor of *Time* magazine in the January 1, 2000 issue:

> The Columbine tapes gave me chills, but not for the politically correct reasons. You see, that was me at 17. I was like those kids on the tapes. I hated everybody at school; I was an outcast loner who mostly stayed at home and listened to gangsta rap. I wanted to kill the school leaders, *the members*, everybody who had screwed me. My plans for mass murder never got beyond the fantasy stage, but under the right circumstances, they could have gone as far as Columbine. How can we stop kids who kill? Many need mental-health intervention. Many simply need someone their own age who gives a damn about them as a person. Teens want approval from their peers, and not getting it can lead to horrible consequences.

There are many factors that contribute to the phenomenon of youth violence, many of which are presented in this book. For some youths, brain impairment and neuropsychological functioning are significant factors resulting in weak social judgment, impulsivity, poor anger control, and acting out behaviors. For other youths, a dysfunctional family unit and a lack of community resources set the stage for future episodes of violence. Abuse, bullying, harassment, the media, and our culture are also critical in completing the picture of youth violence. Many argue that for some individuals, especially those who become hardened criminals, treatment may barely alter the pattern of antisocial behavior. But, for a good many, early intervention, supportive families and communities, and treatment can result in saving the lives of not only the victims but the perpetrators as well. Identifying at-risk children, at-risk families, at-risk schools, and at-risk communities is crucial to reducing the episodes of youth violence in our country.

We know that indeed, over the past few years, youth violence has actually decreased, and that the recent, heightened concern has been accentuated by the isolated outrageous events of school shootings. We also know that death by shootings by youth has increased. Obviously, the youth violence issue is a complex one which nonetheless requires our attention, focus, and action. The loss of one child to violence, whether as victim or perpetrator, is too high a price to pay in exchange for denial, ignorance, or indifference by our families, schools, and communities. As citizens, we each have a responsibility to care for the welfare of our youth, the future of our world. We hope that *Shocking Violence* will allow the reader to gain a greater understanding of the complex problem of youth violence that we face and the need for all of us to work together and integrate our perspectives, knowledge, and tools for the benefit of our communities.

Rosemarie Scolaro Moser
Corinne E. Frantz
Editors

ACKNOWLEDGMENTS

We would like to thank the following individuals and groups who helped make this book a reality:

Our chapter authors who so generously donated their time and expertise in the writing of this book; the New Jersey Psychological Association and its Board members who provided the support and trust in us to produce the landmark, *Shocking Violence Conference 2000*; the NJPA committee members, multiorganizational advisory members, speakers, participants, and donors of the *Shocking Violence Conference 2000*, whose actions reveal their ongoing commitment to our youth; Christopher R. Barbrack, Esq., Ph.D., who donated legal consultation in matters regarding this book; our husbands, Robert B. van Dover, Ph.D. and Robert L. Moser, MD, whose patience, support, and intelligent feedback during the process were invaluable; and our children, Timothy, Christopher, and Geoffrey van Dover and Rachel and Alex Moser, who continuously enlighten and educate us about the importance of our responsibility as parents and as professionals to protect our youth.

CONTENTS

SHOCKING VIOLENCE

Author proceeds from the sale of this book will be donated to the
New Jersey Psychological Association Youth Anti-Violence Projects Fund.

Chapter One

YOUTH VIOLENCE AND VICTIMIZATION: AN INTRODUCTION

CORINNE E. FRANTZ
ROSEMARIE SCOLARO MOSER

THE PROBLEM

ON OCTOBER 1, 1997, a sixteen-year-old boy in Pearl, Mississippi, shot nine students in his high school, killing two, after having killed his mother.

On December 1, 1997, a fourteen-year-old boy in West Paducah, Kentucky, shot eight students in the hallway of his high school, wounding five and killing three.

On March 24, 1998, two boys, eleven and thirteen years old, in Jonesboro, Arkansas, opened fire from the woods and shot fifteen people coming out of their middle school, wounding ten and killing four girls and a teacher.

On April 24, 1998, a fourteen-year-old boy in Edinboro, Pennsylvania, shot and killed a science teacher in front of fellow students at an eighth-grade dance.

On May 19, 1998, an eighteen-year-old honor student in Fayetteville, Tennessee, opened fire in the parking lot of his high school and killed a classmate.

On May 21, 1998, a fifteen-year-old boy in Springfield, Oregon, killed his parents and then opened fire on classmates in his high school, wounding twenty and killing two.

On April 20, 1999, two students in Littleton, Colorado, gunned down twenty-three of their classmates, killing fifteen including themselves. Their intended targets were athletes. The actual victims were a random set of students.

One month later, on May 20, 1999, a depressed fifteen-year-old in Conyers, Georgia, opened fire on his high school classmates, wounding six but killing none.

3

On February 29, 2000, a six-year-old boy took a .32-caliber semiautomatic handgun to his school and shot one of his first-grade classmates, killing her.

These are among the most visible school shootings in recent years, visible because of national media coverage. In the initial shock and subsequent horror that accompanies the reporting of these and similar events, we feel tremendous sympathy for the victims, the victims' families and friends, and horror and disbelief toward the perpetrators of these crimes. It is only weeks or months later, after the heightened media interest subsides, that we learn through other media venues of the protracted suffering that the perpetrators themselves endured prior to their horrific acts of hate, revenge, and despair.

In the spring of 1997, prior to the shootings in West Paducah, Kentucky, Michael Carneal was mentioned in the gossip column of the school newspaper as having "feelings for" a male classmate. Thereafter, he was apparently the victim of repeated and persistent harassment, being called "gay" and "faggot", in the face of which he felt impotent and ineffectual. He experienced suicidal thoughts, was socially isolated, and wrote school essays dealing with graphic, violent themes involving fantasies of revenge. In the fall of the year just prior to shooting his victims, his grades in school precipitously dropped. There is a report that he was plagued by paranoid fears and may have heard voices.

In Littleton, Colorado, Eric Harris and Dylan Klebold were part of a group known as the Trench Coat Mafia, a cluster of high school teens who were routinely picked on and scorned by fellow students and who identified themselves distinctively by dressing in Goth (gothic) style black clothing and wearing long trench coats. In numerous accounts and recollections, Harris and Klebold were regularly called "dirtbags", "faggots" and "inbreeds" by other students with no one, neither fellow students nor faculty, coming to their defense. In one account (Bai, 1999), a classmate was cited as saying, "They'd walk with their heads down, because if they looked up they'd get thrown into lockers and get called a *fag*." In another account (Gibbs, 1999), students reported that some teachers picked on the members of the outcast group, blaming them unfairly and condoning the cruelty and abuse perpetrated at the hands of the jocks. On at least one occasion, rocks and bottles were thrown at Harris and Klebold from a moving car; in turn, on another occasion, Klebold openly brandished a gun from a moving car in the direction of taunters.

Victim turns perpetrator; perpetrator turns victim. The question, "Who deserves our sympathy?" however, is naïve and simplistic, and reveals our own failure to grasp the complexity of the underlying issues. We know that the trio of perpetrator, victim, and silent bystander can give rise to sadistic acts of brutality. We know that those who are hated often learn, in turn, to hate. Sometimes, the hate directed at themselves or people whom they perceive as similar to themselves in some unconscious way can be as vicious as the hate directed at the original perpetrator. Sometimes, the violence of the marginalized group against the perpetrators of abuse is more vicious and intense than the original violence of the group in power. As one recent writer has noted (Sullivan, 1999), despite our ability to provide detailed descriptions of horrific acts of violence, we still know relatively little about the spark which ignites the act itself: Hate.

On the eve of the Littleton, Colorado, shootings, President Clinton spoke at a news conference in Washington. He called on us to teach children how to "express anger and resolve conflicts with words, not weapons," and for those of us who are in contact with our children, "to do more to recognize the early warning signs that are sent before children act violently" (President's Remarks, 1999, p. A17). He also cited Patricia Holloway, 1999 County Commission Chair for Littleton, Colorado, saying, ". . .perhaps now America would wake up to the dimensions of this challenge if it could happen in a place like Littleton" (President's Remarks, p. A17). Littleton is not an inner city where we might rationalize episodes of youth violence as being more common; Littleton is a relatively homogenous, middle class suburb, southwest of Denver. Harris and Klebold were smart, privileged children in an affluent community.

In June 1997, one of the lead articles in *The New York Times Magazine* was entitled, "How Can We Save the Next Victim?" (Belkin, 1997). The article was not about mass school shootings or youth violence, but about fatal medical blunders which have resulted in the tragic deaths of patients. The writer of the article, Lisa Belkin, pointed out that when a patient dies as a result of a medical blunder, ". . .the first question is often, "Who is to blame?" and it is the wrong question!" (p. 28). Ms. Belkin went on to say, ". . .finger-pointing does not provide answers and often no one—no one—is to blame. A cascade of unthinkable things must happen for a patient to die due to medical mistake and it is almost always a failure of a system" (p. 28). It is also a failure of a system when one youth aggresses against another youth, a vastly complex system that includes individual victims, individual perpetrators, families, schools, the larger community, and the culture.

From a need to address the complexity of the system that surrounds expressions of violence, *Shocking Violence*, was conceived as a multidisciplinary contribution that seeks to address the following questions:

1. What role does the media play in influencing youth violence?
2. What are some of the individual predictors or warning signs of violence?
3. What is the relationship between victim and perpetrator in instances of bullying and harassment?
4. What steps for prevention and intervention can be taken by parents, teachers, schools, crisis teams and communities?

5. What are the legal issues that support or deter effective intervention in our schools and communities?

CULTURAL INFLUENCES ON VIOLENCE

The dramatic episodes of mass school shootings in recent years have called our attention to the powerful influence of the media, TV, and video games on our youth today. The perpetrators of violence at West Paducah, Jonesboro, Littleton, and Conyers, for example, shared in common a particular affinity for playing video splatter games, such as *Doom, Quake,* or *Mortal Kombat.* On a scale from 0 to 5, *Time* magazine rated splatter games as 0 in educational content and 5 in violence, providing the following description: ". . . games that put guns in the hands of kids and reward them for blasting everything that moves. Players . . . navigate mazes in first person perspective, picking up ever larger and more lethal weapons" (Cyberguide, 1999, p. 46). Eric Harris and Dylan Klebold apparently became obsessed with playing *Doom* and, at one point, Harris customized *Doom* into a scenario that resembled the actual massacre. He programmed his version to include two shooters with extra guns and unlimited ammunition, facing down helpless victims (Pooley, 1999).

In 1999, the video game industry's revenue was upwards of 6 billion dollars, with splatter games representing a significant portion of the income. With revenue of this magnitude, there is little incentive for the entertainment-software industry to seek regulation. At this time, the industry's own attempts at self-regulation through the use of a rating system is generally accepted as powerless in stopping children from gaining access to whatever software is available, regardless of the degree of the software's violent content. According to one Internet source, Family.com.BigAppleParent (as cited in Assembly Task Force, 1999) ". . . by age five a child will have witnessed over 200 hours of violent images on television; by age fourteen, he or she will have seen over 13,000 separate killings; by age eighteen, the average American will have watched 200,000 violent acts and 40,000 murders" (p. 61).

In 1993, the American Psychological Association (APA) released a summary report from its Commission on Violence and Youth (Assembly Task Force, 1999). The report concluded definitively that viewing media violence had long-term effects on children and adolescents. These long-term effects include: 1) increased aggressiveness and antisocial behavior; 2) increased fear of becoming a victim; 3) increased desensitization to violence and its victims; and 4) an increased appetite for violence in entertainment and in real life. There are many contributing causal factors for an episode of violence perpetrated by an individual. Some of these factors include: 1) temperamental vulnerability; 2) a history of early childhood abuse and severe neglect leading to damaged patterns of adaptation and learned destructive behavior patterns; 3) a biological predisposition, such as neurological injuries giving rise to impulsivity and biologically damaged ego controls; and 4) situational stress. However, when graphic, violent media are added to the presence of underlying vulnerabilities, the likelihood of violent behavior increases dramatically. It has been known for some time in the clinical-scientific literature that certain children are more vulnerable than others to the negative impact of role modeling of violent behavior depicted in the media. These children include those who suffer from low self-esteem and are in some way psychologically unstable.

But what can we do to help our children? There are certain protective factors which help children resist the impact of violence within the culture. These include: 1) a positive and supportive relationship with caring adults within their families, within their community, and with their peers; 2) a sense of belonging within a community which has a high degree of social networks and neighborly support; 3) religious affiliation, particularly when religion is an important, internal aspect of the child's life and is supported by peers and adults who share a similar religious background and set of beliefs; 4) the presence of opportunities to develop and pursue a child's individual interests, talents, and strengths in ways that enhance self-esteem and positive self-regard; and 5) adequate economic security for the basic needs and necessities of life.

The American Medical Association (AMA) and the American Academy of Pediatrics (AAP) (Assembly Task Force, 1999) have recommended to parents the following guidelines for *shared viewing* with their children of TV and entertainment software:

1. Be alert to the programs that your children watch and limit their viewing to no more than two hours each day.
2. Do not use television, videos, video games, or computer games as babysitters for your children.
3. Keep televisions and video players out of your children's bedrooms and do not make the television the focal point of the household.
4. Turn the television off during meals.
5. Learn about new movies and videos, and set guidelines about which ones are appropriate for your child to view.
6. When your children watch television or videos, watch with them and become a critical viewer. Children who are taught to be independent thinkers are more able to resist pressures from peers and the media.

One approach that emphasizes instructing independent thinking about the media is called *media literacy*: teaching children how media violence is created and showing how it contrasts with real-life violence. Two of the goals of media literacy are to demystify the glamorized and unreal images of violence presented to children in the media and to counteract the unrealistic fantasies of power and domination over others presented in images of violence from television, movies, and video games. Children who are seen in the emergency room after having suffered gunshot wounds will often indicate to their attending physician that they were unaware that a gunshot wound hurts!

WARNING SIGNS

As noted, in the fall of the year of the fatal shootings in West Paducah, Kentucky, Michael Carneal's grades precipitously dropped. He also reportedly wrote essays for school detailing graphic fantasies of violent revenge. In one account, writer Lisa Belkin describes an essay, entitled, "The Halloween Surprise", in which " . . . a character named Michael helps to annihilate his fellow students, who are named in the essay and whose deaths are graphically described" (Belkin, 1999, p. 78).

The English teacher of Eric Harris and Dylan Klebold became concerned about the violent nature of the two youths' writings one month prior to the fatal school shootings in Littleton, Colorado. According to one newspaper account, Eric Harris wrote an English essay about an inanimate object in which he described himself as a shotgun shell and his relationship with the gun barrel. His English teacher was quoted as saying, "He often wrote about shotguns" (Brooke, 1999, p. A14). Dylan Klebold wrote an essay describing a killing. The English teacher called these writings to the attention of the parents of both youths. Such events embody important warning signs and prognostic indicators.

The American Psychological Association, in partnership with Music Television (MTV), sponsored a youth anti-violence initiative in 1998 that included the identification of violence warning signs in others and in oneself. This initiative was partly based on the recognition that victims of violence in America today are most likely to be between the ages of twelve and twenty-four. In a recent poll taken by the APA, forty percent of youth said that they have been concerned about a potentially violent classmate (American Psychological Association, 1998). The magnitude and seriousness of the problem is staggering.

According to the APA/MTV program guide (American Psychological Association, 1998), violence is considered a serious possibility with the following *immediate* warning signs: loss of temper on a daily basis, frequent physical fighting, significant vandalism or property damage, increase in the use of drugs or alcohol, increase in risk-taking behavior, detailed plans to commit acts of violence, announcing threats or plans for hurting others, enjoying hurting animals, and carrying a weapon. Michael Carneal carried weapons to school on at least one occasion prior to shooting his victims. As already noted, Dylan Klebold openly brandished a firearm from a vehicle in which he was riding as a passenger. Kip Kinkel in Springfield, Oregon, had a history of torturing animals. Almost every one of the high-profile school shooters told someone that something significant was going to happen at school the next day before the atrocities occurred.

Less immediate, but indicating that a potential for violence is present, are warning signs that may exist *over a period of time*. These include: a history of violent or aggressive behavior, serious drug or alcohol use, membership in a gang or a strong desire to be in a gang, access to or a fascination with weapons (especially guns), threatening others regularly, trouble controlling feelings such as anger, withdrawal from friends and one's usual activities, feeling rejected or alone, having been a victim of bullying, poor school performance, a history of discipline problems or frequent run-ins with authority, feeling constantly disrespected, and failing to acknowledge the feelings or rights of others.

In a seminal work of ego psychology, Fritz Redl and David Wineman (1951) wrote about *Children Who Hate*. These authors pointed out that "...observations gained in the study of diseased behavior [lead to the discovery of] techniques which will safeguard the wise handling of the healthy child" (p. 28). At that time, they opened their treatise with the statement, "Our trouble is that we don't know enough about Hate. Consequently, we don't take it seriously enough" (Redl & Wineman, 1951, p. 17). Over the past fifty years, the incidence of violent crime in America has significantly increased.

In an attempt to understand some of the increase in violence, criminal law in America has recently proposed the distinction between hate crime and ordinary crime: yet, do we know what we mean by *Hate* (Sullivan, 1999)? Andrew Sullivan (1999), writing about a variety of contemporary hate crimes, noted that, " . . . for all our documentation of these crimes and others . . . we seem at times to have no better idea now than we ever had of what exactly they were about . . . About not the violence, but what the violence expresses. About what–exactly–hate is. And what our own part in it may be" (p. 51).

In words that sound disturbingly contemporary, Redl and Wineman (1951) pointed out:

> Among all the troubles that are usually summarized under the term *delinquency*, the most serious seem to be the ones which involve large quantities of *Hate*.

Up till now, so far as the study of children is concerned, even science has literally handled the problem of hate with kid gloves. For a long time we were fooled by the old illusion that hatred is really only some sort of *lack of love* and would happily disappear on its own accord if we just could find ways of always being *nice* to people (p. 20).

What Redl and Wineman (1951) discovered about why treatment approaches and interventions fail in the face of hate, is not the problem of the presence of hatred itself, but "the decomposition of behavior controls which the piled-up aggression has wrought within the personalities of the children [who hate], and the solidification of some of their hatred into an organized department of shrewdly developed defenses against moral implications with the world around them" (p. 26).

We know that a history of brutalization can turn individuals into victims who later become perpetrators of violence against new victims. We also know that the culture we live in has become increasingly open and desensitized to shocking images of vengeful violence and meaningless sexuality. We know that an arsenal of powerful weapons can be easily amassed by youth and adults. However, for interventions to succeed in halting the outpouring of violence and aggression against others, disturbances in behavioral control functions in the individual must be understood and addressed.

INTERVENTION AND PREVENTION

There are many practical suggestions for intervention and prevention with at-risk children, such as the promotion of media literacy and education of children and adults discussed above. In Chapter 2, Lt. Colonel Dave Grossman makes an impassioned plea for national controls on the production and accessibility of media violence to benefit the health of our youth. Similarly, other authors and researchers offer interventions to stop bullying and harassment, to decrease contagion following a traumatic event in a school setting, to proactively identify and treat children at risk in the youngest age groups, and to assist school administrators in effectively implementing policies designed to ensure the safety of students in the school setting.

What Can Teachers Do?

Know the warning signs of the potential for violence in students. Be thoroughly familiar with the policies and procedures established in the school in order to respond most effectively to warning signs of violence and to episodes of bullying and harassment. Be aware of the damaging effects of silently condoning bullying behavior and harassment directed at individual students. Know that mentoring students significantly enhances their young lives. There are also important opportunities available to teachers to creatively implement curricula to promote children's awareness and understanding of the social, political, and economic contexts that support hate and prejudice. Such curricula can also confront the moral challenge involved in learning to integrate feelings of hate with other dimensions of a child's personality, such as knowledge, guilt, self-awareness and behavior control.

One example of the creative use of curricula is evident in Princeton, New Jersey. In 1994, the New Jersey legislature mandated that instruction on the Holocaust and genocide be included in all elementary and secondary school curricula. In response to this mandate, a teacher of fifth-grade students at a public elementary school in Princeton has devised an eight-week history experience in which the Salem witch hunts are used as a historical model for comparison with the Holocaust of Nazi Germany (Escher, 1998).

Researching actual historical accounts of the Salem witch trials and observing parallels across history with Nazi Germany, Constance Escher's pupils draw lessons about the origins and social forces sustaining acts of horrific prejudice and injustice, the perpetration of violence on innocent victims, and the role of the bystander in promoting or deterring such acts. Escher (1998) writes about how her approach renders these issues tangible and real for her students: "Content grabs attention. And no content can match the immediacy and intimacy of original source documents. In these, the student, regardless of background or academic level, hears the clarion voice of an individual who lived what is now history . . . the doomed desperation of an innocent scapegoat . . ." (p. 19). The personal, in-depth engagement of students in the learning process over time helps them develop their skills in thinking about issues of social responsibility which have immediate, present-day relevance for experiences of bullying, harassment, and violence in their own lives.

Understanding Behavioral Control Functions in the Personality

All children and teenagers, no matter how emotionally healthy, need the constant input of important adults in their lives. This is because the various aspects of their personalities are still in the process of formation. Competent baby sitting or competent educational support alone cannot address this need. Children need the consistent care and attention of involved adults who are committed to the task of helping children and youth develop complete, well-functioning personalities. Personality development does not just take place in the first few years of life. It easily spans the first twenty years of development into young adulthood. It can be considered a life-long process as life continues to present the individual with significant challenges. When behavioral control within the personality breaks down, children and teens are likely to reveal aggressive surface behavior. Those individuals who must, on a daily basis, deal with the surface behavior of our children and youth are in need of our support. These individuals are the parents, teachers, police officers, social workers, spiritual leaders, mentors, and employers of youth.

The growing, developing personality of a child is a very complex phenomenon. Modern psychoanalysis has tried to assist in the understanding of this exceedingly complex phenomenon by studying and elaborating on those personality functions which exert behavioral control and which come into existence within the personality over time. Within the psychoanalytic framework, the familiar terms for those aspects of the personality which are concerned with behavioral control are *ego*–which often includes the *ego ideal*–and *superego.*

One of the major tasks of the ego is to perceive reality clearly, both physical reality and social reality, and to keep the individual in effective touch with reality. It is the job of the ego to prevent feelings of hate, revenge, greed, or lust from excessively dominating a person's behavior or actions, that in turn would complicate a person's relationship to reality even further. The ego also has the significant task of preventing certain maladaptive behaviors or actions from taking place which might lead to a serious violation of personal values. If what a person believes in is transgressed, the personality is subjected to excessive guilt, anxiety, and remorse. Thus, the ego must be able to "become aware of the voice of its own conscience" (Redl & Wineman, 1951, p. 64).

Redl and Wineman (1951) studied a small group of seriously delinquent pre-teen boys, aged 8 to 11, for a period of approximately 1 1/2 years. This homogeneous sample of children were selected for participation based on normal-range intelligence and lower socioeconomic status. The children's histories were marked by: 1) extreme lack of consistency in parenting; 2) experiences of severe rejection (brutalization, cruelty, and neglect) in their relationships with adults; 3) severe sibling tension resulting in victimization of the child by other siblings and parents within the family setting; 4) difficulty adjusting in school, including severe patterns of self-defeating behavior giving rise to continuous experiences of failure; and 5) repeated exposure to psychologically traumatic events in their lives.

In the course of their treatment of the children who hate, Redl and Wineman (1951) were able to identify a number of important dysfunctions in the behavioral control system (ego) of the children's personalities. Some of the ego dysfunctions included: 1) an inability to tolerate frustration leading to temper outbursts; 2) an inability to deal with specific anxiety, fear, or feelings of insecurity; 3) an inability to stand up to situations of group psychological intoxication; 4) an inability to relate to situations or objects in terms of a built-in potential for sublimation; 5) a complete inability to know what to do with normal, healthy feelings of guilt; 6) a pervasive tendency to interpret rules or routines in a persecutory way; 7) a failure to learn from experience; and 8) a complete breakdown of behavioral control when confronted with failure, success, or mistakes.

The importance of identifying these and other behavioral control dysfunctions lies in the growing understanding of the many ways in which the ego of the normal, developing child and adolescent needs to be supported by parents and educators. That is, children and teenagers need help in learning to tolerate ever-increasing amounts of frustration; they need strong emotional ties to a beloved person in the face of danger; they need exposure to a secure and accepting environment in order to confront their anxieties and insecurities; they need help in strengthening their ability to resist giving in to tempting gadgets, games, or situations that promise gratification but are not appropriate in the moment (the inability to resist this seduction is one of the great dangers of media, TV, and video games on the developing ego); they need a wide-range of developmentally appropriate experiences, supported by healthy role modeling, to teach them how to make use of and benefit from the inherently gratifying aspects of many constructive situations; and they need to learn what to do with normal guilt feelings when they arise so as to effectively manage such feelings which are vital to a healthy personality.

Of equal importance to understanding children who hate is the description by Redl and Wineman (1951) of the dysfunctional yet successful ways that the delinquent egos of these children ward off guilt and anxiety in order to surrender to impulsive, destructive behavior. This conceptualization has relevance in helping us comprehend the individual acts of violence perpetrated by today's youth. Redl and Wineman (1951) described "the *system of delusions* that [children who hate] have invented in order to talk themselves, so to speak, out of the demands of their own conscience—where it is still intact" (p. 146). Some of these ways include: 1) repressing the actual emotional impact of an incident immediately after it happens, as is reminiscent of those school shooters who said that they did not know why they did it; 2) relieving guilt by "the simple awareness that the guilt-producing behavior was entered in only after somebody else had already openly done what one only intended to do" (p. 148), which may account for the prevalence of copycat behavior after an episode of school violence; 3) using the argument, "but somebody did the same thing to me before" (p. 149), allowing killing "as soon as a specific act can be proved to be 'revenge for an unjustified hurt'"

(p. 150); and 4) eliminating, and rationalizing away, guilt by depreciating the victim or by focusing on experiences of "hostility" from the world outside (p. 153).

As Redl and Wineman (1951) point out, "All children . . . go through certain clearly marked 'developmental phases' with their own tasks and their own problems. In this process, especially in highly 'transitional moments' from one phase to the other, the 'control' system [in the personality] also undergoes changes and finds itself suddenly confronted with an enormous task. We know this especially well from the study of the transition from later childhood to early pre-adolescence, and again at the onset of sexual maturation around puberty . . . *Ego support is one of the primary tasks of the educator* [emphasis added], especially during transitional phases. . . . Beyond this, all children, [also] require 'educational support'" (p. 71.). The authors go on to ask the questions that continue to perplex us today: "What can be done to support the ego . . . to do its educational, aculturational job efficiently? How can the ego be helped to remain in good touch with reality and in good condition in the area of learning which it would have to undergo anyway even though and even while some other part of its pathology is being worked on? Or where are social protective measures needed . . . ?" (p. 72).

We need more knowledge about the specific behavioral control functions of the child's personality at different developmental stages, the conditions that lead to a serious disturbance of the control functions in the personality (such as a history of repeated exposure to cruelty, abuse and brutalization, and/or a complicating history of brain trauma), the behavioral warning signs for when the control functions in a personality are in imminent danger of giving way or yielding to seriously dangerous behavior, and the role that cultural and social influences play in either supporting healthy ego functions or in overtaxing the vulnerable ego of the child or youth in its struggle to achieve its developmental tasks.

PERPETRATORS OR VICTIMS?

In the course of clinical work, we have dealt with tormented, abused, and victimized adolescents whose anger blossoms in fantasies about shooting schoolmates, blowing up the world, knifing parents and teachers. These fantasies are fueled by violent TV, movies, video games, and horror fiction. For these individuals, it is clear to see how they were once victims. Thus, the line between victim and perpetrator becomes blurred. It is easy to blame neglectful parents or insensitive or poorly equipped educators, but this is not always the situation. A case comes to mind of a teen who had been constantly and cruelly harassed and bullied for a number of years in elementary school by his classmates, partly because of his ethnic heritage. By high school, he had joined a crowd of similarly treated peers, what the school system would probably consider a marginal group, all of whom shared fantasies of mass destruction. He isolated himself from his family, hid in his room, and treated his parents poorly. His hard, sinister facade only masked the wounded child who suffered crippling social anxiety and profoundly low self-esteem. After a suicide attempt, he entered intense psychotherapy for a number of years.

Treatment was rocky, with threats of personal harm to the therapist, threats of suicide, anger, and posturing; all efforts to maintain control and harness power in a seemingly cruel and dehumanizing world. Yet, in a consistent, accepting therapeutic relationship, he found a safe place to share his fantasies, which at times had become translated into hearing voices. He began to feel accepted and began to love himself. Slowly, the years of childhood embarrassment and shame that had been cemented into his being began to chip away. He was then able to share his life with others in positive ways as a young adult. He was eventually able to fall in love and start his own family. However, the shadows from his past continue to linger and he is vigilant in maintaining treatment as needed and in managing his stress.

CONCLUSION

We now know a great deal about the identifiable warning signs of violence in our children and our youth. We know that there are ways to prognosticate imminent danger from the warning signs. We have developed tools for intervention and prevention, and we have caring and concerned people in the trenches who interact on a daily basis with our children and youth.

One key factor limiting our ability to respond effectively is fear and a byproduct of that fear is denial. We live in a climate of fear of liability and fear of reprisals. Fear leads to an unwitting denial of the problem. Denial only serves to exacerbate the problem. One way to counteract this fear is to become educated about the legal implications of managing dangerous situations. For those on the front lines, knowledge is power and it enables us to ensure the safety of our children, protect them, and advocate for them, rather than to ignorantly employ denial as a way to avoid our responsibility as adults and citizens. With such knowledge, educators can be equipped to confidently act and react as needed, with the support of their communities.

We believe that it is our duty, our responsibility as adults and citizens, to help make our schools and our communities safe places in which to live. We must work toward developing more accepting, supportive, and caring environments where our youth may develop, grow, and thrive. We have an obligation to protect our hope for the future.

REFERENCES

American Psychological Association. (1998). *Warning signs guide.* Washington, D.C.: Author.

Assembly Task Force on Adolescent Violence. (1999, June 7). *Findings and recommendations.* Trenton, N.J.: New Jersey State Legislature.

Bai, M. (1999, May 3). Anatomy of a massacre. *Newsweek,* pp. 24-31.

Belkin, L. (1997, June 15). How can we save the next victim? *The New York Times Magazine,* pp. 28-33.

Belkin, L. (1999, October 21). Parents blaming parents. *The New York Times Magazine,* pp. 60-100.

Brooke, J. (1999, May 11). Teacher of Columbine gunmen alerted parents. *New York Times,* p. A14.

Cyberguide: A primer for parents on what's out there in the digital world. (1999, May 10). *Time,* pp. 44-46.

Escher, C. K. (1998, August). Can kids love history? *Vassar Quarterly,* pp. 18-23.

Gibbs, N. (1999, May 3). The Littleton massacre. *Time,* pp. 20-36.

Pooley, E. (1999, May 10). Portrait of a deadly bond. *Time,* pp. 26-32.

President's remarks on school shooting. (1999, April 21). *New York Times,* p. A17.

Redl, F., & Wineman, D. (1951). *Children who hate.* Glencoe, Ill.: The Free Press.

Sullivan, A. (1999, September 26). What's so bad about hate? *The New York Times Magazine,* pp. 50-113.

Chapter Two

TEACHING KIDS TO KILL

Lt. Colonel Dave Grossman

A CASE STUDY: PADUCAH, KENTUCKY

MICHAEL CARNEAL, the 14-year-old killer in the Paducah, Kentucky, school shootings, had never fired a real pistol in his life. He stole a .22 caliber pistol from a neighbor, fired a few practice shots, and took it to school.

In the Amadu Dialo shooting, four NYPD officers fired forty-one shots at an unarmed man at point-blank range and hit nineteen times. This is what should be expected from trained shooters. In the L.A. Jewish daycare shooting, the assailant fired seventy shots and hit five of his helpless victims. This is what should be expected from an untrained shooter.

Michael Carneal fired eight shots at a high school prayer group as they were breaking up. Firing at a milling, screaming, running group of kids, in a large high school foyer, he hit eight different kids with eight shots, five of them head shots and the other three upper torso.

I train numerous elite military and law enforcement organizations around the world. I trained the Texas Rangers, the California Highway Patrol, and a battalion of Green Berets. When I told them of this achievement they were stunned. Nowhere in the annals of military or law enforcement history can I find an equivalent achievement.

Where does a fourteen-year-old boy who never fired a gun before get this skill? Video games. His dad was a respected attorney, and he gave Michael everything, including arcade quality video games in his home, and all the access he needed to these murder simulators at the local video arcade. A hundred things can convince someone to want to take a gun and go kill, but only one thing makes them able to kill: practice, practice, practice. Not practice shooting bull's-eyes, or deer, but practice shooting people.

The witness statements state that Michael Carneal stood, never moving his feet, holding the gun in two hands, never firing far to the left or right, never far up or down, with a blank look on his face. He was playing a video game.

Simply shooting everything that popped up on this screen. Just like he had done countless times before.

As an aside, it is interesting to note that it is not natural to fire at each target only once (the norm is to fire until the target drops) but that is what most video games teach you: to only shoot once, since the target will always drop after being hit. And, by the way, many of the games give extra credit for ... head shots.

A MESSAGE FROM JONESBORO, ARKANSAS

I am from Jonesboro, Arkansas. I travel around the world training medical, law enforcement, and military personnel about the realities of warfare. I try to make those who carry weapons aware of the magnitude of the process of killing, helping them to think about who they are and what they're called to do. Hopefully, I am able to give them a reality check.

So here I am, a world traveler, and an expert in the field of *killology*, the study and science of killing, and one of the largest school massacres in American history happens in my hometown of Jonesboro, Arkansas. That crime, as the world now knows, was the March 24, 1998, schoolyard shooting deaths of four schoolgirls and a teacher. Ten others were injured and two boys, ages eleven and thirteen, were convicted of this mass murder. My son attended one of the middle schools in town, so my aunt in Florida called us that fateful day and asked, "Was that Joe's school?" And we said, "We haven't heard about it." My aunt in Florida knew about it before we did!

We turned on the television and, sure enough, the shootings took place down the road from us but, thank goodness, they weren't in Joe's school. There probably weren't any parents in Jonesboro that night who didn't hug their kids and say, "Thank God it wasn't you," as they tucked them into bed. But there was also a lot of guilt because there were a lot of other parents in that city that night who couldn't say that.

I spent the first three days at the Westside Middle School where the shootings took place, working with the counselors, teachers, students, and parents. None of us had ever done anything like this before. I train people how to react to trauma in the military, but how do you do it with kids after a massacre in their school?

I helped train the counselors and clergy the night after the shootings, and the following day we debriefed the students, allowing them to work through everything that had happened. Only people who share trauma together can truly give each other the understanding, acceptance, and forgiveness needed to understand what has happened, and then they can begin the long process of trying to understand *why* it happened.

A VIRUS OF VIOLENCE

To understand the why behind Jonesboro and Springfield and Pearl and Paducah and Littleton and all the other outbreaks of this virus of violence, we need to first understand the overall magnitude of the problems. The per capita murder rate approximately doubled in this country between 1957, when the FBI started keeping track of the data, and 1993 (Statistical Abstracts of the United States, 1957-1997). A better picture of the problem, however, is indicated by the rate at which human beings are attempting to kill one another—the aggravated assault rate. And that rate in America has gone up from around 60 per 100,000 in 1957 to over 440 per 100,000 by the middle of this decade. As bad as this is, it would be much worse were it not for two major factors.

First is the increase in the imprisonment rate of violent offenders. The prison population in America has multiplied nearly fivefold between 1975 and 1999. According to criminologist John J. DiIulio (Grossman, 1996), ". . . dozens of credible empirical analyses . . . leave no doubt that the increased use of prisons averted millions of serious crimes" (p. 301). If not for our tremendous imprisonment rate (the highest of any industrialized nation in the world), the aggravated assault rate and the murder rate would undoubtedly be even higher.

Second, the murder rate would be much worse if it weren't for new medical technology. According to the U.S. Army Medical Service Corps, a wound that would have killed you nine out of ten times in World War II, you would have survived nine out of ten times in Vietnam (Grossman & DeGaetano, 1999). What this means to us is that it is a very conservative statement to say that, if we had a 1930-level medical technology today, the murder level would be ten times higher than it is. The magnitude of the problem has been held down by the development of ever more sophisticated life-saving skills and techniques, such as helicopter medivacs, 911 operators, paramedics, CPR, trauma centers, and antibiotics.

However, the crime rate is still at a phenomenally high level, and this is true not just in America but worldwide (Grossman, 1999b). In Canada, according to their Center for Justice, per capita assaults increased almost fivefold between 1964 and 1993, attempted murder increased nearly sevenfold, and murders doubled. Similar trends can be seen in other countries in the per capita violent crime rates reported to Interpol between 1977 and 1993. During this period, the assault rate increased nearly fivefold in Norway and Greece, and the murder rate more than tripled in Norway and doubled in Greece. In Australia and New Zealand, the assault rate increased approximately fourfold, and the murder rate nearly doubled in both nations. And during the same period, the assault rate tripled in Sweden, and approximately doubled in Belgium, Denmark, England-Wales, France, Hungary, Netherlands, and Scotland, while all these nations had an associated (but smaller) increase in murder. In all of these cases, the gap between murders and attempted murders/assaults is a factor of our ever-improving medical technology saving more lives. In India during this period the per capita murder rated doubled, in Mexico and Brazil violent crime is also skyrocketing, and in Japan juvenile violent crime went up 30 percent in 1997 alone.

So this virus of violence is occurring worldwide. And the explanation for it has to be some new factor that is occurring in all of these countries. There are many, many facets involved, and we should never downplay any of them—for example, the availability of guns in America. But the rise of violence is also happening in many nations with draconian gun laws. And we should never downplay child abuse, poverty, racism, or a thousand other things that must be confronted. But there is only one new variable that is present in every single one of these countries, bearing the exact same fruit in every case, and that is violence in the media being presented as entertainment for children.

KILLING UNNATURALLY

Before retiring from the military, I spent almost a quarter of a century as an Army infantry officer, a paratrooper, a Ranger, and a psychologist, learning and studying how to enable people to kill. Believe me, we are very good at it. It doesn't come naturally, you have to be taught to kill. And just as the Army enables killing, we are indiscriminately doing the same thing to our kids, but without the safeguards.

After the Jonesboro killings, the head of the American Academy of Pediatrics (AAP) Task Force on Juvenile Violence came to town and his primary message was that children don't naturally have the ability to kill. It is a learned skill. The military also knows this. Many people may have the desire to kill, but it takes months and years of rigorous training to build a SWAT team member, or a Ranger, or a Green Beret, or a SEAL, who is truly capable and proficient at killing. And, according to the head of the AAP Task Force, children are learning to kill from abuse and violence as entertainment in television, the movies, and interactive video games.

When considering the violent crime rate, it should give us pause to note that there is a built-in aversion to killing one's own kind. I can best illustrate this from drawing on my own work in studying killing in the military.

We all know that you can't have an argument or a discussion with a frightened or angry human being. What has happened to this person is that vasoconstriction (narrowing of the blood vessels) has literally closed down the forebrain–that great gob of gray matter which makes you a human being (Grossman & Siddle, 1999). This forebrain is what distinguishes you from a dog. When those neurons close down, the midbrain takes over and your thought processes and reflexes are indistinguishable from your dog's. If you've ever worked with animals, you have some understanding of what happens to frightened human beings on the battlefield. The battlefield and the realm of violent crime are the realm of midbrain responses.

Within the midbrain there is a powerful, natural resistance to killing your own kind. When animals with antlers and horns fight one another, they head butt each other in the most harmless possible fashion. But against any other species they go to the side to gut and gore. Piranha will turn their fangs on anything and everything but they fight one another with flicks of the tail. Rattlesnakes will bite anything and everything but they wrestle one another. Every species, with few exceptions, has this hard-wired resistance against killing their own kind in territorial and mating battles.

When we human beings are overwhelmed with anger and fear, we slam head on into that resistance in the midbrain that generally prevents us from killing. Every healthy human being, with the exception of sociopaths, who by definition don't have that resistance, has this innate violence immune system.

What we observe throughout human history is that when humans fight each other there is a lot of posturing. Adversaries make as loud a noise as possible, puffing themselves up, trying to daunt the enemy. There's a lot of fleeing and submission. The ancient battles were nothing more than great shoving matches. It wasn't until one side or the other turned and ran that the vast majority of the killing happened and most of that was stabbing people in the back. All of the ancient military historians report that the vast majority of killing happened in the pursuit after one side had fled.

In more modern times, we know that the average firing rate was incredibly low in Civil War battles. Patty Griffith (1989) in his book, *Battle Tactics of the American Civil War*, revealed that the killing potential of the average Civil War regiment was anywhere from 500 to 1,000 men per minute. The actual killing rate was only one or two men per minute per regiment. At the Battle of Gettysburg, of the 27,000 muskets picked up after the battle from the dead and dying, 90 percent were loaded. This is an anomaly because it took 95 percent of the soldiers' time to load muskets and only 5 percent to fire. But even more amazingly, of the thousands of loaded muskets, over half had multiple loads in the barrel.

The reality is that the average man would load his musket and bring it to his shoulder, but at the moment of truth he could not bring himself to kill. He'd be brave, he'd stand shoulder to shoulder, he'd do what he'd been trained to do, but at the moment of truth he couldn't bring himself to pull the trigger. And so he brings the weapon down and loads it again. One weapon was found with twenty-three loads in the barrel. And of those who did fire, only a tiny percentage fired to hit. The vast majority was firing over the enemy's head.

During World War II, U.S. Army Brigadier General S.L.A. Marshall had a team of researchers studying what the soldiers did in battle. Marshall had a revolutionary idea: for the first time in human history individual soldiers were asked what they did in battle. And what was discovered was that only 15 to 20 percent of the individual riflemen could bring themselves to fire at an exposed enemy soldier. Marshall (1978) in his book, *Men Against Fire*, found that this was consistently true whether the riflemen were involved in enemy action over the period of one, two, or three days.

That's the reality of the battlefield. Only a small percentage of soldiers are able and willing to participate. Men are willing to die, they're willing to give themselves as sacrificial offerings for their nations, but they're not willing to kill. It's a phenomenal insight into human nature, but when the military became aware of that, they systematically went about the process of trying to fix this problem. From the military perspective, a 15 percent firing rate among riflemen is like a 15 percent literacy rate among librarians. And fix it the military did. By the Korean War, around 55 percent of the soldiers were willing to fire to kill. And by Vietnam, the rate rose to more than 90 percent (Grossman, 1999a).

THE METHODS IN THIS MADNESS

How the military increases the killing rate of soldiers in combat is instructive because our culture today is doing the same thing to our children, but without the safeguards of discipline and character development that the military uses. The training methods that the military uses are brutalization, classical conditioning, operant conditioning, and role modeling. I'll explain these in the military context and show how these same factors are contributing to the phenomenal increase of violence in our culture.

Values Inculcation

Brutalization, or *values inculcation*, is what happens at boot camp. From the moment you step off the bus you are physically and verbally abused. Countless pushups, endless hours at attention or running with heavy loads, while carefully trained professionals take turns screaming at you. Your head is shaved, your are herded together naked, and dressed alike, losing all vestiges of individuality. This brutalization is designed to break down your existing mores and norms and to accept a new set of values that embrace destruction, violence, and death as a way of life. In the end, you embrace violence and accept it as a normal and essential survival skill in your brutal new world.

Something very similar to this violent value inculcation is happening to our children through violence in the media, but instead of 18-year-olds, it begins at the age of eighteen months when a child is first able to discern what is happening on television. At that age, a child can watch something happening on television, and then can mimic that action. But, it isn't until the child is six or seven years old that the part of the brain that kicks in that lets the child understand where the information comes from. Children are developmentally, psychologically, and physically unable to sufficiently discern the difference between fantasy and reality prior to that time.

This means that when young children see somebody on TV being shot, stabbed, raped, brutalized, degraded, or murdered, to them it is as though it were actually happening. To have a child of three, four, or five watch a splatter movie in which the child spends 30 minutes learning to relate to a cast of characters and then in the last 60 minutes of the movie watches helplessly as the newfound friends are hunted down and brutally murdered, is the moral and psychological equivalent of introducing your child to a group of new friends, letting him or her play with those friends, and then butchering those friends in front of your child's eyes, one by one. And this happens to our children hundreds upon hundreds of times throughout their lifetimes.

Sure they are told: "Hey it was all a joke, it's all for fun. Look, this is not real, it's just TV." And they nod their little heads and they say okay. But the reality is that they can't tell the difference. Can you remember a point in your life or in your children's lives when dreams, reality, and television were all jumbled together? That's what it's like to be at that level of psychological development. That's what the media are doing to our children.

The *Journal of the American Medical Association* (Centerwall, 1992) published the definitive epidemiological study on the impact of TV violence. The research demonstrated what happens in numerous nations after television makes its appearance, as compared to nations and regions without TV. In the study, two nations or regions were identified as demographically and ethnically identical: only one variable was manipulated—the presence of television. In every single case in the nation, region, or city with television there was an immediate explosion of violence on the playground, and within fifteen years there was a doubling of the murder rate. Why fifteen years? That's how long it takes for the brutalization of a three- to five-year-old to reach the prime crime age. That's how long it takes for you to reap what you have sown when you brutalize, traumatize, and desensitize a three-year-old.

Today, the data that we have linking violence in the media to violence in society are superior to that linking cancer and tobacco. We now have hundreds of sound scientific studies that demonstrate the social impact of this brutalization in the media. The *Journal of the American Medical Association* (Centerwall, 1992), probably the world's most prestigious medical journal, stated in its June 10, 1992, issue:

> It is concluded that the introduction of television in the 1950s caused a subsequent doubling of the homicide rate, i.e., long-term childhood exposure to television is a causal factor behind approximately one half of the homicides committed in the United States, or approximately 10,000 homicides annually . . . if hypothetically, television technology had never been developed, there would today be 10,000 fewer homicides each year in the United States, 70,000 fewer rapes, and 700,000 fewer injurious assaults (p. 3069).

Classical Conditioning

Classical conditioning is like Pavlov's dog. Remember in Psychology 101 how Pavlov's dog learned to associate one thing with another: the ringing of the bell with food? And from that point on the dog could not hear the bell without salivating.

The Japanese were masters at using classical conditioning with their soldiers. Early in World War II, Chinese prisoners were each placed in a ditch with their hands bound behind them on their knees. And one by one, young, unblooded Japanese soldiers had to each go into the ditch and bayonet their prisoner to death. This is a brutal, horrific way to have to kill another human being. Up on the banks there would be an officer who would shoot the Japanese soldiers if they did not kill; and all of their friends would cheer them on in their violence. Afterwards, they were all treated to the best meal they had ever had in months, to sake, and to so-called "comfort girls". The result? They learned to associate committing violent acts with pleasure.

This technique is so morally reprehensible that there are very few examples of it in modern U.S. military training. But there are some clearcut examples of it being used by the media to affect our children. What is happening to our children is a reverse version of the movie, *A Clockwork Orange*. In this movie, a brutal sociopath, a mass murderer, was strapped to a chair and forced to watch violent movies. Unbeknownst to him, a drug was injected into him that made him nauseous and he sat and gagged and retched as he watched the movies. After hundreds of repetitions of this, he began to associate violence with nausea and his ability to engage in violence became limited.

What we are doing is the exact opposite of this: we're having our children watch vivid pictures of human suffering and death and they learn to associate it with what? Laughter, cheers, their favorite soft drink and candy bar, and their girlfriend's perfume.

After the Jonesboro shootings, one of the high school teachers told me about her students' reactions when she told them that someone had shot a bunch of their little brothers, sisters, and cousins in the middle school. "They laughed," she told me with dismay, "they laughed." A similar reaction happens all the time in movie theaters when there is bloody violence. The young people laugh and cheer and keep right on eating popcorn and drinking pop. We have raised a generation of barbarians who have learned to associate violence with pleasure, like the Romans cheering and snacking as the Christians were slaughtered in the Coliseum.

The result is a phenomenon that functions much like AIDS, which I have termed AVIDS–Acquired Violence Immune Deficiency. AIDS has never killed anybody. It destroys your immune system so that other diseases that shouldn't kill you become fatal. Television violence by itself doesn't kill anybody. It destroys your violence immune system and conditions you to derive pleasure from violence. To kill another human being you've got to get through two filters. The first filter is the forebrain. A thousand things can convince the forebrain to kill: racism, politics, religion, anger, greed, and hatred. But, once you're at close range with another human being and it's time for you to pull the trigger, you slam head on into the violence immune system, the midbrain resistance. And that's when this Acquired Violence Immune Deficiency takes over in order to result in killing.

Operant Conditioning

The third method the military uses is operant conditioning, a very powerful procedure of stimulus-response, stimulus-response. A benign example is the use of flight simulators to train pilots. An airline pilot in training sits in front of a flight simulator for endless, mind-numbing hours; when a particular light goes on, he is taught to react in a certain way. When another warning light goes on, a different reaction is necessary. Stimulus-response, stimulus-response, stimulus-response. One day the pilot is actually flying a jumbo jet, the plane is going down, and 300 people are screaming behind him. He's wetting his seat cushion and he's scared out of his wits, but he does the right thing. Why? Because he's been conditioned to respond in a particular way to this crisis situation.

When people are frightened or angry, they will do what they have been conditioned to do. We do it with children in fire drills. When the fire alarm is set off, the children learn to file out of the school in orderly fashion. One day there's a real fire and they're frightened out of their little wits, but they do exactly what they've been conditioned to do and it saves their lives.

The military and law enforcement community have made killing a conditioned response. This has substantially raised the firing rate on the modern battlefield. Whereas target training in World War II used bull's-eye targets, now soldiers learn to fire at realistic, man-shaped silhouettes that pop up in their field of view. That's the conditioned stimulus. The trainees only have a split second to engage the target. The conditioned response is to shoot the target and then it drops. Stimulus-response, stimulus-response, stimulus-response. Soldiers or police officers experience hundreds of repetitions of this. Later, when they're out on the battlefield or a police officer is walking a beat and somebody pops up with a gun, reflexively they will shoot and shoot to kill. We know that 75 to 80 percent of the shooting on the modern battlefield is the result of this kind of stimulus-response training (Grossman & Siddle, 1999).

Now if you're a little troubled by that, how much more should we be troubled by the fact that every time a child plays an interactive point-and-shoot video game, he or she is learning the exact same conditioned reflex and motor skills?

I was an expert witness in a murder case in South Carolina trying to offer mitigation for a kid who was facing the death penalty. We tried to explain to the jury that interactive video games had conditioned this kid to shoot a gun to kill. He had put hundreds of dollars into video games learning to point and shoot, point and shoot. One day he and a buddy decided it would be fun to rob the local, country crossroads quick mart. They walked in and he pointed a snub-nosed .38 pistol at the clerk's head. The clerk turned to look at him, and the defendant shot reflexively from a range of about six feet. The bullet hit the clerk right between the eyes, which is a pretty remarkable shot with that weapon at that range, and killed this father of two children. Afterwards, we asked the boy what happened and why he did it. It clearly was not part of the plan to kill the guy—it was being videotaped from six different directions. The boy said, "I don't know, it was a mistake, it wasn't supposed to happen."

In the military and law enforcement worlds, the right option often is not to shoot. But you never, never put your quarter in that video machine with the intention of not shooting. There's always some stimulus that sets you off. And when he got excited, and his heart rate went up, and the vasoconstriction set in, and his forebrain closed down, this young man did exactly what he was conditioned to do: he reflexively pulled the trigger, shooting and shooting accurately, just like all those times he played video games. This process is extraordinarily powerful and frightening. The result is ever-more, homemade pseudo-sociopaths who kill reflexively and show no remorse. Our kids are learning to kill and learning to like it and then we have the audacity to say, "Oh my goodness, what's wrong."

One of the children allegedly involved in the Jonesboro shootings (and they are just children) had a fair amount of experience shooting real guns. The other kid was a non-shooter and, to the best of our knowledge, had almost no experience shooting. Those two kids between them fired twenty-five shots from a range of over 100 yards, and they hit 15 people. That's pretty remarkable shooting. We run into these situations a lot: kids who have never picked up a gun in their lives pick up a real gun and are incredibly accurate and efficient with that gun. Why? The video games.

The most remarkable example is the Paducah, Kentucky, school shooting outlined at the beginning of this article, in which the boy apparently fired eight shots and got eight hits on eight different milling, scrambling, screaming kids. Five of those eight hits were head shots. Where did he get this phenomenal skill? Well, there is a 130-million-dollar lawsuit against the video game manufacturers in that case, claiming that the violent video games, the murder simulators, gave that mass murderer the skill and the will to kill.

Role Models

In the military you are immediately confronted with a role model: your drill sergeant. He personifies violence, aggression, and discipline. The discipline, along with the fact that it is being done to adults (more mature minds), is the safeguard in the process. Along with military heroes, such as John Wayne, Audie Murphy, Sergeant York, and Chesty Puller, these kind of violent role models have always been used to influence young, impressionable minds.

Today the media are providing our children with role models, and this can be seen not just in the lawless sociopaths in movies and TV shows, but it can also be seen in the media-inspired, copycat aspect of the Jonesboro murders, which is a twist to these juvenile crimes that the TV networks would much rather not talk about.

Research in the 1970s demonstrated the effect of cluster suicides in which the local TV reporting of teen suicides was directly responsible for causing numerous copycat suicides of young, impressionable teenagers. Somewhere in every population there are potentially suicidal kids who will say to themselves, "Well, I'll show all those people who have been mean to me. I know how to get my picture on TV too."

Thus we get the effect of copycat, cluster murders that work their way across America like a virus spread by the six o'clock local news. No matter what someone has done, if you put his or her picture on TV, you have created a celebrity and someone, somewhere, will emulate this person. This effect is greatly magnified when the role model is a teenager, and the effect on other teens can be profound. The copycat lineage of the Jonesboro shootings can first be picked up at Pearl, Mississippi, less than six months before the Jonesboro shootings. In Pearl, a sixteen-year-old boy was accused of killing his mother and then going to his school and shooting nine students, two of whom died, including his ex-girlfriend. Two months later this virus spread to Paducah, Kentucky, where a fourteen-year-old boy was arrested for killing three students and wounding five others.

A very important step in the spread of this copycat crime virus occurred in Stamps, Arkansas, fifteen days after Pearl and just a little over ninety days before Jonesboro. In Stamps, a fourteen-year-old boy who was angry at his schoolmates, hid in the woods and fired at children as they came out of school. Sound familiar? Only two children were injured in this crime, and so most of the world didn't hear about it, but it got great regional coverage on TV, and two little boys in Jonesboro, Arkansas, couldn't have helped but hear it.

And then there was Springfield, Oregon, and finally Littleton, Colorado. Who is next? Is this a reasonable price to pay for the TV network's "right" to turn juvenile defendants into celebrities and role models by playing up their pictures on TV?

One of the local TV news anchors here in Jonesboro told me that the Japanese reporters kept asking her, "Why do you keep putting those kids' faces on TV? Don't you know about copycat crimes? Don't you know that this will inspire other kids to do the same thing?" In Japan and many other democracies around the world it is a punishable, criminal act to place the names and images of juvenile criminals in the media, because they know that it will result in other tragic deaths. But the only justification our TV news anchor could give to these Japanese counterparts was, "Well, if we don't, then our competitors will and they'll eat us up in the ratings."

It is vital that our society be informed about these crimes, but when the visual images of the young killers are put in the media, these youths become role models. The average preschooler in America watches twenty-seven hours a week of television (Grossman & DeGaetano, 1999). The average kid gets more one-on-one communication from the TV than from parents and teachers combined. The ultimate achievement for our children is to get their pictures on TV. The solution is simple and it comes straight out of the suicidology literature: the media has every right and responsibility to tell the story, but it has no right to glorify the killers by presenting their visual images on television.

UNLEARNING VIOLENCE

So what is the road home from the dark and lonely place which we have traveled? One route to follow would be to *just turn it off,* that is, if you don't like what is on television all you have to do is use the "off" button. And yes, turning off the TV and protecting your kids, especially in the first six or seven years, is vitally important. Yet, every single one of the parents of the shooting victims of the numerous school shootings across America could have protected their children from media violence for a lifetime, and it wouldn't have done a bit of good. Because somewhere some other parents didn't just turn it off.

The night of the Jonesboro shooting, clergy and counselors were working in small groups in the hospital waiting room, comforting the groups of relatives and friends of the fifteen shooting victims. Then they noticed one woman who had been sitting alone silently. A counselor went up to the woman and discovered that she was the mother of one of the girls who had been killed. She had no friends, no husband, and no family with her as she sat in the hospital, alone and stunned by her loss. "I just came to find out how to get my little girl's body back," she said. But the body had been taken to Little Rock, 100 miles away, for an autopsy. Told this, in her dazed mind her very next concern was, "I just don't know how we're going to pay for the funeral. I don't know how we can afford it." That little girl was truly all she had in all the world. Come to Jonesboro, my friend, hunt up this mother and tell her how she should just turn it off.

Another possible option to deal with violent crime infringes on civil liberties. We can oppress minorities, take away the freedoms of adults, and extensively regulate our society. One thing that a police state can always truthfully claim is that it can make the streets safe. And if we don't get a grip on violent crime I fear that this is exactly what will happen. But perhaps we can consider regulating what the violence industry is selling to kids, carefully controlling the sale of visual violent imagery to children, while still permitting free access to adults, just as we do with guns, pornography, alcohol, tobacco, sex, and cars.

FIGHTING BACK: LEGISLATION, LITIGATION, EDUCATION

We need to make progress in the fight against child abuse, racism, and poverty, and in rebuilding our families. No one is denying that the breakdown of the family is a factor. But nations without our divorce rates also are having increases in violence. And research demonstrates that one major source of harm associated with single-parent families occurs when the TV becomes both the nanny and the second parent.

Work is needed in all these areas, but there's a new front–taking on the producers of media violence. The solution strategy that I submit for consideration is *legislation, litigation, education.*

Simply put, we ought to work toward legislation which outlaws violent video games for children. There is no constitutional right for children to play interactive video games that teach them weapons-handling skills or that simulates the killing of human beings.

We are very close to being able to do to the networks, through litigation, what is being done to the tobacco industry. The day may also be coming when we should be able to seat juries in America who are willing to sock it to the networks in the only place they really understand–their wallets. As *Time* magazine said in its cover story on the Jonesboro shootings (Lacayo, 1998):

> As for media violence, the debate there is fast approaching the same point that discussions about the health impact of tobacco reached some time ago–it's over. Few researchers bother any longer to dispute that bloodshed on TV and in the movies has an effect on kids who witness it (p. 29).

Most of all, the American people need to be informed, through a comprehensive education campaign, about what is happening. "You shall know the truth and the truth shall set you free." The truth about which people need to be educated is the message I'd like to give you from Jonesboro: Violence *kills;* violence is not a game, it's not fun, it's not something that we do for entertainment.

Every parent in America desperately needs to be warned of the impact of TV and other violent media on children, as we would warn them of some rampant carcinogen. The problem is that our key means of public education in America is the national TV networks using public airwaves we have licensed to them. And they are stonewalling. The folks here in Jonesboro, Arkansas, noticed something interesting about the network TV crews that swarmed in like the second of a series of biblical plagues: The networks have blood on their hands, and they know it, yet they dare not admit it.

As an author and expert on killing, I believe I have spoken on the subject at every Rotary, Kiwanis, and Lions Club in a fifty mile radius of Jonesboro. So when the plague of satellite dishes descended upon us like huge locusts, many people here were aware of the scientific data linking TV violence and violent crime.

The networks will stick their lenses anywhere and courageously expose anything. Like flies crawling on open wounds, nothing is too private nor too shameful for their probing lenses–except themselves, and their share of guilt in the terrible, tragic crime that happened here.

A CBS executive told me his plan. He knew all about the linkage between media and violence. Here's how his own, in-house people have advised him to protect his child from the poison his industry is bringing to America's children: he's not going to expose his child to TV in any way, shape, or form until she's old enough to learn how to read. And then he'll select very carefully what she sees. Now that's a very effective plan. He and his wife plan to send her to a daycare center that has no television and then, when she is old enough to read, he plans to show her age-appropriate videos. That should be the bare minimum with your children and grandchildren: protect them when they are young, later show them only age-appropriate videos, and think very hard about what is age appropriate.

Perhaps, the most benign products you're going to get from the networks are twenty-two minute sitcoms or cartoons providing instant gratification for all of life's problems, interlaced with commercials telling you what a slug you are if you don't ingest the right sugary substances and don't wear the right shoes.

The worst products from the networks are described by Ted Turner and Elliot Moonves, president of CBS. In 1999, Ted Turner publicly stated that , "Television is the single most significant factor contributing to violence in America . . ."(California House of Representatives, 1999, p. 1). And CBS President Leslie Moonves was asked if he thought the Columbine High School shootings in Littleton, Colorado, had anything to do with the media. His answer was: "Anyone who thinks the media has nothing to do with it is an idiot" (Reuters Wire Service, 2000).

Education about the media and violence can make a difference. I was on a radio call-in show in San Antonio, Texas, and a woman called in and said, "I would never have had the courage to do this two years ago. But I was getting the education that you're talking about now. And let me tell you what happened. You tell me if I was right." And she was right.

She said, "My thirteen-year-old boy spent the night with a neighbor boy. After that night, he started having nightmares. I got him to admit to me what the nightmares were about. While he was at the neighbor's house they watched splatter movies all night long: people cutting people up with chain saws and stuff like that."

"I called the neighbors and told them 'Listen to me: you are sick people. I couldn't feel any differently about you if you had given my son pornography or if you would have given him alcohol. And I'm not going to have anything further to do with you or your son–and neither is anybody else in this neighborhood, if I have anything to do with it–until you stop what you're doing.'"

That's powerful stuff. That's what you call censure, not censor. And all of us ought to have appropriate knowledge and the moral courage to stand up and censure people around us who think that violence, especially in television and interactive video games, is legitimate entertainment for children. And education is the key to doing that. Along with a little legislation and litigation, an educated and informed society might just be able to find its way home from the dark and lonely place to which we have traveled.

REFERENCES

California House of Representatives (1999, May). *Resolution on media violence.*

Centerwall, B. (1992). Television and violence: The scale of the problem and where to go from here. *Journal of the American Medical Association, 267,* 3059-3061.

Griffith, P. (1989). *Battle tactics of the American Civil War.* New Haven: Yale University Press.

Grossman, D. (1996). *On killing: The psychological cost of learning to kill in war and society.* New York: Little, Brown, and Company.

Grossman, D. (1999a). Aggression and violence. In J. Chambers (Ed.) *Oxford companion to American military history.* (pp. 10). New York: Oxford University Press.

Grossman, D. (1999b). Weaponry, evolution of. In L. Curtis & J. Turpin (Eds.), *Academic Press encyclopedia of violence, peace and conflict* (pp. 797). San Diego, Calif.: Academic Press.

Grossman, D., & DeGaetano, G. (1999). *Stop teaching our kids to kill: A call to action against TV, movie and video game violence.* New York: Crown/Random House.

Grossman, D., & Siddle, B. (1999). Psychological effects of combat. In L. Curtis & J. Turpin (Eds.)., *Academic Press encyclopedia of violence, peace, and conflict* (pp. 144-145). San Diego, Calif.: Academic Press.

Lacayo, R. (1998, April 6). Toward the root of evil. *Time,* p. 29.

Marshall, S. L. A. (1978). *Men against fire.* Gloucester, Mass.: Peter Smith.

Reuters Wire Service (2000, March 19). CBS airing mob drama deemed too violent a year ago. *The Washington Post.* from http://library.northernlight.com Document ID: HB20000316630000016

Statistical abstracts of the United States, (1957-1997). Washington, D.C.: U.S. Department of Commerce, Bureau of the Census.

Chapter Three

PROFILES OF HOMICIDAL OFFENDERS: MOTIVES, DYNAMICS, AND PROGNOSTIC INDICATORS IN YOUTH MURDER

Louis B. Schlesinger

A N ESSENTIAL FIRST STEP in understanding homicide, or for that matter any aspect of nature, is a classification system with which to organize one's observations. This has been the model that psychiatry has followed since Kraepelin (1896) and to some extent even since Hippocrates. Much of the scientific work on homicide, however, has preceded with little regard for classification. The legal classification is based on the relationship of the murderer to his victim (e.g., parricide, matricide, infanticide) and the degree of intent, both of which ignore the dynamic aspects of the crime. In one study of adolescent parricidal offenders, for example, all the children were considered as a group because all of them had killed a parent (Corder, Ball, Halzlip, Rollins, & Beaumont, 1976). This is not necessarily the most significant parameter, since each of these acts can be stimulated by different psychodynamics, and thus result in a different prognosis.

Over the years, there have been some attempts at classification, although very few with an emphasis on prognostication as a goal. For example, Guttmacher (1973) differentiated six types of murderers: the average murderer with no psychopathology, the sociopath, the alcoholic, the individual who murders to avenge a wrong committed against him, the schizophrenic, and the sadist who kills to achieve sexual pleasure. Brancale (1955) spoke of a simple two-pronged classification including an administrative group and a psychiatric group. The psychiatric group includes those who are psychotic, neurotic, or mentally retarded, and thus should be handled in specialized settings; all other cases (the vast majority) should be handled correctionally.

Tanay (1969) divided homicide into (1) dissociative, (2) psychotic, and (3) ego-syntonic. The dissociative homicide is carried out in an altered state of consciousness and frequently without awareness of motivation. The psychotic homicide is a direct result of an overt psychosis. Ego-syntonic homicides are committed without disruption of ego functions; it is consciously accept-able to the perpetrator and is, in essence, a rational goal-directed act. Halleck's (1971) classification of crime as adaptive or maladaptive is a broad division of antisocial behavior into normal (similar to Tanay's ego-syntonic) and abnormal (similar to the dissociative and psychotic murders). Bromberg (1961) divides homicide into normal and psychopathic; consequently, in the psychopathic category "thrill murder," rape murder, alcoholic murder, and impulsive-bizarre murders are all grouped together in a "kaleidoscope of psychopathy" (p. 134).

One of the few systems of classification, for which some mention of prog-nosis is offered, was proposed by Miller and Looney (1974). They referred to three homicidal syndromes, in their study of adolescent murderers, to be understood in terms of a risk factor. The common denominator is the degree of dehumanization of the victim by the offender. Thus, homicides are divid-ed into (1) high risk with total and permanent dehumanization of the victim, (2) high risk with partial and transient dehumanization, and (3) low risk with transient and partial dehumanization of the victim, requiring consensual val-idation of the peer group. Megargee (1966) divided homicidal offenders into the under-controlled (individuals who respond to frustration with aggression and violence) and the over-controlled (individuals with rigid inhibitions who build up anger which results in explosive violence). Thus, the various sys-tems of classification generally regard homicides as either goal-directed and purposeful, or a result of some type of psychological disturbance, either a psychosis or a disruption of ego-functions.

Reliance on the psychiatric diagnosis per se—except where the offense was a direct outgrowth of a paranoid condition, an organic disorder, or a toxic state—proves unrewarding as a means of classifying and predicting homicide. The majority of research, however, has emphasized the role of psychosis, various demographic factors, certain personality traits, or other signs and symptoms—all with varying degrees of prognostic success (Dershowitz, 1973; Hellman & Blackman, 1966; Rubin, 1972; Smith & English, 1978; Malmquist, 1996).

In search of a common denominator to use as a basis for classification that can be applied to help in prognostication of future violence, Revitch and Schlesinger (1978, 1981, 1989) analyzed the dynamics of the antisocial act itself, and as a result of that analysis, developed the concept of the motiva-tional spectrum as a basis of classification. This classification system views the stimuli that contribute to homicide as spectrally distributed, with purely external (sociogenic) on one end and purely internal (psychogenic) on the other. In moving from the external to the internal, five separate categories of offenses have been specified: (a) sociogenic or environmental, (b) situation-al, (c) impulsive, (d) catathymic, and (e) compulsive. In compulsive offenses, the endogenous pressures are paramount, and external factors play a minimal role. The reverse is true for the environmental offenses. The other categories of offenses have a mixture of endogenous and exogenous factors, depending on the position in the spectrum (see Figure 1). Organic, toxic and paranoid cases form a group of their own which is distinct from our system of classification. Specific criteria used to categorize cases are detailed throughout this chapter and are illustrated by descriptive case studies, primarily with juvenile offenders.

Figure 1
THE MOTIVATIONAL SPECTRUM

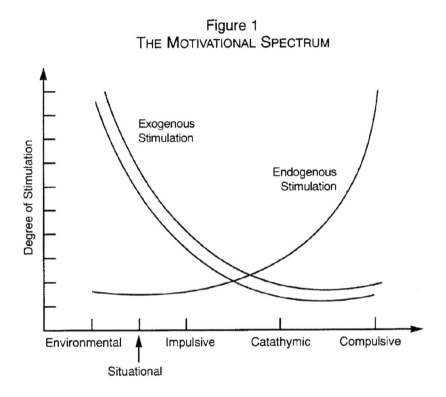

HOMICIDE AS A RESULT OF A PRIMARY PSYCHIATRIC DISORDER: THE ORGANIC, TOXIC, AND PARANOID MURDERS

Murder associated with psychiatric conditions most commonly occurs in the organic, toxic, and paranoid states, and sometimes in a state of psychotic depression. Epilepsy stands out in the organic group, since this is commonly referred to as a possible explanation of sudden murder, and its known presence in an offender may be used as a legal defense. However, epilepsy does not predispose to murder (Lewis, 1975), and epileptics are not more violent than the general population. In fact, homicide committed during an attack of psychomotor seizure or in a postictal state is extremely rare (Walker, 1961).

Various encephalopathies, brain injuries, and brain tumors have all been cited as possible causes of homicide, temper outbursts, and acts of violence. Mark and Ervin (1970) reported a case of homicidal violence which was linked to a tumor in the limbic system; after the tumor was removed, the overt aggression was significantly reduced. In many other cases cited in the literature, all of the above organic pathologies have been regarded as contributory to various types of aggression, as well as in some homicides.

The most common substance associated with aggression is alcohol (Yarvis, 1990). In Marvin Wolfgang's classic 1958 study of homicide, 54 percent of the offenders and 53 percent of the victims were under the influence of alcohol at the time of the offense. Among other agents in the toxic category, amphetamines are statistically the most responsible for assaults and homicide (Ellinwood, 1971). Tinklenberg, Murphy, Darley, and Kopell (1974), however, found secobarbital to be a leading drug in assaults and murders by adolescents. Homicides caused by paranoid delusions are often due to the use of LSD (Reich & Hepps, 1972). Peterson and Stillman (1979) regard phencyclidine (PCP or "Angel Dust") to be the most dangerous drug resulting in assaultive or extremely aggressive behavior. Heroin is not directly a cause of violent crime, but it is a major indirect cause, because many individuals engage in criminal activities, including violence, to obtain money to buy the drug.

The importance of paranoid delusions (particularly delusions of infidelity or delusional jealousy) in homicide has been mentioned in the literature over the years (Lanzkron, 1963; Podolsky, 1956; Silva, Ferrari, Leong & Penny, 1999). Swanson, Bonhart, and Smith (1970) in their review of the paranoid conditions, concluded that pathological jealousy and paranoid delusions are major causes of homicide.

Contrary to popular belief, most crime in general, and homicide in particular, is not an outgrowth of a primary psychiatric disorder. In fact, most crime, according to Pallone and Hennessy (1994) is due to inclination, opportunity, expectation of reward, and expectation of impunity. In only fairly rare instances is homicide a direct outgrowth of a primary mental disorder; however, mental disorders can play a secondary role in terms of weakening inhibitory controls, or by predisposing the offender to an increase in amounts of anger.

The following case is illustrative of murder as a direct result of paranoid psychosis:

Case 1

An eighteen-year-old male, A. A., killed his parents by multiple stab wounds while they were sleeping. Two years earlier, he had become very psychotic and was hospitalized in an acute psychiatric facility. After he stabilized, he was transferred to a long-term treatment program where he stayed for about eighteen months. He was then discharged and he moved back with his parents. Within a short period of time, A. A. discontinued psychotropic medication and developed a belief that his parents were Communists and plotting to kill him. He believed that the bedsprings were serving as radio transmitters that sent him messages, explaining his parents' involvement with the Communist party; he believed he would be killed "for knowing too much." A. A. stabbed both parents to death while they were sleeping. The bodies were discovered several hours later by an older sister who was coming to pay a visit. The offender expressed no remorse, believing his action not only was justified but to be commended "because there is no telling what they might have been up to."

CLASSIFICATION BASED ON THE MOTIVATIONAL SPECTRUM

Without a structure by which to order events, the world would appear chaotic and without relationships. Complex phenomena, such as human behavior, are difficult to classify; therefore, rigid boundaries cannot be established because of fluid borderline cases. Moreover, different examiners may stress different facets of behavior and levels of consciousness, and thus may present different evaluations of the same event (Perr, 1975). The legal approach is to deal with motivational factors, but because only the most superficial and seemingly logical phenomena are considered, what may seem to be premeditation may actually be a compelling irrational need with reasons not conscious to the offender.

In the classification system outlined in this chapter, and described in detail in the following sections, motivational stimuli are emphasized and distinguished between environmental and endogenous influences. A diagrammatic representation of the motivational stimuli, and the relationship to the intensity of exogenous and endogenous factors is presented in Figure 1. For instance, in the compulsive offenses, external factors play a minimal role, while the endogenous pressures are paramount. The reverse is true for the environmental offenses.

Environmentally Stimulated Homicides

Homicide is very frequently due to sociogenic or environmental influences. The breakdown in social order and social stability, rapid social change, feelings of alienation, and strained economic conditions for the poor, provide a background for stimulating murder. There are many historical examples showing that the weakening of social controls and social disintegration itself will foster violence. A recent example is the mass killing in the former Yugoslavia. A historical example is the behavior of the demoralized and undisciplined mercenary armies during the Thirty Years War (Wedgwood, 1957). Political murders in general, even if they are committed by unstable individuals, have a connection with the social mood and pressures. The leadership's attitudes also influence group conduct. For example, atrocities under the Nazi regime were directly sponsored by the leadership, so that angry and sadistic individuals who would otherwise express their aggressive needs in fantasy life, could give vent to their impulses in reality. Several experimental studies by Haney, Banks, and Zimbardo (1973) and Milgram (1963) illustrate the effects of context in influencing fairly normal individuals to participate in fairly aggressive acts.

The violence and audacity of street crime, the senseless murder of aged people, antisocial acts by juveniles, and the behavior of modern political terrorists all can be attributed not only to the personality variables of the offenders, but also to the general weakening of social discipline, values, and restraints. Often what may look like an adaptive or ego-syntonic murder for gain during robbery, may actually be wanton killing, with the robbery serving as a pretext for the murder. Moreover, pathological individuals with a need for violence may be influenced by the social climate which will release, direct, and give meaning to the violent act.

Murders committed by professional criminals for gainful purposes fall under the category of the environmentally stimulated homicides. Sutherland's (1947) theory of differential association (such as criminal behavior learned in interaction with others) also applies to this group of offenders. Thus, individuals with various personality compositions, regardless of the presence or absence of psychopathology, have common environmental influences as the main stimulus to crime and homicide. The most characteristic type of murder stimulated by environmental influences is contract murder committed by members of organized crime for adaptive and logical purposes as far as the needs of their organization are concerned.

The following case of a murder perpetrated within the context of a youth gang, is illustrative of an environmentally stimulated homicide.

Case 2

A seventeen-year-old male, Marvin, was indicted for felony murder as well as aiding and abetting an armed robbery. He described his involvement in the homicide as follows:

> We were at my cousin's house. Steven, Andrew, April, and Renee. I was on my way to go home. Andrew and Steven were talking about going to a liquor store to get beer. I walked out with Andrew; we bumped into Renee and April downstairs. Andrew said to everyone, he wants to rob the man waiting for a bus. I told him "don't do that". He wanted me to watch out for him. I shook my head. He didn't rob him–nothing happened.
>
> Renee told Andrew he should rob the store. I didn't say nothing. Andrew went to open the door at the deli store because the door was locked. We started walking down the avenue. They wanted to rob the deli store and they wanted me to watch out. Andrew said to me 'Let's get these guys.' He said, 'You're not going to help me?' I shook my head, 'No.' He was walking fast. He pulled his mask over his face. He took off to chase the two guys. April went to see what happened. He said 'I am going to get somebody before the night is over.' I just looked at him. I was just watching.

Marvin stated that they then walked up the street when . . .

> Andrew saw a man taking out his garbage. Andrew stopped. He asked me, 'Marvin, are you going to watch out?' I didn't answer him. Then I said, 'Yea, I'll watch out for you'. I met April and Renee; we walked across the street. I crossed the street to watch out for Andrew. He pulled his mask down. He told the man to 'run his pockets'. The man looked at Andrew, then Andrew pulled out a gun. He threw him against the wall. The man grabbed Andrew. The man pushed Andrew in the face, then Andrew pushed the man. He had one hand on the gun; with the other hand he was pushing the man. Then Andrew raised the gun up. The man grabbed the gun; they were struggling.
>
> That's when I ran over there. I put my hand on top of the gun. The man had his hand on Andrew. Andrew was holding the gun. I touched the top of it; the gun went off. The man got shot. The man fell, his eyes were still open. Andrew was checking his pockets and stuff. He snatched me up. We started running up 7th Street.

The offender went to the home of some friends:

> I bumped into April and Renee later on that night. They were asking me 'who shot the man.' I didn't say nothing, I was in shock. Then I went home to my room. I was sitting on my bed thinking about what happened. Thinking about the man, that he got shot. I went to sleep.

The following day when Marvin went to school, he told his girlfriend what had happened. There were a number of eyewitnesses and eventually Marvin and his three cohorts were arrested. There were a number of different conflicting statements given. In fact, two witnesses saw Marvin with the gun shooting the victim.

When questioned why he wanted to rob someone that night, he was unable to offer an explanation stating, "I just wanted to see how it felt. To see how it felt to rob someone." He minimized his involvement stating "I was just there. I was watching out. When I put my hand on top of the gun, it went off. I didn't do anything wrong. I should have went home in the first place."

Comment. Marvin had a history of minor crimes including stealing, some school problems including fighting, and some minor drug abuse. This homicide was stimulated, however, by group pressure and the decision on the part of the group, suggested by Andrew, the dominant figure, that they should rob someone. Marvin explained that he wanted to be viewed by others as someone who was not afraid. He impulsively shot the victim under the general stress of the immediate situation. This homicide was not in any way an outgrowth of any mental disorder such as psychosis or depression, nor did it have any sexual dynamics. It is strictly an impulsive offense within the context of an antisocial peer group who had a plan to commit armed robbery just "to see how it felt." There is also an element of trying to impress the two girls that accompanied the males.

Situational Homicides

Situational homicides are, in essence, a reaction to stressful circumstances. They are mostly committed by individuals with little or no psychopathology, although all types of personality compositions may be involved. The homicide may be adaptive, in the sense that it serves a logical purpose, or maladaptive and committed in a state of fear, anger, or despair. The homicide may be committed impulsively or it may be premeditated or partially premeditated. In situational murders, there is often an element of impulsivity, fear, anger, despair, and occasionally a paranoid tinge to thinking, often with alcohol playing a secondary role in terms of loosening inhibitions.

The following case previously reported (Revitch & Schlesinger, 1978) is illustrative of a typical situational murder.

Case 3

An eighteen-year-old, C. C., without a history of delinquency or disturbed behavior, and raised in a fairly stable working class family, was charged with murder. He was bright and psychological testing did not elicit any serious psychopathology. Shortly before the incident, three new families moved to his block, creating some degree of tension and disrupting life patterns in the neighborhood where his family had lived for many years. Frequent arguments and exchanges took place over the course of months. On the day of the incident, C. C. came home in a bad mood, having been discharged from a part-time job, which he obtained shortly after high school graduation. There was a great deal of screaming and noise in the house next door, and he saw the neighbors throwing garbage out the window. Since he had been threatened previously by one of the new neighbors, he became frightened when he saw one of them holding a stick. He took a gun out of his car and went into their house. He said that the gun went off "by accident" and then he suddenly realized that he had shot someone. He called his girlfriend and was glad to be at the police station since he was afraid of being killed by friends of the victim.

Impulsive Homicides

Impulsive offenders react to various environmental and situational stimuli by antisocial acts. They differ from situational offenders by their history of multiple antisocial acts and by their poor impulse control. Impulsive offenses are usually diffuse, poorly structured, unpremeditated, or perhaps partially premeditated. The life pattern of such offenders is marked by lack of direction and unpredictability. Psychiatric and psychological evaluation typically reveals looseness of personality integration as the main personality characteristic. Impulsive offenses may be aggressive, including homicide, or nonaggressive, or sometimes a combination of both. Revitch (1975) reported the case of a nineteen-year-old with a history of juvenile delinquency including vandalism, breaking and entering, and drug use, who, while babysitting his nineteen-month-old niece, impulsively raped her rectally, causing her death.

The following case of an impulsive offender who committed homicide is also illustrative.

Case 4

A seventeen-year-old male, D. D., with a history of fairly minor antisocial acts including stealing radios, public intoxication, possession of marijuana, and a minor assault on a peer (who said something to his girlfriend) murdered a thirty-five-year-old woman. The offender's background included quitting school in the tenth grade, being teased by peers, as well as learning difficulties. He stated that his biological father left the family when he was ten years old "because I had a growth and he couldn't take it." His stepfather treated him poorly including harsh punishment which involved locking him in the closet and hitting him with a hose. At the time of the homicide, D. D. was living with a friend of his mother since his mother was unable to tolerate his incorrigibility, lack of adjustment, and "back-talk."

D. D. met a fifteen-year-old girl on a telephone party-line. After several weeks of conversation, he eventually met her in person and invited her to stay with him for a long weekend. He got into an argument with the woman (his mother's friend) he was living with. He stabbed the victim multiple times with a kitchen knife causing her death.

The condominium where the homicide occurred was drenched in blood, forcing D. D. to stay up all night in an attempt to clean up. He painted the walls multiple times, cut up the rugs and disposed of furniture which was blood soaked. Early the next day, while driving, he and his girlfriend were pulled over by the police and arrested.

Comment. D. D. revealed a great deal of his inner self through one story on the Thematic Apperception Test, a projective personality test in which the subject is asked to tell stories about pictures that are presented. In describing one of the characters in the pictures, he stated, "Women used to reject him and treat him like dirt and tease him. He hates women because he was teased. He thinks of some kind of revenge. He feels like getting back at the world." Although this murder certainly had a strong situational connotation (triggered by an argument), his impulsive lifestyle with multiple minor anti-social offenses, lack of solid integration of personality, poor school and life adjustment, and deep feelings of inadequacy, all make this an excellent example of an impulsive adolescent offender who committed homicide.

Catathymic Homicides

Wertham (1937) introduced the concept of catathymic crisis into the field of forensic psychiatry. He originally defined his concept in the following way: "A catathymic reaction is the transformation of the stream of thought as the result of certain complexes of ideas that are charged with a strong affect--usually a wish, a fear, or an ambivalent striving" (p. 975). In a subsequent publication (Wertham, 1978), he refined his concept as "delusional thinking with the patient being driven to a violent deed without a rational conscious motive, with the act having a symbolic meaning and the victim not counting as a person, but as part of an overpowering image." Other researchers have used the term catathymic crisis in a variety of different ways (Schlesinger, 1996).

Revitch and Schlesinger (1978, 1981, 1989) were influenced not only by Wertham's conception of catathymic crisis, involving a long-term relationship with the future victim, but also by Satten, Menninger, and Mayman's (1960) conception of sudden violence triggered by an individual whom the perpetrator just met. Revitch and Schlesinger conceived of catathymia not as a clinical entity as such, but as a psychological or psychodynamic process of an acute and chronic form, with differentiating characteristics (see Table 1).

TABLE 1
Differentiating Characteristics of Acute and Chronic Catathymic Process

Activation of Process	Incubation Period	Feeling	Victim	Memory of Events
Acute				
Triggered by a sudden overwhelming affect attached to ideas of symbolic significance	Several seconds or longer	Usually flattening emotion	Usually a stranger	Usually poor
Chronic				
Triggered by a buildup of tension, a feeling of frustration, depression, and helplessness	Days to years	Usually relief	Usually close acquaintances and family members	Usually preserved

An acute catathymic homicide is essentially a sudden unprovoked murder or violent act without apparent motivation. This process should be differentiated from situational homicides and assaults committed in an explosion of anger, fear, or jealousy, or when under the influence of paranoid delusions, drugs, or alcohol. In a catathymic homicide, deeper sources of emotional tension are tapped and released by an overpowering emotion attached to complexes of ideas that are disrupted. In fact, the perpetrator of the assault often cannot give a reasonable explanation for the act and, in many cases, can only partially recall the event. Satten et al. (1960) described a classic case of an acute catathymic attack when a soldier drowned a preadolescent girl without any obvious provocation and with partial amnesia for the homicide. Ruotolo (1968) believes that an injury to the pride system is instrumental in precipitating such violence. Schlesinger (1999) described the case of a sixteen-year-old who committed a sexual matricide (including vaginal and anal necrophilia) following years of mother-son incest. The homicide itself, however, occurred while he was in a dissociative state and best explained as an acute catathymic release whereby there was a sudden discharge of emotion-ally pent-up psychic conflict and tension.

The following case, previously reported by Revitch and Schlesinger (1981), of an eighteen-year-old who committed an acute catathymic homi-cide is illustrative.

Case 5

E. E. was an eighteen-year-old high school senior who worked as a part-time gas station attendant, prior to his anticipated entry into junior college in the fall. He strangled a female nightclub entertainer to death under the fol-lowing circumstances: Shortly before closing time, the victim entered the gas station requesting a dime to make a telephone call. E. E. loaned her the money and when he looked into the telephone room, the woman had her dress lifted and invited E. E. to have sexual relations with her. He was unable to get an erection, prompting the woman to say "go home to your mother." E. E. then grabbed a piece of rubber tubing, wrapped it around her neck, and strangled her. He placed the body in his car, drove to a vacant lot, and left the remains there. He slept well that night and went to school the next day without any recollection of the event.

While he was attending classes, fragments of the offense intruded con-sciousness which resulted in some anxiety. He had some memory of an event, but he thought that it was a dream as opposed to reality. He looked in the trunk of his car, and finding the woman's eyeglasses, at this point, believed that he may have actually committed the murder. Following this, E. E. went to the lot where police officers had just discovered the body. He turned himself in and confessed.

Comment. In this case his memory was preserved, although the incident seemed unreal and dreamlike. He spoke about it with emotional detachment, typical of a flattening of affect found in such offenders, and used as a defense to insulate themselves from experiencing the impact of the reality of what had occurred. The emotional stress leading to the ego disintegration in this case, at least on the surface, was an injury to his pride system (Ruotolo, 1968), as the victim teased him when he was unable to get an erection. The very character of the victim's approach threatened him, and his fragile make-up was unable to deal logically with the situation. Homicide was a primitive reaction to a noxious stimulus where his logic was overwhelmed by the strong emotions attached to unresolved conflicts regarding his sexuality.

The chronic catathymic process is itself divided into three stages: incuba-tion, violent act, and relief. Depressed mood, loose and fluid thinking, as well as obsessive preoccupation with the victim characterizes the incubation period which may last for weeks, months, or even up to a year, in some cases. The individual comes to believe (for some reason) that the only solution to this state of tension is through violence. The thought of committing violence takes on a root-like fixation that cannot be shaken. In retrospect, the act seems ego-alien and of a dreamlike quality. In the early stages of this condition, such individuals will often seek attention through various mental health channels, but the idea of violence is usually dismissed as mere fantasy.

The following case of a chronic catathymic process is illustrative.

Case 6

A nineteen-year-old college freshman shot his girlfriend following a tumultuous two-year relationship. F. F. became romantically involved with the victim while they were both juniors in high school. The relationship became immediately intense. For the first year, the relationship was fairly smooth, but F. F. went into a depression and felt somehow "things are not right." They both planned to attend the same college together but these plans changed at the end of their senior year and she went to a different school, although both were in commuting distance of each other. F. F. began acting rather bizarre, calling her several times a day and making unannounced visits to her school. He denied being jealous, and felt the separation from her left him alone and alienated from his other college friends. He became depressed and began to drink moderately.

Slowly an idea to kill the victim emerged, and at first was rather ego-alien and "ridiculous." After several weeks, the idea "took hold" and eventually "I couldn't shake it loose." He bought a gun and, although he explained that "I never really thought it would happen," he also felt "it was what I had to do." He was unable to explain exactly why he believed violent thoughts emerged. He became obsessed with such thoughts until he actually carried out the act while they were together on spring break. Following the murder itself, he felt some degree of relief, at least, from the tremendous feeling of tension and depression that he experienced for the prior six months; however, he was devastated over what had occurred.

Compulsive Homicides

The compulsive homicides are on the extreme endogenous end of the motivational spectrum. They are entirely determined by inner psychological sources, with little or no environmental influence. The murder may be committed in a specific ritualistic manner or the homicide may be of a more diffuse nature, but in either instance an underlying common need to commit a violent act is present. Fantasies often precede the offense by many years. In some cases, homicides are repeated frequently, in serial fashion, or with intervals of many years between (Schlesinger, in press a). There are numerous examples throughout the literature of individuals who have served long prison sentences only to commit a similar act when on parole. For example, Guttmacher (1951) reported the case of an individual who killed two eleven-year-old girls while on parole from serving a sentence for attacking several women with a penknife. Guttmacher (1963) also reported the case of a forty-year-old man who was released from prison after serving a sentence for the murder and mutilation of a prostitute. Thirteen years later, he served an eighteen-month sentence for threatening a prostitute with a knife, and three years after this incident he killed and beheaded yet another prostitute.

Some compulsive murderers attempt to resist the urge but this frequently induces a great deal of inner tension. William Heirens, famous for his saying, "Catch me before I kill more, I can't help myself," (Freeman, 1955) had headaches when he resisted the urge to kill. He is quoted as saying, "I resisted for about two hours. I tore sheets out of place and went into a sweat. When I got these urges, I would take out plans and draw how to get into certain places. I would burn up the plans. Sometimes this helped" (Kennedy, Hoffman, and Haines, 1947, p. 118). There are other individuals whose homicidal compulsions, normally dormant, are released by disintegration of social order. Compulsive offenders of this type often have a better personality organization than those whose fantasies and impulses break through in violent acts without any environmental trigger. Most, if not all, of the compulsive murders are sexually determined.

In sadistic, compulsive, repetitive sexual homicide, there is very likely a fusion of sex and aggression. Freud (1905) believed that the sexual instinct has many components "some of which detach themselves to form perversions. Our clinical observation thus calls our attention to fusions, which have lost their expression in the uniform normal behavior" (p. 572). Additionally, a neurobiological substraight may underlie compulsive sexual homicide (Miller, in press). According to MacLean (1962), the limbic structures governing feeding and aggression are interconnected with the structures governing sexual functions. As an example, MacLean pointed to the display of genitals in the male squirrel monkey during a fight.

The following case previously reported (Revitch & Schlesinger, 1989) is illustrative of a compulsive sexually motivated adolescent serial murderer:

Case 7

A sixteen-year-old high school student with a history of sexual burglaries and destructive vandalism murdered two women and seriously assaulted a third. The first victim was his high school teacher. The week before the murder he had received an award from her and he stated in the interview, "I really had nothing against her." He described how he woke up at night, laid out his burglar tools, climbed out the window, and went to the teacher's home—allegedly to rob her. When she resisted him, he strangled her, took a few dollars, and ran out of the house. He slept well that night and was even surprised when someone told him the next day that she was found dead. He stated, "I didn't realize it."

The second victim was a sixty-two-year-old woman. He broke into her house and, when he found that she was not in, he waited for her for five hours. When she entered the house, he forced her to give him money. He then tied her up, gagged her, tore off her clothing, and beat her. He finally drowned her in a bathtub comparing this experience with the sadistic drowning of a dog several years before. He added, "I pulled and twisted her breasts. I just wanted to rob her." Following the homicide, he again slept well at night and went to school the next day as if nothing had transpired. He said, "I did not think I did it." In addition to these murders, he assaulted another woman, abusing her brutally for several hours. He twisted her breasts, gagged and blindfolded her, and finally left her for dead in a nearby park; however, she miraculously lived.

This youngster had begun breaking into houses two years prior to the murders. He reported a state of depersonalization during these acts. "It was like I dreamed it. One time while in the house, I thought 'holy cow! What am I doing here?'" A strong voyeuristic compulsion accompanied the break-ins. His life was replete with violence and humiliation at home. In addition to drowning a dog, he fantasized killing his brother and raping women. He was isolated, friendless, lonely, and spent much of his time in his room listening to the radio. When interviewed under the influence of sodium amytal injected intravenously, he revealed sadistic fantasies and a feeling of power and satisfaction when the victims begged him not to kill them.

PREDICTION AND PROGNOSTICATION

The current consensus is that mental health professionals can make some prognostic statements regarding future violence under some circumstances (Litwack & Schlesinger, 1999). Even though what we predict is frequently only a possibility and at times a probability, we should be able to offer some type of prognostic statement to law enforcement, governmental agencies, the courts, and others who are involved with potentially dangerous individuals.

Predictions are based on our classification system. It is clear that the situational offenders have the best prognosis. The sexually motivated compulsive offenders, particularly those with well-defined ritualistic patterns, have the worst prognosis. It is the compulsive offender, particularly the one committing dangerous sexual assaults and murders, who repeats the same offense following years of imprisonment. The prognosis for environmentally stimulated offenders will depend to a great extent on their value system, empathy, associations, and opportunity to commit crimes. Murder in these cases is just incidental and is less likely to be repeated. The impulsive and catathymic offenders have a better prognosis than the compulsive offenders, but not as good as the situational cases. The catathymic homicides usually resolve a conflict stemming from some conflictual relationship and therefore are not likely to be repeated. However, poor ego-integration with aggressive fantasies and compulsive features may on occasions result in a similar act.

Compulsive, catathymic, and many impulsive homicides are pathological and ego-dystonic, so that purely legal action will not deter or rehabilitate, but on the contrary will present a danger to society. These cases should be handled in specialized institutions or in special sections of correctional facilities. The situational and particularly the environmentally stimulated offenders should be treated in accordance with the current correctional model. This type of disposition would be more logical than one based on a sane/insane issue used in the legal system today.

OMINOUS SIGNS OF THE POTENTIAL SEX MURDERER FOUND IN CHILDHOOD AND ADOLESCENCE

Most research conducted in the area of violence risk assessment has been done with mentally disordered offenders with a history of aggressive acting out or who have made recent or distant threats (Monahan, 1981). Risk assessment in cases of a potential sex murderer is quite different in that there is often no overt psychosis or threats. In fact, in some potential sex murder cases, there may even be an absence of any history of interpersonal violence. Offenders who have already committed a sexual homicide have an extremely high likelihood for repetition, despite an absence of psychosis, good prison adjustment, high intelligence, denial of any aggressive ideation, and a display of good insight in psychotherapy. The potential sex murderer—a person who has not yet acted out, but presents serious concerns—represents a much larger group of individuals for whom risk assessment is critical and more complicated. A combination of the following signs (Schlesinger, in press b) have been found in the backgrounds of numerous individuals who have committed one or more sexually motivated compulsive homicides (see Table 2). Although no single sign is determinative, the greater the number present, the greater the tendency, proclivity, or strong probability of dangerousness.

TABLE 2
Ominous Signs When Seen in Combination Indicate Risk
for a Potential Sex Murderer

1. Childhood abuse
2. Inappropriate maternal (sexual) conduct
3. Pathological lying and manipulation
4. Sadistic fantasy with a compulsion to act
5. Animal cruelty, particularly against cats
6. Need to control and dominate others
7. Repetitive firesetting
8. Voyeurism, fetishism, and (sexual) burglary
9. Unprovoked attacks on females, associated with generalized misogynous emotions
10. Evidence of ritualistic (signature) behavior

1. *Childhood abuse.* Severe physical and psychological abuse is very common in the childhood backgrounds of sexual murderers. In the Ressler, Burgess, and Douglas (1988) FBI-sponsored study of thirty-six sexual murderers, all had a history of some type of severe abuse or neglect. Childhood sexual abuse has been shown to have particularly harsh consequences, frequently resulting in the abused becoming the sexual abuser (Burgess, Hartman, & McCormack, 1987).

2. *Inappropriate maternal (sexual) conduct.* Many researchers (Krafft-Ebing, 1886; Brittain, 1970) found sexual murderers to have disturbed relationships with their mothers. The image and behavior of the mother plays an important role in the psychosexual development of adolescent males. Adolescent boys need to have a nonsexual view of their mother; the notion that the mother is sexually promiscuous can be very destabilizing. Revitch and Schlesinger (1981, 1989) and Liebert (1985) found an unhealthy emotional relationship with the mother to be a key component in many cases of gynocide. The mother may be rejecting, punitive, and hated, or she may be overprotective, infantalizing, or seductive.

3. *Pathological lying and manipulation.* The potential sex murderer lies and manipulates. Unlike individuals with common behavior problems, their lying and manipulation is not only to escape responsibility for wrongdoing, but to achieve a sense of control, domination, and mastery over others (Douglas & Olshaker, 1995). Thus, they frequently lie and manipulate when they do not have to, and sometimes the desire to put something over on someone is so strong that they manipulate when it is to their ultimate disadvantage (Bursten, 1972). In many cases (Ressler et al., 1988) skill in

lying and manipulation that develops during adolescence is used in the commission of adult sexual homicides.

4. *Sadistic fantasy with a compulsion to act.* Sexual murderers frequently develop intense morbid fantasies as children and remain deeply immersed in their inner thoughts during their entire life. The fantasies involve themes of domination, control, revenge, and sexually sadistic aggression (Schlesinger, in press a). Ressler et al. (1988) concluded that sadistic fantasies of sexual murderers "begin in childhood, develop and progress until . . . these men are motivated to murder by way of their thinking" (p. 34). It is not uncommon for sadistic fantasies to emerge spontaneously during a routine examination of individuals whose behavior was not initially suspected of being potentially dangerous. While not all individuals who entertain sadistic fantasies act out (Crepault & Couture, 1980), the detection of such fantasy should still be considered a strong red flag since some individuals have entertained fantasies for over thirty years before eventually acting (Revitch, 1965).

5. *Animal cruelty, particularly against cats.* Sexual murderers, as children, frequently displayed early acts of sadism directed towards animals. Four out of nine (44 percent) of Johnson and Becker's (1997) study of adolescents with fantasies of committing sexual homicide, reported severe animal cruelty including one child who killed ten animals a day by lighting them on fire, stabbing, or shooting them. In another study, Myers, Burgess, and Nelson (1998) found a history of animal cruelty in 28 percent of their sample of adolescents who committed a sexual murder.

Revitch and Schlesinger (1981, 1989; Schlesinger and Revitch, 1997) reported many cases where cruelty to cats, in particular, was found in the histories of individuals who committed sexual murders. Felthous (1980) concluded from his research that "cats more than dogs seem to induce a child's sadistic projections and cruel behavior. A number of subjects in the study who had tortured cats admitted an intense dislike of this animal, in particular, but disclosed no insight into the animosity" (p. 175).

6. *Need to control and dominate others.* The need to control others is a significant aspect of sadistic gratification often mentioned by serial murderers and frequently is at the core of their behavior. MacCulloch, Snowden, Wood, and Mill (1983) emphasized the desire to control as the primary motivating force in sadism. Brittain (1970) noted the sadistic murderers' desire to have power over others as an essential part of their abnormality. Such a need for control over others typically first manifests itself in childhood in a variety of different ways. The future sex murderer may directly control other children through acts of play that escalate out of hand, or by threats of violence to intimidate. Ressler, Burgess, and Douglas (1988) found over half of their group of sexual murderers were cruel to their

peers when they were children and adolescents. Johnson and Becker (1997) described several adolescents with fantasies of becoming serial murderers, who expressed a strong need to have "total control over other people" (p. 336).

7. *Repetitive firesetting.* Firesetting has been noted in the childhood backgrounds of many sexual murderers. The sexual dynamics in arson, however, may not always be overt; they may, in fact, be covert, hidden, or less obvious (Banay, 1969) and often missed (Schlesinger & Revitch, 1997). Contrary to popular belief, firesetting by sexual murderers during their childhood does not frequently include an overt display of genitality (such as sexual arousal or masturbation while observing the flames). Thus, sexual motives may be more frequent than they appear because they may not be obvious in just one or two interviews, but may only surface after prolonged therapeutic involvement. A sense of mastery and dominance gained through repetitive firesetting is in many cases covertly eroticized in the same manner as the torture of animals and other sadistic acts. Myers et al. (1998) found 36 percent of their sample of adolescent sexual murderers had a history of firesetting.

8. *Voyeurism, fetishism, and (sexual) burglary.* Voyeurism and fetishism are two paraphilias very important in the risk assessment of sexual homicide. Ressler et al. (1988) demonstrated that sexual murderers had frequently engaged in these paraphilias since childhood; 71 percent of their sample engaged in voyeurism and 72 percent in fetishism. Both voyeurism and fetishism are directly connected to and motivate some acts of burglary. While most burglaries are committed solely for material gain, there is a group of burglars for whom material gain plays a secondary role or is rationalized. These break-ins are symbolic, often ego-dystonic, and sometimes outright bizarre. The more such offenses are compelling, the more likely they are sexually motivated.

The relationship of burglary to acts of aggression, including rape and sexual homicide, has been reviewed by Schlesinger and Revitch (1999) and Schlesinger (in press ©). Both paraphilias begin in late childhood and the burglaries often begin in adolescence. Fetish burglars sometimes soil the premises by urination, defecation, or ejaculation. Voyeuristic burglars are often not recognized by law enforcement or forensic examiners, because the sexual motivation is more covert and often the offender steals some objects of minimal value to rationalize the behavior that he does not understand. Voyeuristic burglary that is sexually motivated is therefore often incorrectly viewed as an unsuccessful burglary for gain.

9. *Unprovoked attacks on females associated with generalized misogynous emotions.* Unprovoked aggression against females, even if relatively minor, frequently precedes sexually motivated homicide. Most commonly, the vic-

tims are battered, choked, or knifed; usually without overt manifestations of genitality, such as rape, attempted rape, erection, or ejaculation (Revitch, 1980). Sometimes the offender may rip female clothes with some expression of sexual arousal or may unnecessarily attack a woman during a robbery, mugging, or quarrel, exerting more force than necessary to accomplish what would seem to be the primary crime. Such violent outbursts, even if they seem minor or insignificant, are often an important indication of underlying homicidal fantasies with a developing compulsion to act.

10. *Evidence of ritualistic (signature) behavior.* Many sexual murderers, particularly serial murderers, exhibit repetitive ritualistic behavior at the crime scene that goes beyond what is necessary to carry out the homicide. Thus, the offender injects an aspect of his personality by leaving his own unique "signature" or psychological imprint (Keppel, 1995). Unlike the offender's modus operandi (M.O.) which can change and develop as the individual learns and perfects techniques to carry out an abduction, rape, or murder, the signature remains relatively constant (Douglas, Burgess, Burgess, & Ressler, 1992). In such cases, committing a murder is not enough to satisfy the offender's psychosexual needs. Such murderers "must often act out fantasies in some manner over and beyond inflicting death producing injuries" (Keppel, 1995; p. 670). Examples of signature behavior include mutilation of the body, overkill, carving on the body, leaving messages, rearranging or positioning the body, engaging in postmortem activity, or making the victim respond verbally in a specified manner (Douglas et al., 1992).

Signature behavior stems from the offender's sexually violent fantasies which have been developing since childhood. Occasionally, early signs of ritualistic behavior emerge in adolescence reflecting the development of dangerous fantasies and the beginning of some form of serious acting out even if it is not initially violent. Revitch and Schlesinger (1981, 1989) reported the case of a 14-year-old who, on different occasions, forced at least two girls to undress and then stuffed tissue paper into their mouths. At age 18, he drove a 15-year-old female school mate to an isolated spot, where he tore off her clothes and stuffed her mouth with tissue paper after he killed her by strangulation. This homicide's pronounced ritualistic element was evident four years earlier by his use of tissue paper with the prior two victims. Thus, any type of behavior that seems odd, unnecessary, unusual or somewhat bizarre, especially when associated with an aspect of interpersonal control or violence, must be thoroughly evaluated with the likelihood of a ritualistic element noted.

TREATMENT AND INTERVENTION

Various techniques and problems encountered in psychotherapy and pharmacotherapy with violence-prone patients have been previously reported (Lion, 1972; Madden, 1977). While there are no specific psychotherapeutic techniques for treating murderers or potential murderers, many of the various psychotherapeutic approaches may be relevant and useful in a given case. Psychopharmacology can also help to reduce various symptoms and, in some cases, reduce the likelihood for acting out, particularly in those cases where symptoms reduce inhibitory controls. Therapeutic rapport and support cannot be overemphasized. The potential murderer needs someone with whom they can connect, someone who is available and willing to listen, and someone who can provide insight at later stages of treatment. Insight is very important, but so is expression of feelings and emotions, because of the cathartic effect (Schlesinger & Revitch, 1990).

The issue of control is also central in treating the potential murderer in an outpatient setting or even in an institution. Family members who might be involved with the potential adolescent offender should, if possible, be made aware of his problem. Often, the offender welcomes such control, as he may also want to control his own behavior. An understanding of the ominous signs and dynamics is very important, as many of these individuals are in treatment before a homicide actually occurs. Additionally, many individuals (except perhaps for the most notorious) are eventually released from prison. Treatment failures are often attributable primarily to the therapist's inability to recognize important prognostic signs prior to the offense, and to establish and maintain rapport and support after the offender has been released from an institution.

The effectiveness of therapy in preventing a sexual homicide is illustrated by a case previously reported by Schlesinger and Revitch (1990).

Case 8

A sixteen-year-old boy broke into and entered a house on three separate occasions. Three months after his first entry he entered the second time, and two weeks later he entered the third time. The first entry occurred early in the evening. He cut the door knob with a hacksaw and entered the premises while the inhabitants were out. During the first entry, the offender defecated on the bed. He later telephoned the home stating "next time you'll get pregnant." The second incident occurred early Sunday morning on his way to church. He found everyone still asleep. He explored and found some beer. After walking around the house carrying the beer bottle, he entered the bedroom of the fifteen-year-old girl (the homeowner's daughter) and hit her on the head with the bottle. He knew the girl from the neighborhood, and had fantasized about her a great deal. She was apparently attractive and popular while he was withdrawn and isolated. The third break-in occurred in the evening. The homeowner's youngest daughter was home, phoned for help, and the youngster was apprehended.

The offender had no previous record of antisocial activities. He was mild mannered, insecure, and his mother described him "as a good boy from the day of his birth." However, he engaged in a bizarre ritual of pillow-fighting with his mother from his childhood through the time of his arrest. In the background of this case is a seductive and overprotective mother and a dominating older brother who made the offender feel weak, inadequate, and shy with girls. The breaking and entering was sexually motivated, involving a fetish for female underwear. He stated that he became somewhat obsessed with the victim's underwear, "I couldn't get it out of my mind." He had daydreams about stabbing girls which had made him feel happy. He was followed in therapy for eleven years and gained insight; he improved in socialization and even got a girlfriend. Because of assets such as a good work history and an optimistic view of the future, his overall prognosis can be considered good.

DISCUSSION

This chapter presents homicide not as a unitary event but as a complex phenomena with different motives, dynamics, and prognoses. Various converging factors may lead to a similar act. The emotionally laden word *murderer* tells us nothing about the individual except that he killed. The legal classification of crime and homicide is a mere abstraction that may serve legal purposes for retribution, but it says little about the crime, and it is a poor and often useless prognostic guide.

Homicide is rarely a direct outgrowth of a primary psychiatric disorder, except in cases where there is an organic or toxic state, or paranoid psychosis where the homicide is a direct response to formed delusions. In search of a common denominator that may be used as a method of classification, the concept of motivational spectrum was developed (Revitch & Schlesinger, 1981). The motivational stimuli of crime in general, and homicide in particular, result in five distinct profiles of homicidal offenders that range from the entirely exogenous—environmentally and socially derived on one end of the spectrum—to the entirely endogenous, subconsciously determined on the other extreme. There will always be borderline conditions, as well as a mixture of stimuli, with one playing the dominant role. For example, a person with an impulsive lifestyle may harbor a compulsive need to commit a specific crime such as homicide. This compulsion may also be found in individuals with an occupationally and even socially stable life pattern. Motivational stimuli may not lead to a criminal act, but only to fantasies of the crime. However, such fantasies may result in acting out after many years of restraint, as was found in at least one case (Revitch, 1965).

Despite the many problems inherent in predicting violent behavior, risk assessment remains an important and necessary aspect of clinical forensic practice. We believe that the possibility, at times probability, and, occasionally, certainty of violence, can be predicted on the basis of our method of classification. The frequent tendency to equate dangerousness with psychosis leads to prognostic failures. In fact, even if an individual is psychotic, the criminal act may be socially determined and therefore the prognosis will depend on the surrounding social network and not on the psychosis. On the other hand, there are many individuals who are not clinically psychotic but who harbor dangerous homicidal compulsions. Such individuals are those who repeat the act after years of imprisonment.

The motivational stimuli of the criminal act should always be evaluated within the context of ego-organization, ethical standards, and capacity for empathy. Frequently the question is asked as to what do we evaluate, the offender or the act? In essence, we evaluate the act itself, but this fuses with the evaluation of the perpetrator. In general, the more we get away from the environmentally/socially stimulated crimes and homicide, the more purely psychogenic subconsciously determined factors play a role in the commission of the offense. The sexually motivated compulsive homicides are due to unresolved sexual conflicts. These offenders present more difficulty, and there are more failures in parole or rehabilitation.

Tanay (1975) has argued that the description of a tendency or probability is frequently confused with the prediction of an actual occurrence of an event. While an exact prophecy of homicide is impossible, some form of prognostic statement can and should be made based, in part, on the motivational spectrum as well as the ominous signs discussed in this chapter; these signs have been found in the backgrounds of scores of homicidal offenders–particularly sexual murderers. A cookbook statistical-like approach, although perhaps desirable (Monahan, 1997), will often miss the essence of the person. We agree with Malamuth (1986) who concluded that prediction should be based on the dynamic interaction, rather than the static summation, of various prognostic signs. He also argued that the evaluation should be viewed along a continuum of differing degrees of the inclination to act aggressively.

The ten ominous signs discussed in this chapter by no means exhaust all of the traits, characteristics, or behaviors of individuals with a potential to commit homicide. These signs, however, are most useful in differentiating the potential sex murderer from other individuals who might engage in other types of criminality. The impact of homicide is devastating, not only for the victims, and their immediate and extended families, but also for the community and even the entire country in highly publicized serial cases. Clinical judgment, an understanding of the various profiles of homicidal offenders discussed, as well as awareness of ominous signs will provide a helpful guide to risk assessment.

Unfortunately, the most experienced therapists often do not want to treat homicidal or potential offenders largely because of the risk of liability. Legal standards that were developed to protect citizens (*Tarasoff v. Regents*, 1976) may actually result in less protection since therapists, out of fear of legal entanglements or reprisals, are avoiding such cases. The potential offender, therefore, will continue without intervention. Hopefully, this situation will change so that mental health professionals become more willing to undertake the treatment of such potentially dangerous adolescents, and thus prevent tragedy.

REFERENCES

Banay, R. S. (1969). Unconscious sexual motivation in crime. *Medical Aspects of Human Sexuality,* Nov., 91-102.

Brancale, R. (1955). Problems of classification. *National Probation and Parole Association, 1,* 118-125.

Brittain, R. (1970). The sadistic murderer. *Medicine, Science and the Law, 10,* 198-207.

Bromberg, W. (1961). *The mold of murder.* New York: Grune & Stratton.

Burgess, A. W., Hartman, C. R., & McCormack, A. (1987). Abused to abuser: Antecedents of socially deviant behavior. *American Journal of Psychiatry, 144,* 1431-1436.

Bursten, B. (1972). The manipulative personality. *Archives of General Psychiatry, 26,* 318-321.

Corder, B. F., Ball, B. C., Halzlip, T. N., Rollins, R., & Beaumont, R. (1976). Adolescent parricide: A comparison with other adolescent murder. *American Journal of Psychiatry, 133,* 957-961.

Crepault, C., & Couture, M. (1980). Men's erotic fantasies. *Archives of Sexual Behavior, 9,* 565-581.

Dershowitz, A. M. (1973). Dangerousness as a criteria for confinement. *Bulletin of the American Academy of Psychiatry & Law,, 11,* 172-179.

Douglas, J. E., Burgess, A. W., Burgess, A. L., & Ressler, R. K. (1992). *Crime classification manual.* San Francisco:, Jossey-Bass.

Douglas, J. E., & Olshaker, M. (1995). *Mind hunter.* New York: Pocket Books.

Ellinwood, E. H. (1971). Assault and homicide associated with amphetamine abuse. *American Journal of Psychiatry, 127,* 1170-1175.

Felthous, A. R. (1980). Aggression against cats. *Child Psychiatry and Human Development, 10,* 169-177.

Freeman, L. (1955). *Before I kill more.* New York: Crown.

Freud, S. (1905). Three contributions to a theory of sex. In: *The basic writings of Sigmund Freud.* A. Brill. Trans. New York: Modern Library.

Guttmacher, M. (1951). *Sex offenses: The problem, causation and prevention.* New York: Norton.

Guttmacher, M. S. (1963). Dangerous offenders. *Crime and Delinquency, 9,* 381-390.

Guttmacher, M. S. (1973). *The mind of the murderer.* New York: Arnow Press.

Halleck, S. (1971). *Psychiatry and the dilemmas of crime.* Berkeley: University of California Press.

Haney, C., Banks, C., & Zimbardo, P. G. (1973). International dynamics in a simulated prison. *International Journal of Criminology & Penology, 1,* 69-97.

Hellman, D. S., & Blackman, N. (1966). Enuresis, firesetting, and cruelty to animals: A triad predictive of adult crime. *American Journal of Psychiatry, 122,* 1431-1435.

Johnson, B. R., & Becker, J. V. (1997). Natural born killers? The development of the sexually sadistic serial killer. *Journal of the American Academy of Psychiatry & Law, 25,* 335-338.

Kennedy, F., Hoffman, H., & Haines, W. A. (1947). A study of William Heirens. *American Journal of Psychiatry, 104,* 113-121.

Keppel, R. D. (1995). Signature murderer: A report of several related cases. *Journal of Forensic Sciences, 40,* 670-674.

Kraepelin, E. (1896). *Psychiatrie.* Leipzig: Johann, Abrosius, Barth.

Krafft-Ebing, R. von. (1886). *Psychopathia sexualis.* Philadelphia: F. A. Davis.

Lanzkron, J. (1963). Murder and insanity. *American Journal of Psychiatry, 119,* 754-758.

Lewis, J. A. (1975). Violence and epilepsy. *Journal of the American Medical Association, 232,* 1165-1167.

Liebert, J. A. (1985). Contributions of psychiatric consultation in the investigation of serial murder. *International Journal of Offender Therapy and Comparative Criminology, 28,* 187-200.

Lion, J. R. (1972). *Evaluation and management of the violent patient.* Springfield, Ill: Charles C. Thomas.

Litwack, T. R., & Schlesinger, L. B. (1999). Dangerousness risk assessments: Research, legal, and clinical considerations. In A. K. Hess & I. B. Weiner (Eds). *Handbook of forensic psychology* 2nd Ed. (pp. 171-217). New York: Wiley.

MacCulloch, M. J., Snowden, P. J., Wood, P., & Mill, H. (1983). Sadistic fantasy, sadistic behavior, and offending. *British Journal of Psychiatry, 143,* 20-29.

MacLean, P. D. (1962). New findings relevant to the evolution of the psychosexual functions of the brain. *Journal of Nervous and Mental Disorders, 135,* 289-301.

Madden, D. J. (1977). Voluntary and involuntary treatment of aggressive patients. *American Journal of Psychiatry, 134,* 553-555.

Malamuth, N. M. (1986). Prediction of naturalistic sexual aggression. *Journal of Personality and Social Psychiatry, 50,* 953-962.

Malmquist, C. P. (1996). *Homicide: A psychiatric perspective.* Washington, D.C. AmericanPsychiatric Press.

Mark, V. N., & Ervin, F. R. (1970). *Violence and the brain.* New York: Harper & Row.

Megargee, E. (1966). Undercontrolled and overcontrolled personality types in extreme antisocial aggression. *Psychological Monographs, General and Applied, 80,* 1-29.

Milgram, S. (1963). Behavioral study of obedience. *Journal of Abnormal and Social Psychology, 67,* 371-378.

Miller, L. (In press). The predator's brain: Neuropsychodynamics of serial killing. In: L. B. Schlesinger (Ed). *Serial offenders.* Boca Raton, Fla: CRC Press.

Miller, D., & Looney, J. (1974). A prediction of adolescent homicide: Episodic dyscontrol and dehumanization. *American Journal of Psychoanalysis, 34,* 187-198.

Monahan, J. (1981). *Predicting violent behavior: An assessment of clinical techniques.* Beverly Hills, Cal.if: Sage.

Monahan, J. (1997). The scientific status of research on clinical and actuarial prediction of violence. In: D. Faigman, D. Kaye, M. Saks, & J. Sanders (Eds). *Modern scientific evidence: The law and science of expert testimony.* St. Paul, Minn.: West.

Myers, W. C., Burgess, A. W., & Nelson, J. A. (1998). Criminal and behavioral aspects of juvenile sexual homicide. *Journal of Forensic Sciences, 43,* 340-347.

Pallone, N. J., & Hennessy, J. J. (1994). *Criminal behavior.* New Brunswick, N.J.: Transaction Publishers.

Perr, I. (1975). Psychiatric testimony and the Rashomon phenomenon. *Bulletin of the American Academy of Psychiatry and Law,* 3, 83-98.

Peterson, R. C., & Stillman, R. C. (1979). Phencyclidine: A review. *Journal of the Medical Society of New Jersey, 76,* 139-144.

Podolsky, E. (1956). The paranoid murderer. *Journal of Forensic Medicine, 3,* 149-151.

Reich, P., & Hepps, R. B. (1972). Homicide during a psychosis induced by LSD. *Journal of the American Medical Association, 219,* 869-871.

Ressler, R. K., Burgess, A. W., & Douglas, J. E., (1988). *Sexual homicide: Patterns and motives.* New York: Free Press.

Revitch, E. (1965). Sex murder and the potential sex murderer. *Diseases of the Nervous System, 26,* 640-648.

Revitch, E. (1975). Psychiatric evaluation and classification of antisocial activities. *Diseases of the Nervous System, 36,* 419-421.

Revitch, E. (1980). Gynocide and unprovoked attacks on women. *Corrective and Social Psychiatry, 26,* 6-11.

Revitch, E., & Schlesinger, L. B. (1978). Murder: Evaluation, classification and prediction. In: I. l. Kutash, S. B. Kutash, & L. B. Schlesinger (Eds). *Violence: Perspectives on murder and aggression.* San Francisco: Jossey-Bass.

Revitch, E., & Schlesinger, L. B. (1981). *Psychopathology of homicide.* Springfield, Ill.: Charles C. Thomas.

Revitch, E., & Schlesinger, L. B. (1989). *Sex murder and sex aggression.* Springfield, Ill.: Charles C. Thomas.

Rubin, B. (1972). Prediction of dangerousness in mentally ill criminals. *Archives of General Psychiatry, 27,* 397-409.

Ruotolo, A. (1968). Dynamics of sudden murder. *American Journal of Psychoanalysis, 28,* 162-176.

Satten, J., Menninger, K. A., & Mayman, M. (1960). Murder without apparent motive: A study in personality disorganization. *American Journal of Psychiatry, 117*, 48-53.

Schlesinger, L. B. (1996). The catathymic crisis, 1912-present: A review and clinical study. *Aggression and Violent Behavior, 1*, 307-316.

Schlesinger, L. B. (1999). Adolescent sexual matricide following repetitive mother-son incest. *Journal of Forensic Sciences, 44*, 736-749.

Schlesinger, L. B. (in press a). Serial homicide: Sadism, fantasy and a compulsion to kill. In L. B. Schlesinger (Ed). *Serial offenders*. Boca Raton, Fla.: CRC Press.

Schlesinger, L. B. (in press b). The potential sex murder: Ominous signs, risk assessment. *Journal of Threat Assessment.*

Schlesinger, L. B. (in press b). Serial burglaries: A spectrum of behavior, motives and dynamics. In L. B. Schlesinger (Ed). *Serial offenders*. Boca Raton, Fla.: CRC Press.

Schlesinger, L. B., & Revitch, E. (1980). Stress, violence and crime. In: I. L. Kutash and L. B. Schlesinger (Eds). *Handbook on stress and anxiety*. San Francisco: Jossey-Bass.

Schlesinger, L. B., & Revitch, E. (1990). Outpatient treatment of the sex murderer and potential sex murderer. *Journal of Offender Counseling, Services and Rehabilitation, 15*, 163-178.

Schlesinger, L. B., & Revitch, E. (1997). Sexual dynamics in homicide and assault. In: L. B. Schlesinger & E. Revitch (Eds). *Sexual dynamics of antisocial behavior*, 2nd Ed., (pp. 203-223). Springfield, Ill.: Charles C. Thomas.

Schlesinger, L. B., & Revitch, E. (1999). Sexual burglaries and sexual homicide: Clinical, forensic and investigative considerations. *Journal of the American Academy of Psychiatry and Law, 27*, 227-238.

Silva, J. A., Ferrari, M. M., Leong, G. B., & Penny, G. (1999). The dangerousness of persons with delusional jealousy. *Journal of the American Academy of Psychiatry & Law, 26*, 607-623.

Smith, J. T., & English, M. J. (1978). Alternatives in psychiatric testimony on dangerousness. *Journal of Forensic Sciences, 23*, 588-595.

Sutherland, E. H. (1947). *Principles of criminology*. Philadelphia: Lippincott.

Swanson, D. W., Bonhert, P. J., & Smith, J. A. (1970). *The paranoid*. Boston: Little Brown.

Tanay, E. (1969). Psychiatric study of homicide. *American Journal of Psychiatry, 125*, 1252-1258.

Tanay, E. (1975). Dangerousness and psychiatry. *Current Concepts in Psychiatry, 1*, 17-26.

Tarasoff v. Regents of University of California, 17 Cal. 3d. 425, 551 P. 2d. 334, 131 Cal. Rptr. 14 (1976).

Tinklenberg, J. R., Murphy, P. L., Darley, C. F., & Kopell, B. S. (1974). Drug involvement in criminal assaults by adolescents. *Archives of General Psychiatry, 30*, 685-689.

Walker, A. E. (1961). Murder and epilepsy. *Journal of Nervous and Mental Disease, 133*, 430-437.

Wedgwood, C. V. (1957). *The Thirty Years War*. Harmondsworth, Middlesex, England: Penguin Books.

Wertham, F. (1937). The catathymic crisis: A clinical entity. *Archives of Neurology and Psychiatry, 37*, 974-977.

Wertham, F. (1978). The catathymic crisis: In I. L. Kutash, S. B. Kutash, & L. B. Schlesinger (Eds). *Violence: Perspectives on murder and aggression.* San Francisco: Jossey-Bass.

Wolfgang, M. E. (1958). Patterns of criminal homicide. Philadelphia: University of Pennsylvania Press.

Yarvis, R. M. (1990). Axis I and Axis II diagnostic parameters in homicide. *Bulletin of the American Academy of Psychiatry & Law, 18*, 249-269.

Chapter Four

YOUTH VIOLENCE AND THE BRAIN

DANIEL E. MCNEILL

T HE COMPLEXITY OF HUMAN aggression and its causes cannot be explained by neurophysiology alone. Thus, our understanding of youth violence requires systematic examination of contributing factors. A large piece of this often puzzling and seemingly senseless behavior includes the relationship between brain functioning and behavior. One level of analysis of this relationship is by way of neuropsychology or neuropsychological examination. Neuropsychology is the measure of brain-behavior relationships and cognitive functioning by examining individual performance on standardized tests. Depending upon an individual's performance on neuropsychological tests, hypotheses can be drawn regarding the integrity of the brain. Areas of cognitive functioning assessed by neuropsychologists include: 1) memory; 2) language skills; 3) sensory, perceptual, and motor skills; 4) visual and spatial abilities; 5) mental speed, efficiency, and flexibility; 6) physical and mental coordination; 7) listening skills; 8) attention and concentration; 9) problem- solving skills; 10) reasoning; and 11) general intellectual functioning.

The following chapter describes the research examining the role of neuropsychological dysfunction in youth violence. It covers five areas of research: first, how youth violence manifests itself across the life span, with a brief discussion regarding the diagnoses of conduct disorder and antisocial personality disorder; second, an examination of the neuropsychology of violence, that is, which brain-behavior relationships are associated with juvenile violence; third, a synopsis of the implicated brain region; fourth, possible causes of neuropsychological deficiencies and theoretical views of how neuropsychological dysfunction interacts with environmental variables to culminate in violent behavior; and finally, violence prevention through the application of our understanding of the neuropsychology of violence.

VIOLENCE ACROSS THE LIFESPAN

Moffitt (1993) cites statistics from the literature indicating that the prevalence rate of antisocial behavior from childhood into adulthood appears to remain stable across development, ranging from 4 to 9 percent. His longitudinal research of 1,037 children found that 5 percent of the sample were considered extremely antisocial by three different raters biennially from ages three to thirteen (Moffitt, 1993). Lahey et al. (1995) found that approximately 50 percent of their sample of boys diagnosed with conduct disorder in the first year of their three-year study were rediagnosed at years two or three. It appears that the younger a child begins to engage in antisocial behavior, the more persistent his or her criminal activity is over the years. Farrington Gallagher, Morley, Ledger, & West (1986) found that boys who begin their criminal careers earlier in life have more arrest convictions than children who first offend when they are older. Moffitt (1993) describes juvenile violent offenders as either being *time-limited incidental* or *persistent and stable* into adulthood. The former classification he terms *adolescence-limited*. The delinquent behavior of these group members tends to be short-lived, and environmental and situational causes best explain the impetus of their antisocial behavior. The latter group members, termed *life-course-persistent*, are more likely to suffer neuropsychological dysfunction (Moffitt, 1993). How antisocial behavior manifests depends upon the age of the child. Difficult temperaments may be evident during infancy. Frequent fights, shoplifting, and lying might highlight the adolescent's criminal activity, and robbery and rape might be the offenses of the young adult. Antisocial behavior is highest during adolescence and decreases with age. Statistics indicate that by early adulthood the majority of former adolescent offenders cease criminal activity altogether (Blumstein & Cohen, 1987).

When examining the variables related to aggressive behavior the group of children and adults often studied have been identified with the diagnosis of conduct disorder and antisocial personality disorder, respectively. The diagnostic criteria from *Diagnostic and Statistical Manual of Mental Disorders,* Fourth Ed. (DSM-IV (American Psychiatric Association, 1994) for conduct disorder describes an enduring pattern of behavior in which the rights of others or societal norms are violated. Acts of aggression toward people or animals, destruction of property, lying or stealing, and disregard for rules exemplify this diagnosis. The diagnosis of Conduct Disorder may persist for people over the age of eighteen years, but the disregard for the rights of others may take on more severe forms in which then the diagnosis of Antisocial Personality Disorder is given. Individuals meeting the criteria for the latter diagnosis continue to disregard the rights of others by breaking the law, deceiving others, behaving impulsively, fighting or assaulting others, disregarding the safety of others, behaving irresponsibly, and lacking remorse for their actions (American Psychiatric Association, 1994). People with Antisocial Personality Disorder have also been identified as psychopaths or sociopaths. However, some authors believe the concept of psychopathy identifies a persistent personality type compared to the more behavioral diagnostic criteria of the DSM-IV (Lynam, 1998).

Identifying children with Antisocial Personality Disorder for research purposes is useful. Psychopathic adults are more likely to commit violent crimes (Hare & McPherson, 1984a; Harris, Rice, & Cormier, 1991). There would be utility in being able to identify these individuals early on as children. Harris, Rice, and Quinsey (1994) suggested the possibility of being able to identify psychopathy in childhood and argued for the construct of childhood psychopathy, and Lynam (1997) found that children identified as psychopathic were the most frequent and aggressive offenders. Interestingly, Raine et al. (1990) found that some children with severe Conduct Disorder have neuropsychological characteristics similar to adults with Antisocial Personality Disorder. It is not surprising that recently Eley, Lichtenstein, and Stevenson (1999) noted that antisocial behavior in children is a strong predictor of adult psychopathic criminality.

NEUROPSYCHOLOGY OF YOUTH VIOLENCE

Research on aggressive behavior and neuropsychological dysfunction has focused primarily on verbal abilities and executive functioning. Researchers of neuropsychological functioning of children identified as delinquents, both of the violent and nonviolent types, have consistently found a discrepancy on the Wechsler Intelligence Scales between Verbal Intelligence (VIQ) and Performance Intelligence (PIQ) in favor of PIQ (Lynam, Moffitt, & Stouthamer-Loeber, 1993; Tarter, Hegedus, Winsten, & Alterman, 1985). The Wechsler scales are commonly used measures of intelligence and consist of verbal and performance subtests. The verbal subtests, which contribute to VIQ, require the examinee to solve problems and give verbal responses using language skills. Performance subtests, on the other hand, which make up the PIQ, require the manipulation of objects (e.g., constructing block designs), have a time limit, and depend mostly upon visual-perceptual and motor skills. Language functions rely mainly upon the dominant left brain hemisphere (Borod, Carper, Naeser, & Goodglass, 1985). Thus, because VIQ tends to be significantly lower than PIQ in juvenile offenders, impaired verbal abilities are believed to be associated with youth violence. Lahey et al. (1995) also found that boys with lower VIQ, and who had a parent with Antisocial Personality Disorder, were more likely to have persistent behavior problems. The relationship between juvenile delinquency and IQ has also been substantiated in the opposite direction in which very high IQ may *protect* at-risk boys from criminal behavior (White, Moffitt, & Silva, 1989).

Differences in language functions have been supported by studies comparing psychopaths with nonpsychopaths on dichotic listening tasks (Hare & McPherson, 1984b; Raine et al., 1990). Dichotic testing involves presenting different stimuli simultaneously to both ears and the subject is required to report which piece of information is more clearly perceived. There is normally a tendency for a strong right-ear advantage because of dominant left hemisphere language processing. Hare and McPherson (1984b) and Raine et al. (1990) found reduced ear asymmetry in psychopathic adult prisoners. They hypothesized that the reduced asymmetry indicates weaker lateralization of language processing in the left hemisphere.

A number of theories attempt to interpret the relationship between impaired language functions and juvenile delinquency. Raine et al. (1990) speculated that language may play an important role in regulating behavior and that "psychopaths are less likely to use cognitive and behavioral strategies that rely on the verbal and sequential operations of the left hemisphere" (p. 274). Luria (1961) who described the importance of speech in controlling one's own behavior would also support this theory. Savitsky and Czyzewski (1978) questioned if verbal limitations impede the delinquent's ability to verbally identify the emotions expressed by others. Or perhaps delinquents are less able to resolve conflicts verbally and, therefore, are more likely to use aggression.

More recent research suggests that the relationship between VIQ and delinquent behavior might be better explained by deficits in executive functions. Executive functions relate to an individual's ability to initiate, monitor, and alter one's behavior as well as anticipate consequences of one's actions. Impulsive, inattentive, and hyperactive behavior have been included within the concept of executive dysfunction (Barkley, 1990; Block, 1995; Lynam et al.,1993; Moffitt & Henry, 1991). Block (1995) used the term *unresilient undercontrol* to describe impulsivity. He argued that VIQ tests require forethought and deliberate self-control. Compromised VIQ scores, therefore, are related to poor mental restraint. White, Moffitt, Caspi, Bartusch, Needles, and Stouthamer-Loeber (1994) also identified impulsivity as contributing to low VIQ in delinquent youth.

Childhood executive dysfunctions of hyperactivity, impulsivity and inattention (HIA) have been strongly linked with Conduct Disorder and Antisocial Personality Disorder (Lilienfeld & Waldman, 1990; Lynam, 1998). For example, Lynam (1998) found that boys with HIA and conduct problems most closely resembled psychopathic adults on various personality and neuropsychological measures when compared to other boys who were identified as either having conduct problems or HIA only. Moffitt (1993) described how the life-course-persistent antisocial youth is impeded by impulsivity and aggression. He theorized that impulse control difficulties can cause a child to engage in troubling behavior because the child desires immediate gratification and fails to anticipate the consequences of his or her actions. These children may also tend to perform poorly academically and socially and, therefore, have less economic opportunities. Consequently, they rely upon more deviant means to meet their needs. White et al. (1994) attempted to improve upon the operational definition of impulsivity. In their factor analysis of impulsivity measures, using a sample of 430 boys, two factors emerged. The first factor was related to a lack of behavioral control, which they identified as *cognitive impulsivity*. The second factor, termed *behavioral impulsivity*, most resembled the mental control that allows a child to switch between cognitive sets. The authors found that both cognitive and behavioral impulsivity were related to delinquency.

Seguin, Pihl, Harden, Tremblay, and Boulerice (1995) studied a large sample of boys to determine if boys with a persistent history of physical aggression could be differentiated by their performance on neuropsychological tests. They concluded that the strongest relationship was between boys with a long stable history of aggression and measures of executive functioning. Luengo, Carrillo-de-la-Pena, Otero, and Romero (1994) analyzed data from a large sample of boys and girls to determine if impulsivity was associated with particular aspects of antisocial behavior. They found impulsivity to be most closely correlated with disregard for rules, vandalism, and aggression. Thus, research has identified a strong relationship between executive dysfunction and youth behavior problems. It is widely believed that the brain region identified as the frontal lobes controls executive functioning.

A series of studies was conducted by Raine and colleagues using positron emission tomography (PET) to link the frontal lobes with violent behavior. PET identifies active brain regions that require energy from glucose during cognitive tasks. Raine, Buchsbaum, Stanley, Lottenberg, Abel, and Stoddard (1994) used PET to study the differences between twenty-two murderers or attempted murderers, who were found not guilty by reason of insanity, and a group of matched controls. They found that the group of murderers had less glucose uptake in the prefrontal cortex of the brain compared to the control group. Raine, Buchsbaum, and LaCasse (1997) expanded upon this study by increasing their subject pool to include forty-one murderers and forty-one control subjects. The group of murderers again had reduced metabolized glucose in the prefrontal cortex. It should be noted, however, that other regions of the brain were also shown to have reduced glucose metabolism, including the superior parietal gyrus, left angular gyrus, and the corpus callosum. Another study by Raine, Stoddard, and Buchsbaum (1998) examined the same forty-one murderers to determine if PET revealed differences between those subjects with histories of psychosocial deprivation (e.g., abuse, neglect, poverty, etc.) and those without such troubled backgrounds. The right orbitofrontal cortex was identified as having lower glucose metabolism in the subjects with psychosocial deprivation.

Studying individuals who have suffered brain injuries has also supported the frontal lobe theory of aggression. For example, Grafman, Schwab, Warden, Pridgen, Brown, and Salazar (1996) studied 279 Vietnam War veterans who had sustained penetrating wounds to the frontal lobes. Subjects with frontal ventromedial lesions were more likely to exhibit aggressive behavior than the control group and those patients who had injuries in other areas of the brain. Thus, the research literature has identified a strong relationship between violence and frontal lobe functioning.

ETIOLOGY OF EXECUTIVE DYSFUNCTION

The literature identifies a number of etiological factors contributing to executive dysfunction and violence. A few studies explored the role of genetic factors. Goodman and Stevenson (1989), for example, studied hyperactivity in monozygotic and dizygotic twins. They reported a concordance rate for hyperactivity at 51 percent for monozygotic twins and 33 percent among dizygotic pairs. The authors concluded that the heritability of symptoms of attention deficit/hyperactivity disorder (ADHD) was 30 to 50 percent. Slutske, Heath, Dinwiddie, Madden, Bucholz, and others (1997) studied 2,682 pairs of twins to determine the heritability of conduct disorder. Their findings indicated an estimated heritability of 71 percent. Eley, Lichtenstein, and Stevenson (1999) also studied monozygotic and dizygotic twins, looking at antisocial aggressive and nonaggressive behavior. They found that aggressive symptoms were related to genetic factors in both boys and girls and to nonaggressive behavior in girls. However, environmental factors had a more powerful influence on nonaggressive boys than did heredity.

Other factors associated with brain dysfunction and violence have been identified. Problems in the developing fetal brain because of maternal smoking (Brennan, Grekin, & Mednick, 1999; Fergusson, Woodward, & Horwood, 1998; Weissman, Warner, Wickramaratne, & Kandel (1999), maternal alcohol abuse (Fast, Conry, & Loock, 1999), and prenatal malnutrition (Neugebauer, Hoek, & Susser, 1999) have been implicated. Other variables studied have included exposure to lead (Masters, Hone, & Doshi, 1998;

Needleman, Riess, Tobin, Biesecker, & Greenhouse, 1996) and brain injury (Anderson, Bechara, Damasio, Tranel, & Damasio, 1999; Andrews, Rose, & Johnson, 1998; Rosenbaum, Hoge, Adelman, Warnken, Fletcher, et al., 1994). Research has revealed an association between child abuse and neuropsychological difficulties. Palmer and colleagues (1999) found that their sample of twenty abused children, compared to twenty nonabused children, had weaker VIQ scores and poorer performance on a measure of attention. Tarter et al. (1984) compared twenty-seven juvenile offenders who suffered child abuse with seventy-four delinquents without abuse. The abused group scored more poorly on tests related to verbal and attentional skills. In summary, neuropsychological dysfunction associated with youth violence can, in part, be explained by heredity and prenatal and postnatal factors. Barkley (1990) concludes:

> In the case of ADHD, it would seem that hereditary factors play the largest role in the occurrence of these symptoms in children....The condition can be exacerbated by pregnancy complications, exposure to toxins, or neurological disease, and by social factors (p. 104).

NEUROPSYCHOLOGICAL DEFICITS AND ENVIRONMENT

A child's neuropsychological difficulties interact with the interpersonal social environment in the development of antisocial traits. Moffitt (1993) presented a developmental taxonomy that describes how a child's neuropsychological difficulties predispose him or her toward antisocial behavior and aggression. Although he described two developmental paths towards antisocial behavior, adolescent-limited and life-course-persistent, it is the latter that has greater implications for neuropsychological functioning. Moffitt explained that subtle neuropsychological abnormalities in the infant can lead to the development of a difficult temperament. The neuropsychological problems and difficult temperament increase parental stress. Parents of such children may be psychologically handicapped themselves or unable to provide for many of the infant's needs. Thus, adverse conditions may emerge as the parents are ill equipped to rear a difficult child. Moffitt (1993) reported that "many sources of neural maldevelopment co-occur with family disadvantage or deviance" (p. 682).

The interaction of a vulnerable and problematic child evokes negative responses from the parents. Persistent antisocial behavior, according to Moffitt, develops as negative parental responses exacerbate the child's problems. The child develops a negative repertoire of interpersonal behaviors, which result in conflict with those around him. The child who has difficulty managing impulsivity and aggression is likely to be rejected by others. Opportunity to learn appropriate social skills diminishes as the difficult child anticipates rejection. In response to the expected rejection, the child may withdraw or act out aggressively. Behavior problems lead to poor academic performance, and educational and vocational advancement becomes more difficult.

SUMMARY

This chapter has described the role of neuropsychological functioning in youth violence by focusing primarily on delinquent children identified as having Conduct Disorder or Antisocial Personality Disorder. Such children are most likely to behave aggressively. A number of studies link executive dysfunction with violence and impaired performance on neuropsychological measures. Executive dysfunction also describes the symptoms in children with ADHD, such as impulsivity and poor anticipation of consequences. From studies of executive dysfunction and aggression, we recognize the importance of the role of the frontal lobes of the brain in executive functions and violent behavior. The causes of neuropsychological impairment in violent youth have been identified as both genetic and environmental. Studies of twins have found that hyperactivity, Conduct Disorder, and aggressiveness can be inherited. Other potential causes of neurological impairment involve neonatal and postnatal exposure to neurotoxins, injury to the brain, and traumatic stress. A theory of developmental taxonomy was reviewed to suggest how the negative interaction between neuropsychological impairment and interpersonal environment leads to antisocial personality.

INTERVENTIONS

Understanding the relationship between neuropsychological factors and youth violence can guide us in the application of prevention strategies. Because violent offenders with antisocial personalities are difficult to treat, primary prevention is necessary at all stages of a child's development. Appropriate prenatal care is imperative to prevent developmental difficulties. Economic policies that assist vulnerable families at risk for neurological impairment because of impoverished environments should be supported. Providing services in the community to promote a safe and healthy environment for expectant mothers is an important step toward preventing youth violence. Early intervention for children with impulsivity and attentional difficulties coupled with parenting training and parent support groups is also helpful. Using the assessment skills of neuropsychologists in pre- and elementary schools can help facilitate the early identification of at-risk children.

REFERENCES

American Psychiatric Association (1994). *The diagnostic and statistical manual of mental disorders–Fourth edition.* Washington, D.C.: American Psychiatric Association.

Anderson, S. W., Bechara, A., Damasio, H., Tranel, D., & Damasio, A. R. (1999). Impairment of social and moral behavior related to early damage in human prefrontal cortex. *Nature Neuroscience, 2* (11), 1032-1037.

Andrews, T. K., Rose, F. D., & Johnson, D. A. (1998). Social and behavioural effects of traumatic brain injury in children. *Brain Injury, 12* (2), 133-138.

Barkley, R. A. (1990). *Attention-Deficit Hyperactivity Disorder: A handbook for diagnosis and treatment.* New York: Guilford.Block, J. (1995). On the relation between IQ, impulsivity, and delinquency: Remarks on the Lynam, Moffitt, and Stouthamer-Loeber (1993) interpretation. *Journal of Abnormal Psychology, 104* (2), 395-398.

Blumstein, A., & Cohen, J. (1987). Characterizing criminal careers. *Science, 237*, 985-991.

Borod, J. C., Carper, M., Naeser, M., & Goodglass, H. (1985). Left-handed and right-handed aphasics with left hemisphere lesions compared on non-verbal performance measures. *Cortex, 21*, 81-90.

Brennan, P. A., Grekin, R. R., & Mednick, S. A. (1999). Maternal smoking during pregnancy and adult male criminal outcome. *Archives of General Psychiatry, 53*, 215-219.

Eley, T. C., Lichtenstein, P., & Stevenson, J. (1999). Sex differences in the etiology of aggressive and nonaggressive antisocial behavior: Results from two twin studies. *Child Development, 70* (1), 155-168.

Farrington, D. P., Gallagher, B., Morley, L., St., Ledger, R. J. & West, D. J. (1986). *Cambridge study in delinquent development: Long term follow-up.* Unpublished annual report, Cambridge University Institute of Criminology, Cambridge, England.

Fast, D., Conry, K. J., and Loock, C. A. (1999). Identifying fetal alcohol syndrome among youth in the criminal justice system. *Journal of Developmental and Behavioral Pediatrics, 20* (5), 370-372.

Fergusson, D., Woodward, L. & Horwood, L. J. (1998). Maternal smoking during pregnancy and psychiatric adjustment in late adolescence. *Archives of General Psychiatry, 55*, 721-727.

Goodman, R., & Stevenson, J. (1989). A twin study of hyperactivity: II. The aetiological role of genes, family relationships, and perinatal adversity. *Journal of Child Psychology and Psychiatry, 30*, 691-709.

Grafman, J., Schwab, K., Warden, D., Pridgen, A, Brown, H. R., & Salazar, A. M. (1996). Frontal lobe injuries, violence, and aggression: A report of the Vietnam Head Injury Study. *Neurology, 46* (5), 1231-1238.

Hare, R. D., & McPherson, L. M. (1984a). Violent and aggressive behavior by criminal psychopaths. *International Journal of Law and Psychiatry, 7*, 35-50.

Hare, R. D., & McPherson, L. M. (1984b). Psychopathy and perceptual asymmetry during verbal dichotic listening. *Journal of Abnormal Psychology, 93*, 141-149.

Harris, G. T., Rice, M. E., & Cormier, C. A. (1991). Psychopathy and violent recidivism. *Law and Human Behavior, 15*, 223-236.

Harris, G. T., Rice, M. E., & Quinsey, V. L. (1994). Psychopathy as a taxon: Evidence that psychopaths are a discrete class. *Journal of Consulting and Clinical Psychology, 62* (2), 387-397.

Lahey, B. B., Loeher, R., Hart, E. L., Frick, P. J., Applegate, B., Zhang, Q., Green, S. M., & Russo, M. F. (1995). Four year longitudinal study of conduct disorder in boys: Patterns and predictors of persistence. *Journal of Abnormal Psychiatry, 104* (1), 83-93.

Lilienfeld, S.O. & Waldman, I.D. (1990). The relationship between childhood attention deficit hyperactivity disorder and adult antisocial behavior reexamined: the pull of heterogeneity. *Clinical Psychology Review, 10*, 699-725.

Luengo, M. A., Carrillo-de-la-Pena, M. T., Otero, J. M., & Romero, E. (1994). A short-term longitudinal study of impulsivity and antisocial behavior. *Journal of Personality and Social Psychology, 66* (3), 542-548.

Luria, A. R. (1961). *The role of speech in the regulation of normal and abnormal behavior.* New York: Basic Books.

Lynam, D. R. (1997). Pursuing the psychopath: Capturing the fledgling psychopath in a nomological net. *Journal of Abnormal Psychology, 106*, 425-438.

Lynam, D. R. (1998). Early identification of the fledgling psychopath: Locating the psychopathic child in the current nomenclature. *Journal of Abnormal Psychology, 107* (4), 566-575.

Lynam, D., Moffitt, T., & Stouthamer-Loeber, M. (1993). Explaining the relation between IQ and delinquency: Class, race, test motivation, school failure, or self-control? *Journal of Abnormal Psychology, 102*, 187-196.

Masters, R. D., Hone, B., & Doshi, A. (1998). Environmental pollution, neurotoxicity, and criminal violence. In J. Rose (Ed.), *Environmental toxicology* (pp. 13-48). Newark, N.J.: Gordon and Breach.

Moffitt, T. E. (1993). Adolescence-limited and life-course-persistent antisocial behavior: A developmental taxonomy. *Psychological Review, 100* (4), 674-701.

Moffitt, T. E. & Henry, B. (1991). Neuropsychological studies of juvenile delinquency and juvenile violence. In J. S. Milner (Ed.), *Neuropsychology of aggression.* Boston: Kluwer Academic.

Needleman, H., Riess, J., Tobin, M., Biesecker, G., & Greenhouse, J. (1996). Bone lead levels and delinquent behavior. *Journal of the American Medical Association, 275* (5), 363-369.

Neugebauer, R., Hoek, H. W., & Susser, E. (1999). Prenatal exposure to wartime famine and development of antisocial personality disorder in early adulthood. *Journal of the American Medical Association, 282* (5), 455-462.

Palmer, L., Frantz, C., Armsworth, M., Swank, P., Copley, J., & Bush, G. (1999). Neuropsychological sequelae of chronically psychologically traumatized children:

Specific findings in memory and higher cognitive functions. In L. M. Williams & V. L. Banyard (Eds.), *Trauma and memory* (pp. 229-244). Thousand Oaks, Calif.: Sage.

Raine, A., Buchsbaum, M., & LaCasse, L. (1997). Brain abnormalities in murderers indicated by positron emission tomography. *Biological Psychiatry, 42*, 495-508.

Raine, A., Buchsbaum, M. S., Stanley, J. Lottenberg, S., Abel, L., & Stoddard, J. (1994). Selective reductions in prefrontal glucose metabolism in murderers. *Biological Psychiatry, 36*, 365-373.

Raine, A., O'Brien, M., Smiley, N., Scerbo, A., & Chan, C. J. (1990). Reduced lateralization in verbal dichotic listening in adolescent psychopaths. *Journal of Abnormal Psychology, 99* (3), 272-277.

Raine, A., Stoddard, S. B., & Buchsbaum, M. (1998). Prefrontal glucose deficits in murderers lacking psychosocial deprivation. *Neuropsychiatry, Neuropsychology, and Behavioral Neurology, 11* (1), 1-7.

Rosenbaum, A., Hoge, S. K., Adelman, S. A., Warnken, W. J., Fletcher, K. E., & Kane, R. L. (1994). Head injury in partner-abusive men. *Journal of Consulting and Clinical Psychology, 62* (6), 1187-1193.

Savitsky, J. C., & Czyzewski, D. (1978). The reaction of adolescent offenders and nonoffenders to nonverbal emotional displays. *Journal of Abnormal Child Psychology, 6*, 89-96.

Seguin, J. R., Pihl, R. O., Harden, P. W., Tremblay, R. E., & Boulerice, B. (1995). Cognitive and neuropsychological characteristics of physically aggressive boys. *Journal of Abnormal Psychology, 104* (4), 614-624.

Slutske, W., Heath, A., Dinwiddie, S., Madden, P., Bucholz, K., Dunne, M., Statham, D., & Martin, N. (1997). *Journal of Abnormal Psychology, 106* (2), 266-279.

Tarter, R. E., Hegedus, A. M., Alterman, A. L., & Katz-Garris, L. (1984). Neuropsychological, personality, and familial characteristics of physically abused delinquents. *Journal of the American Academy of Child Psychiatry, 23*, 668-674.

Tarter, R. E., Hegedus, A. M., Winsten, N. E., & Alterman, A. I. (1985). Intellectual profiles and violent behavior in juvenile delinquents. *The Journal of Psychology, 119*, 125-128.

Weissman, M., Warner, V., Wickramaratne, P. J. & Kandel, D. B. (1999). Maternal smoking during pregnancy and psychopathology in offspring followed to adulthood. *Journal of the American Academy of Child and Adolescent Psychiatry, 38*, (7), 892-899.

White, J. L., Moffitt, T. E., Caspi, A., Bartusch, D. J., Needles, D. J., & Stouthamer-Loeber, M. (1994). Measuring impulsivity and examining its relationship to delinquency. *Journal of Abnormal Psychology, 103* (2), 192-205.

White, J. L., Moffitt, T. E., & Silva, P. A. (1989). A prospective replication of the protective effects of IQ in subjects at high risk for juvenile delinquency. *Journal of Consulting and Clinical Psychology, 57* (6), 719-724.

Chapter Five

BULLYING AND HARASSMENT IN SCHOOLS

MICHAEL B. GREENE

ALTHOUGH THE PHENOMENON of bullying has been described in anecdotal reports since the eighteenth century (Aries, 1962), the scientific study of bullying and harassment, and corresponding attempts to establish and promote prevention and intervention strategies, have been undertaken only recently (Ross, 1996). With limited exceptions, these studies have been conducted in the Scandinavian countries, England, Australia, Canada, and recently in the United States.

The impetus for establishing the first systemic prevention and intervention program was the suicide in 1982 of three Norwegian boys between the ages of 10 and 14, suicides that were attributable to their being subject to chronic and severe bullying (Olweus, 1993a). Dan Olweus, who had begun an ongoing longitudinal study of bullying in the early 1970s, was asked by the Norwegian Ministry of Education in 1983 to oversee the implementation of a National Campaign Against Bullying (Olweus & Limber, 1999; Ross, 1996). Virtually all of the subsequent work in the field has been influenced by Olweus's initial and continuing writing and research.

In this chapter, I will summarize the literature on bullying and harassment in schools, highlighting and interpreting those aspects of the literature that have a direct bearing on prevention and intervention strategies. The chapter will be organized into four sections: 1) the nature and extent of bullying and harassment; 2) individual, interpersonal, and familial characteristics of bullies and victims; 3) the influence of peers and adults; and 4) preventive and intervention strategies.

Consistent with definitions in the literature, I use the terms *bullying* and *harassment* interchangeably. In general, bullying is a term that is applied to and used by younger children while harassment (or *diss'n* in common youth parlance) is a term that is typically used by adolescents and commonly, though not exclusively, associated with aggression that is sexual in nature.

NATURE AND EXTENT OF BULLYING AND HARASSMENT

In this section, I will present the essential components of bullying, elucidate varying types of bullying, and review data on the prevalence of bullying in schools. While adults certainly can bully one another in the school setting, this chapter will focus on situations in which students are victims of bullying by other students or adults in the school system, as well as students who bully their peers or otherwise participate in school-based bullying. Bullying behavior among children and youth, it should be noted, is most common at the school and on school grounds, more so than on the way to or from school (Olweus, 1993b).

Components

While there are some differences in emphasis among experts in the field about the components that constitute bullying, most acknowledge, either explicitly or implicitly, that there are five central features (Arora, 1996; Bjorkvist, Lagerspetz, & Kaukiainen, 1992; Bowers, Smith, & Binney, 1994; Craig, 1998; *Davis v. Monroe County Board of Education,* 1999; Farrington, 1993; Madsen, 1996; Olweus, 1993b; Olweus & Limber, 1999; Ross, 1996; Salmivalli, Lagerspetz, Bjorkqvist, Osterman, & Kaukiainen, 1996; Stephenson & Smith, 1989). Bullying, first and foremost, is a form of aggression in that the bully intends to cause harm to, or induce distress or fear in, the victim. Second, aggressive acts can be classified as bullying only if the aggression is unprovoked by antecedent verbal or physical aggression. Third, aggressive acts can only be classified as bullying if the aggressive behavior occurs repeatedly (either toward the same victim or by the same aggressor). Fourth, aggressive acts can only be classified as bullying if the bully has, or is perceived by the victim to have, more power than his or her victim (physically, status-wise, or intellectually). Bullying, therefore, is a type of aggression akin to child abuse in that there is always an imbalance of power between the bully and victim. Finally, bullying always occurs in relatively small social groups in which the members of the group know, or are familiar with, one another, for example, schools, families, prisons, units of the armed forces, or work settings.

While these five defining components have been used by researchers in the field, children's understanding of bullying is not nearly so inclusive. Five- and six-year-olds, for example, define bullying in very broad terms, such as, "bullying is something bad done to someone else" (Madsen, 1996, p. 15) and the idea of bullying as a repetitive form of aggression is first recognized by some but not all children at about age eleven (Madsen, 1996). Furthermore, parents and teachers frequently do not include all five components in their definitions, often excluding the notion of intentionality and repetition (Madsen, 1996; Boulton, 1993). Finally, high school-aged students tend to think of bullying as a physical form of aggression (Olweus, 1993b), as distinct from verbal harassment, and they associate bullying with younger children.

Because of these discrepancies between researchers on the one hand, and students, teachers, and parents on the other hand, some writers have suggested that the term *bullying* should not be used in surveys and peer or teacher nomination scales (Arora, 1996; Bosworth, Espelage, & Simon, 1999; Swain, 1998). Rather, these researchers argue that a more accurate assessment of prevalence rates can be derived from instruments that refer to concrete behaviors that explicitly or implicitly include the five components articulated above.

Types of Bullying

Bullying is generally defined to include physical, verbal, psychological, and gestural forms of aggression (Olweus, 1993b; Olweus & Limber, 1999). A small number of studies have reported on differential prevalence rates of verbal and physical forms of bullying. Some studies have found that verbal forms of bullying are significantly more common than physical forms among elementary and middle school children (Atlas & Pepler, 1998; Juvonen, Nishina, & Graham, in press; Rivers & Smith, 1994). Other studies suggest that physical forms of bullying are more common than verbal forms among male but not among female preschool and elementary school children (Craig, 1998; Crick, Cass, & Hyon-Chin, 1999; Perry, Kusel, & Perry, 1988). Developmentally, physical forms of bullying decrease as children move from the elementary to high school years (Boulton & Underwood, 1992; Craig, 1998; Olweus, 1993a; Perry, et al., 1988; Rivers & Smith, 1994).

Other than prevalence rates and overall developmental changes, we know very little about the differential dynamics, sequencing, and effects of verbal and physical bullying. There is, however, some evidence as well as anecdotal reports from the field, that verbal forms of bullying can evolve, for both the perpetrator and the victim, into physical forms of aggression (Boulton, 1993; Boulton & Hawker, 1997). Boulton (1993), for example, found that of all physical fights that were directly observed on a school playground, one-quarter appeared to be caused by *teasing.* Similarly, results from focus groups with middle and high school students in five New Jersey School Districts suggest that physical fights typically evolve from verbal disputes (L. Hirsch, personal communication, February 2, 2000). The students, moreover, stated that they neither possess nor use skills that would help them de-escalate verbal conflicts. The potential for explosive retaliatory behavior among chronic victims of verbal bullying was tragically illustrated in Columbine High School on April 20, 1999. Systemic longitudinal and ethnographic studies need to be undertaken to establish the nature, contexts, dynamics, and frequency of such sequential patterns.

There is an even greater paucity of discussion or analysis of the dynamic contributions of sexism, of antagonism toward developmental and learning disabled students, of racism, of homophobia, and other forms of bias in the bullying literature (McMaster, Connolly, & Craig, 1997; Ross, 1996; Sjostrom & Stein, 1996). Given the extraordinarily high documented rates of sexual harassment in the schools (American Association of University Women, 1993) and documented as well as suspected rates of bias-based harassment among children and teenagers (Bodinger-deUriarte, 1991; Kelly & Cohn, 1988), the near-absence of articulation between these two literatures should be addressed. Moreover, students may not encode or understand sexual harassment as a form of bullying, despite the fact that sexual harassment clearly fulfills the criteria for bullying behavior (McMaster, et al., 1997). One way to address bias-related harassment is through the establishment of school-based policies and regulations (Bodinger-deUriarte, 1991; U.S. Department of Education, Office of Civil Rights, 1999; *Davis v. Monroe County Board of Education,* 1999; also see section Preventive and Intervention Strategies).

By far the most frequently discussed and researched distinction between types of bullying is that between *direct* and *indirect* bullying (Atlas & Pepler, 1998; Craig, 1998; Crick & Bigbee, 1998; Crick & Grotpeter, 1995; Crick, et al., 1999; Graham & Juvonen, 1998; Lagerspetz, Bjorkqvist, & Peltonen, 1988; Olweus, 1993b; Olweus & Limber, 1999; Rivers & Smith, 1994). Direct bullying is a form of overt aggression that includes physical assaults (hitting, kicking, pushing), verbal or gestural threats to the physical well-being of the victims (often contingent on the victim giving something to or doing something for the bully), or verbal harassment or disrespectful comments about the victim (including racist or sexist remarks or remarks about what the bully perceives as an undesirable physical characteristic). Indirect bullying, sometimes characterized as *relational victimization,* is intended to harm a victim's social or friendship network or undermine a victim's social status. This form of bullying can occur through shunning, maligning, spreading derogatory rumors, and social exclusion and it may or may not occur through face-to-face interactions.

There is empirical support for distinguishing between direct and indirect bullying in that those who regularly engage in bullying behavior tend to adopt one but not both styles of bullying (Crick & Bigbee, 1998). Furthermore, there is evidence that indirect bullying has an increased and negative impact upon social adjustment, above and beyond the impact of direct bullying (Crick & Bigbee, 1998; Crick et al., 1999). Additionally, indirect bullying, as well as indirect victimization, is significantly more common among girls than boys (Batsche & Knoff, 1994; Bijttebier & Vertommen, 1998; Crick et al., 1999; Crick & Bigbee, 1998; Lagerspetz et al., 1988; Olweus, 1993b; Rivers & Smith, 1994; Sharp & Smith, 1991). This difference is not surprising given girls' greater concern with connection and relationships and boys' greater concern with dominance and assertion (Finnegan, Hodges, & Perry, 1998). Nevertheless, there is some evidence that gender differences in direct and indirect forms of bullying disappear or at least are narrowed during the adolescent years (Bijttebier & Vertommen, 1998; Rigby, 1998; Rivers & Smith, 1994).

Prevalence

There is little doubt that bullying is the most common form of aggression among school children. Nevertheless, rates of bullying and harassment in schools, as documented in the literature, vary tremendously, depending upon the instruments used to measure prevalence, the time period covered, the frequency rate of bullying that is used as the criterion (from several times each week to ever having happened), the age or grade of the population studied, and the particular setting.

Most of the large-scale surveys conducted in Scandinavia, England, and in the United States have used Olweus's Bullying/Victim Questionnaire (Olweus & Smith, 1995). In this questionnaire, bullying is defined through brief examples of physical and verbal, as well as direct and indirect forms of bullying, and students are asked a variety of questions about the frequency and circumstances of the bullying events. This survey, then, relies on students to consistently retain the definition presented. As suggested above, students may revert to their own definitions, ones that are likely to be more inclusive or at least different than the standard defined in the questionnaire. Alternatively, they may use varying definitions throughout the survey.

Other researchers have used self-report surveys in which subjects are asked to indicate how often they have engaged in specific behaviors that fulfill the researchers' criteria of bullying behavior (Bosworth, Espelage, & Simon, 1999; Juvonen, Nishina, & Graham, in press; Rigby & Slee, 1993). Still others have used peer nomination questionnaires or inventories. These can take one of two forms: 1) students are given a definition of bullying behavior with examples and asked to rate their peers on whether they have bullied or have been victims of bullying, and 2) students are asked to rate their peers on whether and to what degree they have engaged in, or been subject to, specific behaviors that the researcher believes to constitute bullying behavior (Juvonen, Nishina, Chang, & Ross, 1999; Perry, Willard, & Perry, 1990; Salmivalli, Karhunen, & Lagerspetz, 1996).

Teacher nominations of those who bully or who have been bullied are employed in still another type of measurement tool (Crick & Dodge, 1996). This type of instrument, however, may not be particularly useful since much bullying is perpetrated when adults are not present (Bosworth et al., 1999; Olweus, 1993b). Finally, a group of researchers in Canada have used video and audio recordings of children in natural settings, from which judgments are made about which behaviors constitute bullying (Atlas & Pepler, 1998; Pepler & Craig, 1995).

The most widely cited estimate of bullying behavior is derived from Olweus's surveys in Norway and Sweden of more than one-half million elementary and middle school children (ages seven to sixteen). Fifteen percent of the surveyed students were involved in bullying incidents during the prior semester; 9 percent as victims (35 to 40 percent of whom were bullied by a single individual), and 7 percent as bullies, with 1 1/2 percent classified as both a bully and a victim (Olweus, 1993b; Olweus & Limber, 1999).

Olweus & Limber (1999) noted that in the largest survey of bullying in the United States completed by Melton and others (cited in Olweus & Limber, 1999), middle school students in rural South Carolina reported signficantly higher rates of bullying behavior than in Scandinavia, despite using a stricter cut-off criterion: 23 percent had been frequently bullied (several times or more during the prior three months) and 20 percent reported that they had frequently bullied others. In a study of sixth and seventh graders in Los Angeles, Juvonen and her colleagues reported rates of bullying similar those in Olweus's surveys (using a peer nomination instrument): 11 percent had bullied others and 12 percent had been bullied (Juvonen et al., 1999). Other studies of bullying in the United States have documented rates of bullying and victimization as high as 70 to 80 percent (Bosworth et al., 1999; Clarke & Kiselica, 1997; Juvonen,et al., in press; Hoover, Oliver, & Hazler, 1992). Because researchers have used different instruments and criteria to assess the prevalence rates of bullying and victimization; we cannot determine whether or to what degree the variations in prevalence rates cited above are attributable to population-based sociodemographic, peer group, family, school, or communitywide ecological and economic differences.

Despite these wide-ranging prevalence estimates, some common patterns have emerged. First, with increasing age (from middle school through high school) the percentage of bullies remains relatively constant while the percentage of victimized students decreases precipitously (Boulton & Underwood, 1992; Hoover et al., 1992; Olweus & Limber, 1999; Salmivalli, Lappalainen, & Lagerspetz, 1998; Whitney & Smith, 1993). Second, the percentage of victims tends to be higher than the number of bullies throughout the elementary and middle school years (Olweus, 1993b; Ross, 1996). Third, a relatively small percentage of students—fewer than 10 percent—are bullied or bully frequently, usually defined as several times a week (Bosworth, et al., 1999; Olweus, 1993b; Olweus & Limber, 1999; Perry et al., 1988; Randall, 1995). And finally, a very small percentage of students—commonly estimated as less than 10 percent—are on both the giving and receiving ends of bullying behavior (Boulton & Smith, 1994; Duncan, 1999; Olweus, 1993a; Pellegrini, Bartini, & Brooks, 1999).

INDIVIDUAL, INTERPERSONAL, AND FAMILIAL CHARACTERISTICS OF BULLIES AND VICTIMS

While there have been only a handful of longitudinal studies to assess the within-individual stability of bullying behavior and victimization status, these studies suggest that those who bully continue to bully and those who are victimized by bullying continue to be victimized (Boulton & Smith, 1994; Egan & Perry, 1998; Juvonen et al., in press; Olweus, 1992; 1993b; Pulkkinen & Pitkanen, 1993; Salmivalli et al, 1998). This is not to suggest that once a bully or victim, always a bully or victim. As will be discussed in the next sections, there are both programmatic interventions as well as naturally-occurring factors and dynamics that can alter such trajectories. For example, there is some evidence that female victimization patterns are less stable than they are for males (Pulkkinen & Pitkanen, 1993; Boulton & Smith, 1994).

Given the relative stability within individuals of bullying-associated behavior, it is not surprising that the literature is filled with studies aimed at discovering common individual traits and family dynamics of bullies and victims. With respect to these characterizations, please note that here and throughout this chapter, I have referred to children and youth who bully and those who are the targets of bullying as *bullies* and *victims*, respectively. I have done this for purposes of conventionality and readability; however, these terms more properly should be used as adjectives to describe a portion of the circumstances and behavior of these children. I also want to point out that as social scientists, we tend to look at statistically significant differences among and within groups of individuals, differences which do not in any way imply thoroughgoing homogeneity. This is particularly true with respect to the characterizations summarized below; not all bullies and not all victims precisely fit these profiles and, in fact, for nearly every generalization there is at least one study with contradictory findings. The profiles can best be understood as trends that can help frame prevention and intervention strategies.

Bullies and Bully-Victims

Contrary to what one might expect, most studies suggest that children and youth who bully others do not differ from their non-bullying peers in their levels of self-esteem, anxiety levels, or in the degree to which they engage in pro-social behavior (Graham, & Juvonen, 1998; Olweus, 1993b; Pepler, Craig, & Roberts, 1993; Rigby & Slee, 1993). The four central psychological characteristics that typify bullies are: 1) an elevated need for dominance and control; 2) adeptness in selecting and manipulating submissive victims (highlighting the fact that bullies are not indiscriminately aggressive); 3) an elevated valuation of aggression as a method to resolve conflicts; and 4) a tendency to attribute hostile intentions in ambiguous situations (Batsche & Knoff, 1994; Bernstein & Watson, 1997; Bosworth et al., 1999: Graham & Juvonen, 1998; Juvonen et al., 1999; Lochman & Dodge, 1994; Olweus, 1993a). Temperamentally, bullies have been characterized as hot-tempered and impulsive (Bosworth et al., 1999; Olweus, 1978, 1993b). An important caveat to these findings is that these characterizations are most typical of male bullies who engage in direct (in contrast to indirect) aggression.

Several studies have examined how bullies fare in their social interchanges with their peers. Bullies tend not to be popular among their peers, particularly in middle school and high school, but, not surprisingly, they do maintain friendships and are popular with aggressive peers or peers that support aggressive behavior, the so-called birds-of-a-feather hypothesis (Clarke & Kiselica, 1997; Olweus, 1991; Pellegrini et al., 1999; Salmivalli, Huttunen, & Lagerspetz, 1997; Schwartz, Dodge, Pettit, & Bates, 1997). Juvonen and her colleagues (1999) found that while bullies tend to be popular with respect to their social status, they are not particularly well-liked by their peers. Finally, bullies tend to think of themselves as more popular than peer nominations would suggest (Graham & Juvonen, 1998; Zakriski & Coie, 1996).

Aside from studies conducted by Olweus, which, again, focus on direct bullying among male children, very little work has been undertaken to examine the family rearing practices or family dynamics among bullies. In terms of parenting styles, bullies tend to come from families that are permissive in that the parents do not set and enforce clear limits with respect to their children's aggressive behavior. When the parents do impose their authority, they do so with authoritarian methods, including physical punishment (Olweus, 1993b; Rigby, 1993). The parents of bullies also tend to be psychologically detached from, and uninvolved with, their children. Not surprisingly, these children do not feel particularly close to their parents (Olweus, 1993b). Finally, children who bully other children at school have higher than average rates of bullying involvement with their siblings (as bullies or victims) and, similarly, appear to be more concerned than are non-bullies with sibling power relationships (Bowers et al., 1994; Duncan, 1999).

The small subgroup of bullies who also are victimized by their peers (designated as bully-victims or aggressive victims in the literature) present a different, and significantly more dire, psychological and interpersonal profile. They differ from bullies in that their aggression toward peers is reactive or retaliatory in contrast to the skillfully manipulative and instrumental aggression that bullies tend to employ (Olweus, 1978; Pellegrini, 1998; Schwartz et al., 1997; Sutton, Smith, & Swettenham, 1999). In addition, these children—more so than bullies, victims, and those not involved in bullying behavior—are at heightened risk for depression and suicidal ideation, tend to be emotionally labile, manifest more behavioral problems at school, are unpopular among their peers, and have more contentious relationships with their siblings (Duncan, 1999; Juvonen et al., 1999; Kaltiala-Heino, Riittakerttu, Marttunen, Rimpela, & Rantanen, 1999; Olweus, 1978, 1991, 1993b; Perry, Kusel, & Perry, 1988; Schwartz et al., 1997). There is also some evidence that these children tend to come from physically abusive families (Bowers et al., 1994; Schwartz et al., 1997).

Victims

Victimization, unlike bullying, is not a volitional act; no one wants to be bullied. Furthermore, victims of bullying, as suggested above, are not randomly selected by their victimizers. While there have been no ethnographic or observational studies that document the process through which bullies identify their victims, a process that has been suggested is that bullies initially *sample* likely victims from among their peers and then narrow the field to those whom they continue to bully based upon whether bullying a particular child will accrue benefits and pose few risks (Perry et al., 1990). This implicit risk-benefit analysis, according to several researchers, leads to the selection of peers who are submissive and can be easily coerced. These victims are peers who blame themselves for their victimization, whose victimization will increase the bullies' social status (i.e., bullies do not pick on very popular or highly valued students), and who are easily distressed (Coie, Dodge, Terry, & Wright, 1991; Egan & Perry, 1998; Juvonen et al., in press; Olweus, 1993b; Pellegrini, 1998). Salmivalli and her colleagues (1996) found that it is not the most submissive children who are continuously victimized. Rather, bullies tend to target peers who initially respond aggressively but are relatively easy to subdue. The bully's status, therefore, is derived from beating off someone who fights back ineffectively. The most effective or constructive method to fend off continuing harassment, Salmivalli found, is a nonchalant response, a response that would seem to provide little in the way of increased status or satisfaction to the bully.

Given the foregoing selection process, it is not surprising that different teams of researchers in different continents and countries have uncovered a reasonably consistent profile of victims. Most concisely, victims of bullying (excluding the bully-victims described above and provocative victims described below) have been characterized as having internalizing psychological problems. These include depression, anxiety, shyness, insecurity, submissiveness, low self-esteem, and loneliness (Crick & Bigbee, 1998; Duncan, 1999; Egan & Perry, 1998; Graham & Juvonen, 1998; McMaster et al., 1998; Olweus, 1993a; Rigby & Slee, 1993; Kaltiala-Heino, et al., 1999; Slee, 1995).

There is some evidence that low self-regard, particularly low self-perceived social competence, is not only associated with victimization but also increases the likelihood that a child will continue to be victimized (Egan & Perry, 1998; see also Hodges, Malone, & Perry, 1997). Conversely, displays of enhanced self-regard function as a protective factor against subsequent victimization. It appears that positive self-regard somehow signals to bullies that a child is not, or is no longer, a good target for bullying. Furthermore, other studies suggest that continued victimization fuels pre-existing internalizing problems (Crick & Bigbee, 1998; Kochenderfer & Ladd, 1996). The relationship between victimization and internalizing problems is, therefore, bidirectional, and can best be conceptualized as a reciprocal and ever-engulfing negative feedback loop. Longitudinal studies, however, are required to verify this thesis.

Consistent with a pattern of internalizing problems, victims of bullying tend to maintain few friends, lack social competence and pro-social skills, and are generally rated low in popularity (social status) and peer acceptance (likeable, having close friendships) (Egan & Perry, 1998; Juvonen et al., 1999; Perry et al., 1988). Hodges and his colleagues (Hodges, Boivin, Vitaro, & Bukowski, 1999; Hodges, Malone, & Perry, 1997), however, found that reciprocated friendships can serve as a protective factor against psychological maladjustment among victims, moderating the link between victimization and internalizing problems. Furthermore, friendships tend to reduce the degree and extent of victimization. These protective functions, however, accrue primarily from friendships with higher status, nonvictimized children (Pellegrini et al., 1999).

In addition to the profile of victimized children presented thus far, there is a subgroup of victims who have been designated as *provocative* victims by Olweus and others (Olweus, 1978; 1993b; Ross, 1996; Stephenson & Smith, 1989). While the term provocative victim does convey the fact that these children are experienced by others as annoying, the term should be used cautiously as it could be construed as placing blame on the victim. Indeed, this term has been inappropriately and ominously applied to some female victims of dating, rape, and intimate partner violence. The so-called provocative victims typically violate one or more traditional social mores; for example, repeatedly interrupting discussions with tangentially related and self-centered stories or other forms of behavior that are perceived to be uncommonly obnoxious. The children who fit this designation tend to be anxious, have high levels of arousal, and a significant proportion of them manifest some or all of the diagnostic criteria for Attention Deficit Hyperactivity Disorder (see Whitney, Nabuzoka, & Smith, 1992). A dual approach is needed with such children: 1) assisting them in understanding, in a nonjudgmental and nonaccusatory manner, how they may provoke others and teaching them appropriate interpersonal skills; and 2) changing the school climate so that peers and school personnel become more understanding and more empathic with such children.

Research on the family characteristics and family dynamics of male as well as female victims provides some insight into the early establishment of personality characteristics that may render children likely targets of bullying. In general, these studies suggest that parents of victims adopt intrusive, unresponsive, and demanding parental styles that inhibit opportunities for assertion and age-appropriate strivings for autonomy (Ladd & Kochenderfer-Ladd, 1998). At the same time, these parents tend to be overprotective of, and overinvolved in, the lives of their children, thus creating enmeshed family systems (Bowers et al., 1994).

Additional studies have pinpointed gender differences with respect to the family dynamics of victims. These studies suggest that the parents of female victims tend to be coercive and unresponsive, with the mother perceived as rejecting, critical, and bossy (Finnegan et al. 1998; Rigby, 1993). The parents of male victims, on the other hand, tend to be overprotective (particularly so for mothers) and emotionally enmeshed (Bowers et al., 1994; Finnegan et al., 1998; Ladd & Kochenfenderfer-Ladd, 1998; Olweus, 1978). Not surprisingly, all of the parenting styles that are associated with peer victimization function to inhibit the age-appropriate development of negotiating and conflict resolution skills, making it difficult for these children to fend off bullies.

THE INFLUENCE OF PEERS AND ADULTS

Up to this point, I have focused almost exclusively on the nature of bullying and on the characteristics of bullies and victims. In this section, I will review what we know about the social and contextual influences that facilitate, if not stimulate, bullying behavior (the inhibitory forces will be discussed in the next section on prevention and intervention strategies). First, it is important to recognize that bullying behavior nearly always occurs in the presence of other students (Craig, 1998; Pepler, Craig, & Roberts, 1993). Indeed, the child who bullies typically receives social sustenance through the explicit or tacit support of many of their peers as well as from some adults (Atlas & Pepler, 1998; Clarke & Kiselica, 1997; Graham & Juvonen, 1998; Olweus & Limber, 1999; Pellegrini, 1998). Such support occurs through attitudes, norms, and through behavioral responses.

A number of studies have examined the attitudinal structure among students that supports bullying behavior. In a survey of Australian high school students, nearly half indicated that such behavior was "none of their business" and one in five indicated that they do not intervene because they fear being "picked on in return" (Slee, 1995). In another study, nearly one quarter of the children reported that they were "amused" by bullying incidents portrayed in a video (Boulton & Flemington, 1996). In yet another study, one-fifth of the students stated that they might join in if they saw someone being bullied (Whitney & Smith, 1993), and in still another study 29 percent said they would do nothing although they thought they should help (Boulton & Underwood, 1992). These studies and additional studies (Rigby & Slee, 1993; Randall, 1995) suggest that children who encourage bullying behavior, or at least refrain from actively objecting to it, do so both out of a relief that they themselves are not being victimized and/or with a disdain for the victimized children (see also Oliver, Hoover, & Hazler, 1994, and Perry et al., 1990).

Olweus and Limber (1999) have postulated a seven-point continuum of behavioral roles with respect to bullying behavior in what they call the *bully circle*: 1) initiating the bullying behavior, 2) actively supporting the bully (follower or henchman), 3) less actively supporting the bully, 4) passively supporting the bully, 5) disengaged onlooker, 6) showing disdain for the bully, and finally 7) defending the victim. For a slightly different categorization, see Sharp (1996).

There is some empirical support for such a continuum. Christina Salmivalli and her colleagues have developed and used the Participant Role Questionnaire (Salmivelli, Karhunen, & Lagerspetz, 1996; Salmivelli, Lagerspetz, & Bjorkvist, Osterman, & Kaukiainen, 1996; Salminvalli, Lappalainen, & Lagerspetz, 1998) in order to study the roles adopted by children with respect to bullying behavior. This peer nomination instrument includes a comprehensive definition of bullying and a series of questions that reflect the full range of responses embodied in the bully circle. Children are given a list of names of their classmates and they are asked to rate how often each engages in each of the described behavioral pattern (e.g., joins the bully when someone else has started it). Through this work, as well as the work of Sutton and Smith (1999), four roles, in addition to those of bully and victim, have been empirically derived: reinforcer (actively supporting and further provoking the bully, for example, through laughing or shouting support), assistant or follower (joins in once the bullying has started, acting more as an assistant than provocateur), defender (supportive or consoling to the victim), and outsider (doing nothing or staying away).

Several pertinent findings have emerged from these studies. First, individuals' self-rated scores, though generally correlated with peer nominations, tend to place the children in a more positive light than that suggested by the peer nominations. For example, those who are rated by their peers as bullies rate themselves as reinforcers and assistants (Salmivalli, Lagerspetz et al., 1996). Second, girls are more frequently rated by their peers as defenders than are boys and, conversely, boys tend to be rated by their peers as adopting the roles of assistant and reinforcer roles more so than girls (Salmivalli, Lagerspetz, et al., 1996). The research of Sutton and Smith (1999) supported these trends, as well as that of Randall (1995) who found that girls are more sympathetic to victims than are males. Third, Salmivalli and her colleagues (1998) found that those children most likely to defend the victim have friends who also tend to defend the victim.

In the single observation study that examined peer roles, Atlas and Pepler (1998) also observed significant involvement of peers in bullying incidents. They found that peers actively supported bullies in one-third of the bullying incidents (parallel to reinforcers in Salmivalli's classification), peers were onlookers in 13 percent of the incidents (parallel to Olweus's disengaged onlooker), and peers attempted to intervene on behalf of the victim in 10 percent of the incidents (though sometimes this was done inappropriately by aggressively attacking the bully).

In addition to the roles played by peer bystanders, teachers can play an influential role in facilitating or inhibiting bullying behavior (Batsche & Knoff, 1994; Clarke & Kiselica, 1997; Madsen, 1996). Some evidence of their inhibitory role derives from findings that bullying tends to occur most often in situations and locations in which teachers are not present or in settings in which the children can easily avoid observation (Atlas & Pepler, 1998; Bosworth et al., 1999; Olweus, 1993b). In addition, as Olweus points out, the deterence effect of a teacher's presence is weakened if teachers do not intervene in bullying incidents that they do observe, thus conveying to students their silent acceptance of such behavior (Olweus, 1993a; see Sharp, 1996).

In fact, several studies suggest that a significant proportion of teachers do not intervene in response to bullying incidents that they observe and, consequently, are not perceived by children and youth as helpful or responsive to their concerns or experiences with bullying behavior. In one study, for example, one-quarter of the teachers reported that it is "sometimes helpful to ignore the problem" (Stephenson & Smith, 1989). Boulton and Hawker (1997) found that teachers are particularly unresponsive to verbal, in contrast to physical, forms of bullying, viewing such interactions as a sort of rite of passage (see Clarke & Kiselica, 1997). Similarly, Olweus (1993a) noted that 40 percent of elementary school students and 60 percent of middle and high school students reported that teachers tried to "put a stop to it only once in a while" or "almost never" (p. 20).

In a study of twelve- to eighteen-year-olds in the Midwest, two-thirds of the self-reported victims indicated that school officials responded "poorly" to bullying behavior (Hoover et al., 1992). In Boulton and Underwood's study (1992) of eight to twelve year-olds in Great Britain, one-third of the students reported that teachers tried to intervene "sometimes" or "almost never" in one-third of such incidents. Even more dramatically, Atlas and Pepler (1998), in their observational study of classroom bullying, found that teachers intervened in only 18 percent of the bullying episodes.

Finally, there is some anecdotal evidence that teachers' lack of responsiveness may be exacerbated by their own active participation in bullying behavior. Middle school children often report that some teachers bully them through put-downs and other forms of degrading remarks, by blaming the victim, and through preferential treatment of certain groups (e.g., athletes and star students) over others (J. Fielder, personal communication, October 26, 1999; Ross, 1996). Clearly, much work needs to be done in educating and helping teachers and other school personnel to effectively address bullying and harassment in schools.

Parents also can play a significant role in addressing school-based bullying and harassment. Unfortunately, there is a dearth of information about how parents respond to or inquire about bullying behavior. Boulton and Underwood (1992) found that 42 percent of self-reported victims and 40 percent of self-reported bullies indicated that their parents had spoken to them about bullying. Interestingly, both figures were higher than corresponding figures for teachers' talking to the children. Olweus (1993b) reported slightly higher rates of parents speaking to their children about bullying than did Boulton and Underwood (1992), although he also found that the majority of parents did not engage their children in such discussions. These studies, however, include no information on what the parents said about bullying. Some of the parents may, in fact, have provided perspectives and advice regarding bullying and harassment but were less than helpful to their children.

PREVENTIVE AND INTERVENTION STRATEGIES

While several antibullying strategies have been presented in the literature, the most well-established program, and the only one that has been proven to be effective through rigorous evaluation research, is Olweus's Bullying

Prevention Program (BPP) (Olweus, 1993a; Olweus & Limber, 1999), which is presented below. Given the socially-embedded context in which bullying occurs and through which it is generally supported, most commentators have advocated that preventive and intervention strategies need to be implemented and coordinated on several levels: schoolwide, within each classroom, with parents and other family members, and with the students themselves. Correspondingly, representatives from each group need to be involved in the establishment of such strategies.

The first step in establishing preventive and intervention strategies entails consciousness-raising about the significance and importance of addressing bullying and harassment in a school or school district, a critical feature of BPP. The starting point for such a process can take the form of a guest lecture or workshop for teachers, administrators, and parents. Or, it could take the form of discussions in classrooms to ascertain the perspectives of students. Without awareness of the problem and corresponding commitment to address it by all parties, the program is likely to fail, if not in the short run, then certainly in the long run (Eslea & Smith, 1998; Ross, 1996; Sharp, 1996).

A critical component of BPP is a formal assessment of the nature and extent of bullying in each school. The primary methods for conducting such an assessment are an anonymous student self-report instrument (the most frequently used and psychometrically sound is Olweus's Bullying/Victim Questionnaire (Olweus & Smith, 1995) or a peer nomination instrument. The two most frequently used and psychometrically sound peer nomination instruments are are the Peer Nomination Inventory (Perry et al., 1990) and the Participant Role Questionnaire (Salmivalli, Lagerspetz et al., 1996).

These formal assessments need to be supplemented by informal and qualitative methods, e.g., focus groups, classroom discussions, parent group discussions, key stakeholder interviews, and thorough methods such as suggestion boxes. Students can also play a key role in the investigation and understanding of bullying and harassment, as well as in suggesting strategies to address these kinds of behavior (Collins, 2000; Kenney & Watson 1998; Sharp, 1996). The purpose of these informal and qualitative methods is to determine more specifically the contexts in which bullying occurs: where it occurs, who is present, the range of responses to the bullying by peers and adults, the power relationships between the bullies and the victims (physical, social or class status, intellectual), and the form or subtext of the bullying behavior. This subtext is represented by bias or exploitation based upon factors such as ethnicity, gender, social or physical characteristics, religion, sexual orientation, financial extortion, social gain, and so on.

Results from both formal and informal assessments can be used in conjunction with initial consciousness-raising efforts and should serve as the empirical foundation for establishing and implementing appropriate strategies. The assessments also should provide a basis for establishing overall goals, as well as short- and long-term objectives. The formal assessment should be used as a baseline measure to assess the impact of the program(s).

The next step is the establishment of an ongoing planning or coordinating committee that includes representatives from each of the key stakeholder groups, e.g., teachers, counselors, administrators, parents, and students (some would suggest that this should be the first step). Eslea and Smith (1998), based upon their three-year evaluation of the Bullying Prevention Program in England, strongly recommend that a "dedicated senior member of the staff" should serve as the leader or coordinator of this group in order to sustain the committee's work over time (see Olweus & Limber, 1999, p. 53, for a list of coordinator responsibilities). The tasks of this ongoing group are to assess and interpret the data, set priorities, articulate preliminary goals and objectives, formulate policies and procedures, discuss viable strategies and programs, establish a preliminary implementation time-line, and from time to time, assess the group's progress.

The key strategies that have been articulated in the literature, most of which are incorporated in the BPP, include

1. establishment of school policies and procedures,
2. training and/or workshops for school personnel,
3. regular classroom discussions,
4. social skills training programs and classroom-based curricula,
5. enhanced adult supervision of bullying "hot spots,"
6. family meetings and family counseling,
7. counseling for victims, bullies, and bystanders, and
8. ongoing assessment and corresponding strategy modification.

It is important to note that these are complementary strategies, none of which can be effective without the adjunct support of at least some of the other strategies. In short, bullying prevention and intervention requires a multidimensional strategy and involvement of multiple stakeholders.

Establishment of School Policies and Procedures

A key task and product of the bullying coordinating committee is the formulation of school or districtwide policies and procedures with regard to bullying and harassment. This should take two forms: 1. a policy statement and 2. a set of more elaborated procedures and processes. The policy statement should define what is meant by bullying and harassment including indirect forms of bullying and the various subtypes of bullying such as sexual and racial harassment. It should also articulate the general purpose of the policies and include a set of applicable rules and regulations as well as a statement of rights and responsibilities.

The policy statement should be as simple and straightforward as possible and ideally formatted for easy posting in key places throughout the school. Olweus, for example, recommends the adoption of four simple rules: 1) "We will not bully other students," 2) "We will try to help students who are bullied," 3) "We will make it a point to include all students who are easily left out," and 4) "We will tell a teacher and an adult at home when we know someone is being bullied" (Olweus & Limber, 1999, p. 31). Whatever policy statement is adopted, it is critical that it is widely distributed, displayed, and discussed. Unless all members of the school community are knowledgeable about the policy statement, problems will arise with respect to adherence and enforcement. Olweus (1993b) has also recommended the convening of a full-day school conference to discuss the policies and the corresponding procedures that are adopted.

The more elaborated set of procedures for reporting and responding to instances of bullying should include a series of graduated sanctions that are imposed when the rules and regulations are violated. These sanctions may range from a simple verbal reprimand to school suspension and, in severe cases, to police involvement. Olweus has outlined several guidelines for framing such sanctions, suggesting that they should be easy to administer, adapted to the developmental level of the student, and focused on the behavior and not the child (Olweus & Limber, 1999). Maines & Robinson (1992) has also recommended guidelines for responding to violations of rules against bullying through a system he calls the No Blame Approach. Several models of statewide policies to address harassment and hate crimes in schools, as well as instructive guidelines for developing such policies, have been included in a publication entitled *Protecting Students from Harassment and Hate Crime: A Guide for Schools* (U.S. Department of Education, 1999). The majority ruling by the Supreme Court in it's landmark decision regarding student-on-student sexual harassment, *Davis v. Monroe County Board of Education* (1999), is also very instructive.

The set of procedures should also include information about process. For example, it should designate who is responsible for receiving reports of bullying and harassment and who is responsible for imposing and monitoring the sanctions. Additionally, it should include basic due process provisions such as appeal rights and procedures, and include language that allows for some flexibility or discretion in interpreting the rules. The procedures, of course, need to be consistently and fairly enforced (Clarke & Kiselica, 1997; Olweus & Limber, 1999; Sharp, 1996) and the rules and regulations need to apply to teachers, counselors, and administrators as well. Because of the volatility associated with bullying and harassment, policies and procedures should be adopted that ensure the protection of victimized students as well as of nonvictimized students and teachers who report bullying and harassment incidents to school authorities (Atlas & Pepler, 1998; Olweus, 1993a). The fully elaborated set of procedures, as well as the policy statement, may be included as part of the school's disciplinary handbook or codes of conduct, or a separate booklet may be created..

In addition to negative sanctions specified in the policy, informal methods for rewarding or praising students for compliance and support of the policies should be suggested and discussed (see Olweus & Limber, 1999, p. 33). Similarly, it is important for teachers to model the kind of nonaggressive behavior that the policies are designed to promote. Indeed, the policies should be designed as much to promote positive, cooperative behavior as to deter negative behavior.

The goal is to change the outcome structure so that bullying and harassment are not reinforced, and so that cooperative, supportive behaviors are promoted (Sutton et al., 1999). Finally, the set of policies and procedures should be regularly reviewed and revised, with input from all of the key stakeholders. Without the involvement and full support of representatives from all these sectors, the impact and implementation of the established policies and procedures are unlikely to succeed (Eslea & Smith, 1998; Randall, 1995; Sharp, 1996).

Training and Workshops for School Personnel

Boulton (1997) surveyed teachers about their perceived capacity to respond appropriately to bullying situations. His finding, that the vast majority of teachers were not confident about their ability to respond appropriately to bullying and that 87 percent wanted more training in this area, speaks to the need for specific training for school staff. Olweus (1993b) recommends that small groups of teachers, five to ten per group, meet regularly to talk about bullying in their school, to share ideas and experiences, and to discuss the application of the school's policies and procedures and supplementary programs. He also recommends study groups for teachers and parents to discuss articles, books, and videos about bullying. Olweus (2000) has prepared a teacher handbook to help in these activities. Some of the recommendations, while desirable in school settings in the United States, may not be altogether practical nor realistic.

Three particularly important areas of training are 1) distinguishing playful teasing and rough-and-tumble play from bullying behavior (Boulton, 1993; Boulton & Hawker, 1997; Olweus, 2000; Ross, 1996); 2) promoting a classroom and school climate that undercut the typical social support that bullies receive (Clarke & Kiselica, 1997); and 3) identifying and responding to indirect bullying, which tends to be more hidden than direct bullying (Eslea &

Smith, 1998). Neese (1989) further recommends that school counselors conduct workshops for school personnel whose behavior may at times constitute bullying or harassment. This, of course, is a very sensitive topic, requiring clear and strong administrative support (Clarke & Kiselica, 1997). From a practical point of view, outside consultants may be better suited for this work.

Regular Classroom Discussions

The classroom provides an opportunity for all students to engage in discussions with their teachers about their experiences with, and observations of, bullying and harassment. These discussions can serve as vehicles to promote understanding about the nature and consequences of bullying and harassment and about various participant roles that peer bystanders adopt. Discussions can also provide the opportunity to experiment with classroom-based strategies to better address the specific forms of bullying and harassment experienced and observed.

In addition, the classroom discussions can provide a forum for discussing and elaborating upon the established school policies and procedures with respect to bullying. For example, it is often difficult for children and youth to report rule violations that they observe to adults in authority since this kind of behavior is often viewed as tattling on other students. Yet, most policies encourage such telling (Atlas & Pepler, 1998). Ross's (1996, pp.123-124) description of *the telling school* adds additional insight into this situation. Teachers can be helpful in facilitating discussions about the dilemma of tattling or telling. It is even more difficult for students to report instances in which they are bullied or harassed by teachers or other adults in the school. The policies, procedures, and corresponding protections must be crystal clear on this matter of reporting incidents.

The students might also choose to engage in classroom discussions about cliques, other forms of peer networks, and the possible roles these groups play in bullying and harassing behaviors (Salmivalli et al., 1998; Sharp, 1996). Teachers can help organize such discussions to encourage "outsider" children and youth to be paired with "in-group" children and youth for participation in cooperative, group projects. This may promote and develop friendship patterns, or at least empathy, across cliques and break the tendency for aggressors to associate with aggressors and victims to associate with victims (Salmivalli et al., 1998). Changing the group compositions and dynamics can begin to fracture the peer networks that actively or passively support bullying behavior.

In general, if students raise concerns about the policies and procedures, such as viewing them as unclear or inconsistently enforced, these concerns should be submitted to the ongoing bullying coordinating committee. Students may also want to make recommendations, based upon their classroom discussions, with regard to the policies and procedures. If the students raise concerns or make recommendations, it is important that these comments are addressed, or at the very least, that the students receive timely feedback from the coordinating committee.

Social Skills Training Programs and Classroom-Based Curricula

A variety of programs and strategies have been established to help students better cope with bullying and harassment. These may be organized into two types: social skills training programs and curricular approaches. Nearly all curricula that have been developed address deficits in the social skills of students, particularly conflict resolution techniques. Curricula, in contrast to training programs, tend to be much more structured and prescriptive, including a specific number of lesson plans. In addition, most curricula are designed for primary prevention, in which all students are addressed regardless of their involvement in bullying and harassment. In contrast, social skills training programs can be tailored to specific subgroups of students which can be adapted as secondary and tertiary prevention efforts.

Social Skills Training Programs

Several programs and strategies that have been discussed in the literature involve techniques that victimized and potentially victimized students can use to deter bullies (Ross, 1996; Sharp, 1996). Most of these have been designed to address direct verbal bullying. On the most general level, these programs teach fundamental assertiveness and interpersonal skills. While this approach with victimized or potentially victimized students has not been evaluated with respect to bullying and harassment, it does address deficits that have been articulated in the literature. Nevertheless, such training requires sustained and long-term commitment and, in many cases, should be supplemented with individual or group counseling.

Programs that are more specifically tailored to bullying have also been formulated (Boulton & Hawker, 1997; Perry et al., 1990; Ross, 1996; Sharp & Cowie, 1994). These programs are generally based on the principle of nonreward, not giving the bully what he or she wants. More particularly, such programs help children learn how to ignore taunting verbal assaults (Kellerman, 1991). Theoretically, the approach to ignore seems appropriate, particularly in light of Salmivalli's finding that a nonchalant response is reasonably effective in deterring such behavior (Salmivalli, Karhunen, et al., 1996). Nevertheless, a response of nonchalance, or even assertiveness, may be difficult for victimized children to muster in the face of their own limited interpersonal adeptness and the manipulatively skilled bully (Boulton & Hawker, 1997).

Other approaches have focused on teaching peers who witness bullying to come to the defense of students who are being bullied, thus undercutting and crippling the social support that many bullies enjoy. Sharp (1996) has discussed several strategies, emphasizing the importance of rehearsal and role-play to reinforce verbal defensive strategies. Similarly, Sharp and Cowie (1994) have recommended training peer helpers to intervene on behalf of victimized children. Strategies like these derive from a philosophical premise that the norms of the entire school should be channeled against bullying and harassment, drawing on the entire student body, not just victimized children, to make this happen.

On a more general level, at least two organizations have prepared tip sheets on how to combat racial harassment and other forms of bias-related behavior (Anti-Defamation League, 1999; Southern Poverty Law Center, 1998). Tip sheets are useful primarily in conjunction with an information campaign to address and stamp out discriminatory behavior.

Unfortunately, the potential of tailoring skills training to particular groups of children and youth, such as those who both bully and are bullied, has not generated much in the way of programmatic strategies. Tailoring programs for subgroups of students does pose the risk of stigmatization for participating students which should be addressed.

Classroom-Based Curricula

Several curricula have been developed to counteract general and specific forms of bullying. For example, a series of three curricula have been developed by Nan Stein and her colleagues (Stein & Sjostrom, 1996; Sjostrom & Stein, 1996; Stein & Copello, 1999). Other curricula include: 1) the Bullying Prevention Program companion curriculum (though not formally a part of Olweus's Bullying Prevention Program) developed by Sue Limber (1999); 2) Slaby's Aggressors, Victims & Bystanders curriculum (Slaby, Wilson-Brewer, & Dash, 1994); 3) Facing History (Strom & Parsons, 1982); 4) The Holocaust & Genocide (New Jersey Commission on Holocaust Education, undated); and 5) A World of Difference (Anti-Defamation League, undated). Unfortunately, none of these curricula have been adequately evaluated.

Several factors should be considered in choosing the best curriculum for each specific school or school district. First, the curriculum should encourage the students themselves, through active learning and creative processes, to come to an understanding about the nature and consequences of bullying and harassment. Second, the lesson plans should be founded on sound theory and a sound understanding of the bullying and harassment literature, including a focus on bystander behavior. Third, lesson plans should have sufficient flexibility to allow teachers and students to address the specific kinds of bullying and harassment problems that have been documented in the targeted school or district. Fourth, the curriculum should be consistent with the specific policies and procedures adopted by the school or district. Fifth, the lessons should be age and culture appropriate to the setting in which they will be used. Finally, the lessons should be engaging and stimulating for the students. Preferably, all students in the school should receive at least partial exposure to the curriculum.

Enhanced Adult Supervision of Bullying Hot Spots

Several studies have focused on the school playground as a place where a good deal of bullying occurs, primarily because adult supervision is generally less adequate than elsewhere in the school, with the notable exceptions of bathrooms and stairwells (Boulton, 1992, 1993; Olweus, 1993a; Pepler et al., 1993). Consequently, Olweus includes enhanced adult supervision as a core component of the BPP (Olweus & Limber, 1999; Olweus, 1993b). The determination of where enhanced supervision is needed should be dictated by data from the initial formal and informal assessments. Of course, as stated above, the teachers need to be trained in both the identification of bullying behavior and in the appropriate procedures established for intervention. If bullying incidents are perpetrated regularly on school playgrounds, school personnel and students should also examine how activities can be structured to better engage students and reduce opportunities for bullying.

Family Meetings and Family Counseling

Given the powerful influence that parental behavior and parenting styles exert on children, the finding that bullies and victims tend not to talk to their parents about bullying (Olweus, 1993b), and the mirroring of school-based bullying in the home setting (Batsche & Knoff, 1994; Duncan, 1999), no preventive and intervention program would be complete without involving and engaging parents. Additionally, it is critical that parents understand and support school policies and procedures with regard to bullying and harassment because parents can easily undermine both the philosophical underpinnings and operation of a bullying prevention program. For example, a parent might encourage a victimized child to physically strike out at his tormentor, or might have a very limited and inaccurate conception of what constitutes bullying, or might not view bullying as a problem (Madsen, 1996).

Olweus suggests three forms of parental involvement (Olweus, 1993b; Olweus & Limber, 1999). First, as noted above, he recommends parental representation on the planning or coordinating committee. Second, he recommends that parents should be fully informed about the program through meetings, telephone conversations, and through written materials. One key aspect the school policy should address is how the school communicates with the parents. For example, what are the procedures that the school has adopted in notifying the parent of a child who has been bullied, or has bullied? What are the steps that follow such notification? Correspondingly, parents need to be informed about who they can call at the school if they hear from their child that he or she has been bullied or has bullied others. Third, Olweus provides specific recommendations to parents about how they can work with their children to support the overall Bullying Prevention Program (Olweus & Limber, 1999).

In some instances, therapeutic family interventions need to be undertaken to address the family dynamics and the possible family dysfunction that can contribute to the perpetuation of school-based bullying and harassment. Unfortunately, very limited work has been conducted in this area (Morgan & Piccos, 1997; Oliver, Oaks, & Hoover et al., 1994). Nevertheless, two family therapy-oriented programs, functional family therapy and multisystemic therapy, have been shown through rigorous evaluation research to be effective in reducing aggressive behavior among youth, although they were not designed to address the specific problems of bullying and harassment (Alexander et al., 1998; Henggeler, 1998).

Short of professional therapeutic interventions, at least two groups have formulated suggestions or tips for parents in addressing bullying and victimization (National Crime Prevention Council, undated; Kidscape, undated). These sets of suggestions provide a supportive guide for helping parents help their children and for responding to their children's questions and concerns. If such supportive guides are adopted, telephone numbers of professionals who can further assist parents should also be provided, particularly for situations when severe problems emerge.

Counseling for Victims, Bullies, and Bystanders

Given the nature and extent of psychological problems experienced by chronically victimized students, professional counseling, individual as well as group, should be made available to such children and youth. The kinds of internalized psychological issues that need to be addressed in such cases are not atypical of those commonly addressed and treated by child and family counselors. On the other hand, bullies generally do not experience their behavior and general psychological well-being as problematic and, consequently, are less likely to voluntarily enter into treatment. Nevertheless, if the climate of a school shifts to one of disrespect for bullying behavior, this may serve to create the kind of psychological dissonance that is a prerequisite for treatment. Indeed, the effectiveness of counseling around bullying issues can be significantly enhanced if it is supported by such climate changes (Robson, 1997).

Therapeutic or self-help support groups, preferably with a trained facilitator, have also been suggested as a means through which students can come together to address the psychological and social issues related to bullying and harassment. However, there are some risks involved with such groups, such as stigmatization and exploitation of vulnerable children. These same concerns apply to peer counselor or peer listener approaches, which tend to place a great deal of responsibility on the counselor or listener. At a minimum, facilitators or peer counselors should be carefully screened, trained, and supervised.

The one type of counseling that is not considered appropriate is peer or adult-led mediation. As Olweus and Limber (1999) point out, bullying is a form of abuse in which a child's rights are violated; it is not a conflict among equals. The potential for stimulating feelings of humiliation and shame within the victimized child and the potential for subsequent retaliation renders such an approach irresponsible.

Ongoing Assessment

Rigorous evaluations of multidimensional bullying prevention programs are extraordinarily expensive and beyond the scope of expertise of most schools and school districts. While collaborations with university partners are desirable and helpful, full-fledged evaluations are still costly and require grant support. Nevertheless, yearly monitoring of programs is not only desirable, it is critically important. The most straightforward method of assessing progress is through the annual administration of the formal assessment instrument that is used to make the initial assessment. This method can inform all of the key stakeholders about how much progress has been made and whether progress has been made equally with regard to different forms of bullying and for different groups of students.

This kind of formal assessment, however, needs to be supplemented by regular and ongoing feedback from students, teachers, counselors, administrators, and parents. Through this feedback, the separate components of the program can be informally assessed. As in all endeavors designed to tackle complex human problems, the prevention and intervention strategies should evolve with greater understanding, experience, and progress. Formal and informal assessments need to guide this evolutionary process.

REFERENCES

Alexander, J., Barton, C., Gordon, D., Grotpeter, J., Hansson, K., Harrison, R., Mears, S., Mihalic, S., Parsons, B., Pugh, C., Schulman, S., Waldron, H., & Sexton, T. (1998). *Functional family therapy.* Boulder, Colo.: Institute of Behavioral Science, Regents of the University of Colorado.

American Association of University Women. (1993). *Hostile hallways: The AAUW survey on sexual harassment in America's schools.* Washington, D.C.: American Association of University Women Educational Foundation.

Anti-Defamation League. (1999). *Prejudice: 101 ways you can beat it.* New York: Author.

Anti-Defamation League. (undated). *A world of difference.* New York: Author

Aries, P. (1962). *Centuries of childhood.* New York: Vintage Books.

Arora, C.M.J. (1996). Defining bullying: Towards a clearer general understanding and more effective intervention strategies. *School Psychology International, 17,* 317-329.

Atlas, R. S. & Pepler, D. J. (1998). Observations of bullying in the classroom. *Journal of Educational Research, 92*(2), 86-100.

Batsche, G. M., & Knoff, H. M. (1994). Bullies and their victims: Understanding a pervasive problem in the schools. *School Psychology Review, 23*(2), 165-174.

Bernstein, J. Y., and Watson, M. W. (1997). Children who are targets of bullying. *Journal of Interpersonal Violence, 12*(4), 483-498.

Bijttebier, P., & Vertommen, H. (1998). Coping with peer arguments in school-age children with bully/victim problems. *British Journal of Educational Psychology, 68,* 387-394.

Bjorkqvist, K. L., Lagerspetz, K.M.J., & Kaukiainen, A. (1992). Do girls manipulate and boys fight? Developmental trends in regard to direct and indirect aggression. *Aggression Behaviour, 18,* 117-127.

Bodinger-deUriarte, C. with Sancho, A. R. (1991). *Hate crime: A sourcebook for schools confronting bigotry, harassment, vandalism, and violence* (ERIC # ED 334 523). Los Alamitos, Calif.: Southwest Regional Laboratory.

Bosworth, K., Espelage, D. L., & Simon, T. R. (1999). Factors associated with bullying behavior in middle school students. *Journal of Early Adolescence, 19* (3), 341-362.

Boulton, M. J. (1992). Participation in playground activities at middle school. *Educational Research, 34,* 167-182.

Boulton, M. J. (1993). Proximate causes of aggressive fighting in middle school children. *British Journal of Educational Psychology, 63,* 231-244.

Boulton, M. J. (1997). Teachers views on bullying: Definitions, attitudes, and ability to cope. *British Journal of Educational Psychology, 67*(2), 223-233.

Boulton, M. J., & Flemington, I. (1996). The effects of a short video intervention on secondary school pupils' involvement in definitions of and attitudes toward bullying. *School Psychology International, 17*, 331-347.

Boulton, M. J., & Hawker, D. (1997). Verbal bullying—the myth of "sticks and stones" In D. Tattum & G. Herbert (Eds.), *Bullying: Home, school and community* (pp. 53-63). London: David Fulton Publishers.

Boulton, M. J., & Smith, P. K. (1994). Bully/victim problems in middle-school children: stability, self-perceived competence, peer-perceptions and peer acceptance. *British Journal of Developmental Psychology, 12*, 315-329.

Boulton, M. J., & Underwood, K. (1992). Bully/victim problems among middle school children. *British Journal of Educational Psychology, 62*, 73-87.

Bowers, L., Smith, P. K., & Binney, V. (1994). Perceived family relationships of bullies, victims and bully/victims in middle school. *Journal of Social and Personal Relationships, 11*, 215-232.

Clarke, E. A., & Kiselica, M. S. (1997). A systemic counseling approach to the problem of bullying. *Elementary School Guidance & Counseling, 31*, 310-324.

Coie, J. D., Dodge, K. A., Terry, R., & Wright, V. (1991). The role of aggression in peer relations: An analysis of aggression episodes in boy's play groups. *Child Development, 62*, 812-826.

Collins, K. (2000). No place for bigotry. *Teaching Tolerance, 17*, 26-27.

Craig, W. M. (1998). The relationship among bullying, victimization, depression, anxiety, and aggression in elementary school children. *Personality and Individual Differences, 24*(1), 123-130.

Crick, N. R., & Bigbee, M. A. (1998). Relational and overt forms of peer victimization: A multiinformant approach. *Journal of Consulting and Clinical Psychology, 66*(2), 337-347.

Crick, N. R., Cass, J. F., & Hyon-Chin, K. (1999). Relational and physical forms of peer victimization in school. *Developmental Psychology, 35*(2), 376-385.

Crick, N., and Dodge, K. (1996). Social information processing mechanisms in reactive and proactive aggression. *Child Development, 67*, 993-1002.

Crick, N. R., & Grotpeter, J. K. (1995). Relational aggression, gender and social-psychological adjustment. *Child Development, 66*, 710-722.

Davis v. Monroe County Board of Education, slip o. 97-343. dec. (May 24, 1999).

Duncan, R. D. (1999). Peer and sibling aggression: An investigation of intra- and extra-familial bullying. *Journal of Interpersonal Violence. 14*(8), 871-886.

Egan, S. K., & Perry, D. G. (1998). Does low self-regard invite victimization? *Developmental Psychology, 34*(2), 299-309.

Eslea, M., & Smith, P. K. (1998). The long-term effectiveness of anti-bullying work in primary schools. *Educational Research, 40*(2), 203-217.

Farrington, D. P. (1993). Understanding and preventing bullying. In M. Tonry (Ed.)., *Crime and justice: An annual review of research*. (Volume 17). Chicago: University of Chicago Press.

Finnegan, R. A., Hodges, E. V. E., & Perry, D. G. (1998). Victimization by peers: Associations with children's reports of mother-child interaction. *Journal of Personality and Social Psychology, 75*(4), 1076-1086.

Graham, S., & Juvonen, J. (1998). A social cognitive perspective on peer aggression and victimization. *Annals Child Development, 13*, 21-66.

Henggeler, S. W. (1998). *Multisystemic therapy.* Boulder, Colo.: Institute of Behavioral Science, Regents of the University of Colorado.

Hodges, E. V., Boivin, M., Vitaro, F., & Bukowski, W. M. (1999). The power of friendship: Protection against an escalating cycle of peer victimization. *Developmental Psychology, 35*(1), 94-101.

Hodges, E. V., Malone, M. J., & Perry, D. G. (1997). Individual risk and social risk as interacting determinants of victimization in the peer group. *Developmental Psychology, 33*(6), 1032-1039.

Hoover, J., Oliver, R., & Hazler, R. J. (1992). Bullying: Perceptions of adolescent victims in the midwestern USA. *School Psychology International, 13*, 5-16.

Juvonen, J., Nishina, A., Chang, J., & Ross, J. (1999). *The "cool" and "wimpy" in middle school: A comparison of the social adjustment of bullies and victims.* Paper presented at the Bi-Annual Meeting of the Society for Research in Child Development, Albuquerque, N.M.

Juvonen, J., Nishina, A., & Graham, S. (In press). Peer harassment, psychological adjustment, and school functioning in early adolescence. *Journal of Educational Psychology.*

Kaltiala-Heino, R., Riittakerttu, M., Marttunen, M., Rimpela, A., & Rantanen, P. (1999). Bullying, depression, and suicidal ideation in finish adolescents: School Survey. *British Medical Journal, 319*, 348-351.

Kellerman, J. (1991). *Helping the fearful child.* New York: Norton.

Kelly, E., & Cohn, T. (1988). *Racism in schools: New research evidence.* Stoke-On-Trent: Trentham Books.

Kenney, D. J., & Watson, T. S. (1998). *Crime in the schools: Reducing fear and disorder with student problem solving.* Washington, D.C.: Police Executive Research Forum.

Kidscape (undated). *Preventing bullying – A parents guide.* http://www.uncg.edu/edu/ericcass/bullying/DOCS/kids3.htm.

Kochenderfer, B. J., & Ladd, G. W. (1996). Peer victimization: Cause or consequence of school maladjustment? *Child Development, 67*, 1305-1317.

Lochman, J. E., & Dodge, K. A. (1994). Social-cognitive processes of severely violent, moderately aggressive and nonaggressive boys. *Journal of Consulting and Clinical Psychology, 62*(2), 366-374.

Ladd, G. W., & Kochenderfer-Ladd, B. (1998). Parenting behaviors and parent-child relationships: Correlates of peer victimization in kindergarten? *Developmental Psychology, 34*(6), 1450-1458.

Lagerspetz, K.M.J., Bjorkqvist, K., & Peltonen, T. (1988). Is indirect aggression typical of females? Gender differences in aggressiveness in 11- to 12-year-old children. *Aggressive Behavior, 14*, 403-414.

Limber, S. (1999). *The Bullying Prevention Program: Supplemental lesson plans.* Clemson, S.C.: Clemson University, Institute on Family and Neighborhood Life.

Madsen, K. C. (1996). Differing perceptions of bullying and their practical implications. *Educational and Child Psychology, 13*(1), 14-22.

Maines, B. & Robinson, G. (1992). *The no blame approach.* Bristol: Lucky Duck.

McMaster, L. E., Connolly, J., & Craig, W. M. (1997). *Peer-to-peer sexual harassment in early adolescence: A developmental perspective.* Paper presented at the meeting of the Canadian Psychological Association, Toronto.

McMaster, L. E., Connolly, J., Pepler, D., & Craig, W. M. (1998). Sexual harassment victimization and mental health among early adoelscents. Poster session at the Biennial Meeting of the Society for Research on Adolescence, San Diego, Calif.

Morgan, A., & Piccos, J. (1997). Working with parents to manage children's behavior. In D. Tattum & G. Herbert (Eds.), *Bullying: Home, school and community* (pp. 17-28). London: David Fulton Publishers.

National Crime Prevention Council (undated). *Bullies: A serious problem for kids.* http://www.ncpc.org/10adu3.htm.

Neese, L. A. (1989). Psychological maltreatment in schools: Emerging issues for counselors. *Elementary School Guidance & Counseling, 23,* 194-200.

New Jersey Commission on Holocaust Education (undated). *The Holocaust & genocide.* Trenton, N.J.: Author.

Oliver, R., Hoover, J. H., & Hazler, R. (1994). The perceived roles of bullying in small-town midwestern schools. *Journal of Counseling and Development, 72,* 416-420.

Oliver, R., Oaks, I. N, & Hoover, J. H. (1994). Family issues and interventions in bully and victim relationships. *School Counselor, 41,* 199-202.

Olweus, D. (1977). Aggression and peer acceptance in adolescent boys: Two short-term longitudinal studies of ratings. *Child Development, 48,* 1301-1313.

Olweus, D. (1978). *Aggression in the schools: Bullying and whipping boys.* Washington, D.C.: Hemisphere.

Olweus, D. (1991). Bully/victim problems among school children In D. Pepler & K. Rubin (Eds.), *The development and treatment of childhood aggression,* Hillsdale, N.J.: Erlbaum.

Olweus, D. (1992). Victimization by peers: Antecedents and long-term outcomes. In K. H. Rubin & J. B. Asendorpf (Eds.), *Social withdrawal, inhibition, and shyness in childhood* (pp. 315-141). Hillsdale, N.J.: Erbaum.

Olweus, D. (1993a). Bullies on the playground: The role of victimization. In C. Hart (Ed.), *Children on the playground: Research perspectives and applications* (pp. 411-448). Hillsdale, NJ: Erbaum.

Olweus, D. (1993b). *Bullying at school.* Malden, Mass.: Blackwell Publishers.

Olweus, D. (2000). *Olweus's core program against bullying and antisocial behavior: A teacher handbook.* Bergen, Norway: Author.

Olweus, D., & Limber, S. (1999). *Bullying prevention program.* Boulder, Colo.: Center for the Study and Prevention of Violence.

Olweus, D., & Smith, P. K. (1995). *The Bully/Victim Questionnaire (English version).* Oxford: Blackwells.

Pellegrini, A. D. (1998). Bullies and victims in school: A review and call for research, *Journal of Applied Developmental Psychology, 19*(2), 165-176.

Pellegrini, A. D., Bartini, M., & Brooks, F. (1999). School bullies, victims, and aggressive victims: Factors relating to group affiliation and victimization in early adolescence. *Journal of Educational Psychology, 91*(2), 216-224.

Pepler, D. J., & Craig, W. M. (1995). A peer behind the fence: Naturalistic observations of aggressive children with remote audiovisual recording. *Developmental Psychology, 31*, 548-553.

Pepler, D. J., Craig, W., & Roberts, W. (1993). *Aggression on the playground: A normative behavior*. Paper presented at the Annual Meeting of the Society for Research in Child Development, New Orleans.

Perry, D. G., Kusel, S. J., and Perry, L. C. (1988). Victims of peer aggression. *Developmental Psychology, 24* (6), 807-814.

Perry, D., Willard, J., & Perry, L. (1990). Peers' perceptions of the consequences that victimized children provide aggressors. *Child Development, 61*, 1289-1309.

Pulkkinen, L., & Pitkanen, T. (1993). Continuities in aggressive behavior from childhood to adulthood. *Aggressive Behavior, 19*, 249-263.

Randall, P. (1995). A factor study on the attitudes of children to bullying. *Educational Psychology in Practice, 11*(3), 22-26.

Rigby, K. (1993). Some children's perceptions of their families and parents as a function of peer relations. *The Journal of Genetic Psychology, 154*, 501-513.

Rigby, K. (1998). The relationship between reported health and involvement in bully/victim problems among male and female secondary school children. *Journal of Health Psychology, 3*(4), 465-476.

Rigby, K., & Slee, P. T. (1993). Dimensions of interpersonal relations among Australian children and implications for psychological well-being. *Journal of Social Psychology, 133*(1), 33-42.

Rivers, I., & Smith P. K. (1994). Types of bullying behaviour and their correlates. *Aggressive Behavior, 20*, 359-368.

Robson, M. (1997). Developing pupil counseling and peer support initiatives. In D. Tattum & G. Herbert (Eds.), *Bullying: Home, school and community* (pp. 88-89). London: David Fulton Publishers.

Ross, D. (1996). *Childhood bullying and teasing.* Alexandria, Va.: American Counseling Association.

Salmivalli, C., Huttunen, A. & Lagerspetz, K. M. J. (1997). Peer networks and bullying in schools. Scandinavian Journal of Psychology, 38, 305-312.

Salmivalli, C., Karhunen, J., & Lagerspetz, M. J. (1996). How do the victims respond to bullying? *Aggressive Behavior, 22*, 99-109.

Salmivalli, C., Lagerspetz, K.M.J., Bjorkqvist, K., Osterman, K. & Kaukiainen, A. (1996). Bullying as a group process: Participant roles and their relation to social status within the group. *Aggressive Behavior, 22*, 1-15.

Salmivalli, C., Lappalainen, M., & Lagerspetz, M. J. (1998). Stability and change of behavior in connection with bullying in schools: A two-year follow-up. *Aggressive Behavior, 24*, 205-218.

Schwartz, D., Dodge, K. A., Pettit, G. S., & Bates, J. E. (1997). The early socialization of aggressive victims of bullying. *Child Development, 68*(4), 665-675.

Sharp, S. (1996). The role of peers in tackling bullying in schools. *Educational Psychology in Practice, 11*(4), 17-22.

Sharp, S., & Cowie, H. (1994). Empowering pupils to take positive actions against bullying. In P. K. Smith & S. Sharp (Eds.), *School bullying: Insights and perspectives* (pp. 108-131). London: Routledge.

Sharp, S., & Smith, P. K. (1991). Bullying in UK Schools: The DES Sheffield Bullying Project. *Early Childhood Development and Care, 77,* 47-55.

Sjostrom, L., & Stein, N. (1996). *Bullyproof: A teachers guide on teasing and bullying.* Wellesley, Mass.: Wellesley College Center for Research on Women.

Slaby, R. G., Wilson-Brewer, R., and Dash, K. (1994). *Aggressors, victims and bystanders: Thinking and acting to prevent.* Newton, Mass.: Education Development Center.

Slee, P. T. (1995). Bullying: Health concerns of Australian secondary school students. *International Journal of Adolescence and Youth, 5,* 215-224.

Southern Poverty Law Center. (1998). *Ten ways to fight hate.* Montgomery, Ala.: Author.

Stein, N., & Capello, D. (1999). *Gender violence/gender justice.* Wellesley, Mass.: Wellesley College Center for Research on Women.

Stein, N., & Sjostrom, L. (1996). *Flirting or hurting?* Wellesley, Mass.: Wellesley College Center for Research on Women.

Stephenson, P., & Smith, D. (1989). Bullying in the junior school. In D. P. Tattum & D. A. Lane (Eds.), *Bullying in schools.* Stoke-on-Trent, England: Trentham Books.

Strom, M. S., & Parsons, W. S. (1982). *Facing history and ourselves: Holocaust and human behavior.* Watertown, Mass.: International Educations.

Sutton, J., & Smith, P. K. (1999). Bullying as a group process: An adaptation of the participant role approach. *Aggressive Behavior, 25,* 97-111.

Sutton, J., Smith, P. K., & Swettenham, J. (1999). Socially undesirable need not be incompetent: A response to Crick and Dodge. *Social Development, 8*(1), 132-134.

Swain, J. (1998). What does bullying really mean? *Educational Research, 40* (3), 358-364.

U.S. Department of Education, Office of Civil Rights, (1999). *Protecting students from harassment and hate crimes: A guide for schools* (ERIC # ED 422 671). Washington, D.C.: Author.

Whitney, I., Nabuzoka, D., & Smith, P. K. (1992). Bullying in schools: Mainstream and special needs children. *Support for Learning, 7,* 3-7.

Whitney, I., & Smith, P. K. (1993). A survey of the nature and extent of bullying in junior/middle and secondary schools. *Educational Research, 35,* 3-25.

Zakriski, A. L., & Coie, J. D. (1996). A comparison of aggressive-rejected and nonaggressive-rejected children's interpretations of self-directed and other-directed rejection. *Child Development, 67,* 1048-1070.

Chapter Six

WHEN YOUR CHILD IS MOLESTED BY A YOUTH: FIGHTING DENIAL

MARIA LUISA BRIONES

IN THE FOLLOWING CHAPTER, I hope to directly address not only the professionals and adults who work with children who have been sexually abused by juvenile perpetrators, but also the parents (I use this term generally to refer to all primary caretakers) of these child abuse victims. The information shared here may also be useful to all families and their children who have been sexually molested by anyone.

There are children who have great confidence in their parents and are able to reveal to them incidents of sexual molestation. Most, however, have difficulty doing so, while others would prefer never to speak of these incidents altogether. I write this for those children, those silent and precious gifts, who have every right to be protected by their parents but are not because of fear, embarrassment, uncertainty, or simply because their parents are unaware of their rights as parents to protect their precious gifts. There are other parents who confuse keeping quiet with *civil behavior*.

REACTIONS AND REVELATIONS

A phone rings:

Mom, remember what you said about good touch and bad touch?

Yes. Why?

Well…I had the bad touch.

Are you okay? What happened? Who did it? When? Why?

All these questions ensue. Like many other children, there is very little information given, minimizing the extent and type of abuse. Then the child begins to defend the abuser:

…but, he's my best friend, Mom!

Best friends don't do such things!

The conversation continues with much listening and brief questioning on the part of the mother. She is reassuring and calm, although completely shocked with what she is hearing. Her son on the other end of the phone line is downplaying the account for fear of being taken out of the boarding school, separated from his friends, and returned home. The mother wants to end the conversation immediately to make reservations for the first flight in the morning to see her son, to be with him and reassure herself. She ends the conversation telling him: "We'll talk more about it when I see you . . . I love you. God bless you." Unknown to the child, this mother is taking the first flight out the next day just to be able to hug her child, love him, and see with her own eyes that he is fine.

Another phone rings. Another child calling from a boarding school telling his mother an older boy in school sexually molested him:

Mom, I have to tell you something that happened to me here in school.

He proceeds to tell her how and by whom. Like most mothers, she is shocked and stunned. She doesn't know what to do or say but is able to calmly give her child a very reassuring and most important statement: *I love you.* She continues:

I'll wait to hear from school about this incident and see what they will do. However, we can't do much because we are poor, you are on scholarship, and we owe the school a lot of favors.

This time no phone rings. It is a father talking to his son after learning of the sexual molestation incidents that occurred in his son's dorm.

Son, is it true that you were sexually molested?

Yes, Dad.

With great sadness in his eyes, the boy tells his dad what happened. Again, the victim must relive the fear and embarrassment as he discloses the abuse to his father. To have been sexually molested is traumatic enough. To confess the molestation to a parent can be just as traumatic, especially if the parent doubts or, in a classic attempt at denial, believes that maybe the child misinterpreted the alleged abuser's actions. These disclosures are extremely painful for children to initiate, much less to admit that the abuse occurred. The boy's father reassures his son that everything will be fine and adds: "Do not tell your mom anything about this. She will be devastated. No one is to know about it. You don't have to talk to anyone and I am not talking to anyone about it either." The father proceeds to quote Scripture:

Things that make people fall into sin are bound to happen,
but how terrible for the one who makes it happen! It would be better
for him if a large millstone were tied around his neck and he were
thrown into the sea than for him to cause one of these little ones to sin
(Luke 17:1-2).

Each of the revelations above certainly provokes the requisite emotions of anger, outrage, disbelief, and devastation. These are the very normal emotions. Yet, some of these emotions may be difficult to admit to oneself. Which parents want to admit that at the initial moment, when their child has first disclosed the abuse, when it has first registered, they felt a moment of overwhelming disbelief–that they doubted their child? Denial and initial doubt can be human responses to situations of threat or trauma. However, what happens next is critical: Will the parent accuse the child of lying, of making up stories? In the above vignettes, all of the parents acted with love, warmth, calm, and lack of condemnation. They reassured their children, that regardless of the horror they experienced, these children would still be loved, cherished, and, most significantly, accepted. Despite the commonality of reassurance and love, the ultimate reactions of the parents to these situations varied from action to inaction to suppressed anger.

Discovering the abuse also produces grief, an emotion similar to what one experiences in a divorce, after the death of a loved one, or with any significant loss. In *When Your Child Has Been Molested,* Kathryn B. Hagans and Joyce Case (1988) describe in detail the grief process that most parents experience after learning of their child's sexual molestation. The grief process includes the stages of denial, anger, guilt, depression, bargaining, and acceptance.

SHOCK AND THE AFTERMATH

Robert Townley, author of *Safe and Sound: A Parent's Guide to Child Protection* (1985) writes: ". . . for your child's sake: feel the outrage, but don't disbelieve (p. 178)." Yes, feel the outrage, the shock, but please believe in your child. Townley further writes that disbelief can only retraumatize a child. Not believing, or even being indifferent or noncommittal, can only be harmful. Young children have a difficult time fabricating stories about molestation because of their very limited knowledge and vocabulary regarding sexual acts. Lying is unlikely. Very few victims exaggerate what has happened to them. Most likely, they minimize their descriptions. Fear of punishment, fear of making the parent angry, or fear of being called a liar are some of the risks taken by a child who reports. The chances that a child is exaggerating are slim.

Most parents know their children well enough to be able to determine when lying is taking place. Unfortunately, it is often as a result of shock that we react with disbelief. This disbelief or denial is a mechanism or effort to protect ourselves from the emotional violation we may experience when we hear of the physical and sexual violation of our own flesh and blood. We must educate ourselves and be very clear about the harm of disbelief. Believing the victim is vital to emotional recovery and mental health.

Hagans and Case (1988) also describe how most often sexually molested children are terrorized by their predators in order to remain silent. So any disclosure is a risk and a major step for the child. Taking this risk and then not being believed can result in abuse of the child from both sides, creating feelings of isolation and self-doubt. However, children risk more than further punishment from the abuser. What they fear most are the social repercussions, reactions of people other than their family members, people who are not necessarily expected to love the child unconditionally. As victims, sexually abused children may fear being branded homosexual or as possible future molesters.

Furthermore, blaming or scapegoating can only be disastrous. Humans often exhibit a tendency to see the problem outside of themselves, to externalize, rather than to jump right into the situation and take responsibility. It is too easy to blame the victim. Hagans and Case (1988) offer very sound advice, "Be there for your child, right from the time you first learn of the molestation. Sexual abuse is a burden your child should not have to carry alone" (p. 31).

When parents listen openly and actively, when parents are receiving and accepting, they strengthen their children's trust in them. Parents also reinforce the certainty of their own right to protect their precious gifts. When children confide this very delicate information to their parents, what they are really communicating is, "Help. I need your protection and your support." It takes a great deal of courage for a child to share this information, and a great deal of courage for a parent to fight denial, secrecy, and her or his own embarrassment. But, bottom line, it is the parent, the adult, who must provide the empowering words, actions, reassurance, protection, and love.

DENIAL

It is a grave understatement to say that sexual molestation is not a parent's dream for her or his child. A good parent wants nothing more than the best for her or his child. The idea of the possibility of any form of sexual abuse is foreign. In sexual molestation, after the initial shock, a parent's reaction may be denial: a refusal to accept and come to terms with the fact her or his son or daughter has been sexually molested. It is a refusal to see the truth. Just as victims may refuse to think about having been abused, so do their parents. Most often parents agonize over the thought and the fantasized images of this molestation. The pain and the suffering endured by the child is experienced by the parents. The child's helplessness at the hands of the abuser is a stabbing reality. A temporarily effective, yet ultimately dysfunctional, way of dealing with these thoughts is to escape the truth, to not think about it, stash it in the back of one's mind, and forget it ever happened. Yet, we know that we never truly forget.

When the child and the family members do not receive treatment or professional guidance, it is difficult for healing to begin. Such is the case of the father who misguidedly advises his son to never speak of the abuse again, to become a partner with him in denial. He believes he is sparing his wife the emotional pain. He places a greater burden on the child to keep the secret from his mother. Such a plan is destined to backfire. The father is withholding vital information regarding the child's health and welfare, information that not only impacts the child's relationship with his mother and other people, but impacts the child's physical/medical care. Shouldn't the pediatrician know? Will the child need testing for sexually transmitted diseases? If so, for how long? Will he experience mixed feelings when he approaches puberty? How will he adjust to his future sexual experiences as an adult? Furthermore, the father's request for silence and denial provides a model for the child to use in similar situations of loss and pain. If we don't think about it, don't talk about it, it didn't happen. Suppressing the child's ability to freely express feelings stifles the child and kills her or his voice.

Denial is an unwillingness to see the need for outside help and the need to talk about it. There is the desire to keep the information away from family members and friends because of shame. But where should the shame be placed, on the victim or the abuser? Wasn't it the abuser who committed the shameful act? Yet, denial implies that the victim should feel shameful.

Another reaction to denial can be an urge to remove the abused child from her or his current environment, the school or community, to escape. What is better, however, and more to the point, is to remove the child from the source or situation that promotes this abuse. Uprooting a child from her or his happy surrounding can be very detrimental to her or his self-confidence and is disruptive and destabilizing. If you remove the child, then you may be punishing her or him for being truthful. Instead, eliminating further exposure to the perpetrator should be the action of choice. Whatever actions are taken, they should be perceived by the child as reactions to the abuse, not to the disclosure. Removing the situations that expose the child to the abuser should be immediate and swift. This relieves the child of the burden of having to face the abuser, making it easier to talk freely.

Parents, while needing to be loving and reassuring, must also delicately question, and communicate with, the child. A careful explanation to the child of the reasons for the questions, for the need to gather more information about the event(s), is important. Furthermore, honesty and openness with feelings set the stage for the processing of fear, guilt, and shame. Communicating unconditional acceptance helps to keep the door open and will encourage the child to feel comfortable enough to further disclose. Yet, keep in mind that children don't always want to talk about the same event or topic, over and over again. Thus, parents should balance their need for information with the needs of the child. Parents must "get it right the first time" and be sure that they exactly understand what the child is saying. Parents should also offer feedback and check with the child to be sure that all was understood correctly. In some conversations with your child, you may want to include close, immediate family members to talk about what has happened in a slow, gradual, yet open way. When your child slips into silence, be attuned to her or his need for a private space and a certain comfort level. Help make your child feel that the world at home is still intact and safe. It will take time and patience for all involved as the child is bruised, embarrassed, and in the process of healing.

In this delicate process, parents should never overrule their gut feelings. Never overrule your intuition! These personal detectors, these transmitters, warn you to put up your guard and protect your child. They are your traffic light, signal to stop, proceed with caution, and then, Go! Gavin de Becker (1999) illustrates the importance of intuition:

> Understand, however, that intuition about your children is always right in at least two ways: It is always based on something, and it always has your child's best interests at heart. While some question the accuracy of intuition, nobody can doubt its intent, particularly when it comes to violence. It is there to keep you and your children safe (pp. 26-27).

Denial is not only a problem for the victim or the victim's family. Professionals who have responsibility for children, like school administrators, teachers, and physicians have all too often also engaged in denial. As so keenly put by David Hechler (1988), a New York City investigative reporter, " For parents or children to deny the horror of their experience is one thing. But denial by professionals who have a responsibility for children is another" (p. 18). Professionals, like school administrators, teachers, physicians, and religious leaders, who are so-called mandated reporters, are required by law in all fifty states to report a suspicion of child abuse. It is an ethical responsibility to protect child victims. But, not only is there a requirement to report, there is the possibility of prosecution for failure to report. Hechler (1988) describes a scandal of non-reporting:

> . . . few administrators informed of allegations ever report them, even though by law they must do so. Noteworthy because it is an exception, a high-ranking Los Angeles school district administrator was convicted of failing to report suspected child molestation, a misdemeanor, in July, 1986. It was the first successful prosecution in the area . . . (p. 20).

Any kind of denial is unacceptable in that the lives of children are endangered. The law does not require the mandated reporters to investigate; they are only obliged to report their suspicions. This can be done anonymously and the reporters cannot be held civilly liable for the consequences of their reports. If the alleged abuser is the child's parent or caretaker, investigations may be conducted by social workers. If not, police may conduct the investigations.

Parental denial can sometimes be the result of lack of information and understanding of the rights of parent and child. Frequently, parents are unaware of the law. In the case of exposing a school or other organization, parents may be afraid of being branded the betrayer and having their family and child ostracized and alienated from the mainstream. The parents of other children may also demonstrate denial and may perceive the abused child's parents as troublemakers. Thus, the social pressure to stay quiet and keep the secret is powerful. This pressure is also placed on school personnel, church workers and other group members when they have knowledge of abuse. Too often, rather than reporting to the authorities, an organization, such as a school, may attempt to conduct its own private investigation only to conclude that there was not enough evidence. Furthermore, professionals may tend to support and protect their colleagues and buy into denial as a way of not having to deal with the repercussions of the truth. Ultimately, this denial must be stopped.

ANGER AND THE NEED FOR TREATMENT

Once denial dissipates, there is an awakening and then anger sets in. Anger can be defined as a feeling resulting from injury or mistreatment and is usually shown in a desire to lash out at something or someone else. When anger becomes uncontrolled, it may become translated into violence or aggressive acts. When one is utterly violated personally or by an attack on a vital significant person, such as one's child, the depth of rage may be symbolically summed up in one word: "Kill!" To feel anger is certainly acceptable. Anger is a natural body signal that lets us know that something bad has happened to us. It tells us to be on guard, to protect ourselves, and to avoid the threat.

To feel anger and rage after hearing of your child's molestation is an important, necessary step toward ultimate resolution and healing. However, if the anger is manifested and expressed by violent, aggressive, retaliative behavior, the result will not only promote greater harm and destruction, but may instill greater fear and guilt on the part of the child. The child is looking for support, protection, and healing. This should not be confused with retaliation, aggression, and violence. Aggressive, demonstrative reactions by the parent may only serve to increase the child's unwillingness to volunteer any more information, taking a posture of silence.

According to psychologists, participating in psychotherapy as soon as possible can help to diffuse the anger. The child, as well as family members, significantly benefits from discussing feelings, worries, and concerns with a trained mental health professional with particular expertise in the area of sexual abuse. But how do you select a therapist?

Each state has its own department that deals with child abuse. The names of these state departments may vary such as Department of Social Services, or Department of Youth and Family, etc. You can also call the licensing and certification boards or the professional membership societies of the various mental health professionals in your state. These mental health professionals can include psychologists, social workers, violence counselors, family therapists, and psychiatrists.

No matter whom you choose, involve your child in the selection of the therapist. Once a therapist is chosen with whom your child and you feel comfortable, stay with that person. Changing therapists creates insecurity and emotional upheaval for your child. A therapeutic relationship takes time and the development of trust. To rebuild the trust already established and to repeat the disclosure of the same molestation over and over again can be retraumatizing. In choosing a therapist, Hagans and Case (1988) suggest:

> The first priority of the therapist should be the continued protection of your child. Try to work with a therapist who wants to see that the molester is treated fairly, but who puts your child's welfare first. A therapist with this emphasis helps see that your child is protected by an even broader system of support than just your family (p. 85-86).

In your choice of therapist be sure to ask about specialized training, degrees, certifications, and years of experience. It is reasonable to ask where the therapist received her or his formal education as well as postgraduate training in family counseling. Has the therapist continued training by attending workshops on sexual abuse? How long has the therapist worked with individuals who have been sexually abused? What portion of the therapist's practice is devoted to victims and families of sexual abuse? Don't be surprised if you find that few therapists have had more than a few years of training or experience in this area, since, as a specialty, sexual abuse treatment is relatively new.

Once you have found your therapist, remember to be honest and open. Your therapist won't be judging your feelings as right or wrong, rather your feelings are accepted as your reality. Also remember that you and your family are not crazy, hopeless, or stupid. You are simply experiencing the expected reactions to a trauma, loss, and violation. Finally, there is no predetermined length of time for healing. It can take three or 103 sessions to complete the family's healing process (Hagans & Case, 1988, pp. 86-87).

GUILT

When parents are unable to protect their children from predators, the feeling of guilt immediately takes over. Parents blame themselves for not being watchful enough, and, because of this perceived lack of cautiousness, also blame themselves for the resulting abuse. They feel responsible for the harm done to their child. In addition to outright self-blame, guilt may be expressed in a variety of ways. Parents may overcompensate by showering the child with expensive gifts, excessive attention and care, privileges not normally given, and special treatments with the hope that all these things will ease the parent's sense of guilt, erase the hurt. Yet, this overcompensation unwittingly provides a false sense of healing. Parents must be aware of this phenomenon and not let the guilt overcome them. Allowing this to happen will only distract parents from the true needs of their child. Instead, telling the child that you will protect her or him, that the family will accompany her or him to treatment are responsible actions.

Victims feel guilty too. They feel they must have done something wrong for the abuse to have happened. They may feel that they were bad and are being punished, perhaps by God. The "what ifs" and the "maybes" abound. Because of this guilt, victims may even refuse to identify the abuser. This erroneous but prevasive sense of guilt is best processed in the therapeutic counseling relationship with the assistance of a caring and direct, well-informed therapist who can attack the irrational beliefs of guilt and support the underlying self-confidence and goodness of your child.

DEPRESSION

Victims of sexual abuse may suffer long-term and deep-seated emotional effects. When these negative effects remain unaddressed, victims continue to suffer with little hope for progress and recovery. When the feelings of sadness, pain, anger, shame, or guilt about the sexual abuse persist, it may lead to depression and thoughts of suicide. Although some victims react with these internal negative emotions, others may also act outwardly in antisocial ways. For example, it is not uncommon for a child to begin showing behavior problems in school, and getting in trouble at home. Victims may have difficulty trusting people and may begin to experience problems in relationships. Some may cry easily and their sadness can become agonizing and acute. Essentially, the victim is grieving and this grief is deep. We know that grief can be caused by misfortune, sorrow, pain, or loss. For the victim of sexual abuse, the intense emotional anguish, suffering, or grief is viewed as depression.

Parents are victims too and grieve over the loss of their child's innocence, over the suffering their child endured. Grief and depression limit the ability to feel joy and be alive. The sadness can become overpowering and the pain as cutting as a knife plunged into the heart. David Hechler (1988) cites Flora Colao, a therapist and specialist in treating children who are assault victims. Ms. Colao notes that the grief of parents who are secondary victims is "particularly acute because (their feelings) cannot be expressed in front of their children, for whom they must be strong, and it is not easily shared with friends or even family (p. 90)." Grief, if suppressed, can lead to depression; whereas if families and victims are encouraged to grieve and release their feelings, relief can occur.

BARGAINING AND ACCEPTANCE

Well, maybe if you straighten out your thoughts, are a good citizen, become a better parent, increase your cautiousness, and pray daily to God, all of this will go away—soon. Bargaining does not work. It does not speed the healing process, it does not take the place of therapy. It does not erase what has happened. It does not prevent the possibility of future losses. At some point, the abused child, the parents/caretakers, and the family members must face the reality and begin the process of acceptance. Acceptance is not synonymous with approval. It does not mean that what happened was OK. Rather, it is the process by which we realize that the past cannot change and that its effects on the present need to be dealt with. After being humiliated, defiled, and reduced to helplessness, the victim-child needs to become reempowered. Parental support and understanding equate with love which is an extremely powerful, strong antidote for a child's battered self-esteem. This is where psychotherapy can also be instrumental in enhancing self-esteem for the child as well as for the family. Treatment offers the family the opportunity to feel whole again. If you are in therapy and your doctor recommends medication, strongly consider taking it. Also, begin treatment as soon as possible rather than waiting to hit "rock bottom". The sooner you intervene, the shorter your treatment may be.

In addition, other avenues of activity can be therapeutic for you and your child. The arts can be a wonderful way to restore beauty and goodness to your environment. Musical and artistic expression allow for the human voice to express and rejoice, to nurture the spirit and heal the soul. Martial arts can promote self-discipline and self-confidence, enhance the ability to protect the self, and reduce feelings of helplessness.

CONCLUSION

In a family in which a child has suffered sexual abuse by a youth or any other outside perpetrator, parents often suppress their own feelings in an attempt to keep the focus and attention on the child. Parents often feel unreasonable guilt for having somehow allowed the abuse to happen to their child. While this guilt is natural and even understandable, parents should know, should accept, that nothing they did or didn't do provoked the abuse of their child. Parents should also realize that they cannot suppress their own emotions and yet expect their own healing to occur.

To the parents: remember, while the attack may have been on your child, it will take the whole family to heal your child, which also means that the entire family must learn to heal as well. Do not be afraid if sometimes the controlled and calm façade you have developed for your child cracks. You are allowed to experience your emotions whatever they are. You are human. Just know that when your child reveals the abuse to you, she or he does not expect you to just show love as you always do. Your child expects more. Your child expects an affirmation that regardless of the abuse she or he suffered, you will still accept her or him as you always have. At the heart of it all, acceptance and belonging is what we all yearn for.

REFERENCES

De Becker, G. (1999). *Protecting the gift: Keeping children and teenagers safe (and parents sane)*. New York: Dial Press.

Hagans, K., & Case, J. (1988). *When your child has been molested: A parent's guide to healing and recovery*. Lexington, Massachusetts: Lexington Books.

Hechler, D. (1988). *The battle and the backlash: The child sexual abuse war*. Lexington, Massachusetts: Lexington Books.

Townley, R. (1985). *Safe and sound: A parent's guide to child protection*. New York: Simon and Schuster.

Chapter Seven

RELIGIOUS AND SPIRITUAL FACTORS IN YOUTH VIOLENCE

REVEREND J. WILLIAM WAUTERS, JR.
AND
ROSEMARIE SCOLARO MOSER

WHO IS GOD? What is God? These profound questions will not be addressed here. Rather, this chapter will begin with the understanding that we may each define the construct of God based on our own personal, spiritual, and faith traditions. What will be addressed is how our relationship with God, or lack thereof, can influence both the manifestation of violent behavior in our culture and the vulnerability of our youth.

VIOLENCE AS DOMINATION

Violence is that in our human experience which tries to dominate or impose itself on others in a variety of different ways. It is often a response to an internal fear an individual may experience that may not be consciously identified as fear. From a religious perspective, it is a result of alienation from God. Given that we are born with free will, we may decide that our carnal desires are more important than following what God has asked of us. Violence is a splitting of the ways, which for many, was initially described, and is dogmatically known, as "original sin." Much of the violence we experience in society is a product of our alienation from others within our societal group. If we are created in the image and likeness of God, then ultimately, we are alienated not only from these others, but from God and from ourselves. Thus, this domination, the need to have power over others, these acts of violence, can be viewed as human reactions against the creatorship of God.

As Genesis tells us, God empowers us by bestowing upon us the ability to think and reason and therefore be co-creator with God. There is a relationship established between God and ourselves. In that relationship, we are placed in a position where, if we so choose, we may try to assume the entirety of the relationship. We may attempt to possess all the power and control rather than share it with God and others, resulting in the distorted belief that we are the only creators, the most important beings. This distortion is the basis for the division between God and ourselves, and between ourselves and our community. It reinforces narcissism and the lack of the greater perspective of our place in the world, amongst fellow humans, and in our faith communities. God empowers us. It is our choice and our free will that determine whether we use that power within the context of our relationship with God, or whether we use it outside of that context, for other more materially-based, destructive, non-life-enhancing purposes.

THE PHENOMENON OF SCAPEGOATING

Historically, across faith traditions, there has always been a connection between violence and the sacred. Sacrificial acts, the slaughtering of lambs, the Old Testament's depiction of Abraham's readiness to sacrifice his son, and ritualistic human sacrifices in some cultures were symbolic vehicles for a community's expression of violence in controlled, religiously acceptable ways. An outgrowth of this displacement of violence is the phenomenon of scapegoating, a process by which we place the burdens of our own alienation onto someone else. We hear of scapegoating daily in our society when children are abused or women are raped. When a husband engages in domestic violence, he places his fears onto his wife and therefore makes her the scapegoat of all that is not perfect in his life. She is to blame. It is frightening that this scapegoating is so pervasive in our present-day culture. Is it any wonder that nearly two-thirds of all incarcerated youths have experienced violence in their own homes?

In a broader sense, it is our culture that is unknowingly scapegoating our children. We, in the American culture, promote a façade of success, comfort, and convenience. Yet, not all of us are so privileged or so safe. Thus, the unacknowledged needs and anxieties of our culture become manifest in our children. Our youth see the inequities among groups of peoples, the poverty, the prejudice, and the dire needs. Our culture expects our youth to be the hope of our future, to succeed, to be better than their parents, to achieve higher SAT scores, to earn more money. Yet, our culture continues to fail in finding solutions to our social and global ills. Will there be an ozone layer? Will the fighting stop in Kosovo? Will there be an atomic World War III? Statements of chemical and biological warfare and nuclear disaster seed an underlying fear and anxiety about whether the world will continue to exist. Our youth see little hope for change and thus nihilism sets in. "So, if it doesn't make any difference what I do in my life, then I might as well do whatever I feel." It is difficult for youth to see their place and their future in society. They feel alienated. They feel unsupported. They believe no one is listening. They lack a sense of purpose. In turn, just as youth become the scapegoats of our culture, youth resort to scapegoating each other. We observed this in Columbine, in the retaliation against the scapegoaters or the jocks, orchestrated by the scapegoated, the trenchcoats. We observe this in gangs, among ethnic groups, and between the old vs. newcomer students in a school. In a sense, the greater anxieties of our culture filter down to our children who exhibit the symptoms of violence and who express the acts of aggression in an effort to gain some control in the midst of their chaos. However, society has established a set of strict legal and moral rules and consequences to help govern the behavior of adults. In contrast, children are typically less responsible, less accountable, and less clearly structured. The burden of their moral upbringing and guidance is placed on the greater adult community.

ALIENATION AND THE NEED FOR COMMUNITY

It is not just our youth who are alienated. The greater adult community also experiences this alienation. Our culture's values tend to be defined by material success and the mediating institutions that support these values and surround individuals are no longer morally strong and consistent. Today, the major institutions in one's life include political and economic networks, material possessions, and the ever-changing media representations of beauty, wealth, and celebrity. It is the mediating institutions that define the community. Thus, with fleeting, fickle institutions, a sense of a stable, enduring community is lacking.

Historically, it was the church, synagogue, temple, or other place of worship that symbolized God's call to humans to join a community. The connection between the individual and God's community provided stability, structure, support, and acknowledgment of the individual as an integral part of a larger context. A relationship with God and the community provided a sense of belonging, meaning, and purpose to the individual. If our culture lacks this sense of purpose, which had been fostered by a relationship with God, then it is not surprising to see how our youth may wander aimlessly without a sense of purpose, lacking hope. This disconnection from God, this lack of a relationship with God, is at the crux of our alienation, our fear and anxiety, and our acts of aggression toward one another. We may choose material success as most important in our lives. We may choose to live in the stunning, gargantuan home in the upscale development. Yet we gate this development/community out of fear and we barely know our neighbors. The anxiety is apparent and the sense of belonging is absent.

THE ROLE OF PROPHETS

Biblically, it has been the role of the prophet to call people back into the community, into the right relationship with God, and into the God-created order. In the twentieth century, we experienced a number of prophets, one of whom had a profound impact on American culture. Martin Luther King, Jr. was a remarkable prophet, not only for the people of the South, but for all people. He challenged us to overcome the fear of people who are different from ourselves. His practice was one of nonviolence and his mentor was Mahatma Ghandi, who revealed the importance of respect for life and for others. The victory that is won is not *over* somebody but *through* somebody. Rather than seeking a victory of black over white, Martin Luther King, Jr. directed his efforts to the transformation of people through prayer and non-violence, amidst the firehoses, the police dogs, and the violence around them. He helped to transform blacks by increasing their confidence in God and confidence in themselves to overcome the inequities. As whites viewed this respect of God and the nonviolence stance, they too underwent a trans-formation, realizing that their own fears were unjustified. The wounds with-in the souls of both Southern blacks and whites began to heal. The nonvio-lence and the prayer touched these wounds and made them apparent, the first step toward reconciliation and healing. In contrast, the North was marked by violent responses and riots which only served to reinforce the fears, anxieties, and differences of both groups. Further, Martin Luther King, Jr. believed in the biblical concept of the Beloved Community. As he described in the well-known "I Have A Dream," it is not the color of one's skin but the content of one's character that will define the new, Beloved Community of God. His theology echoed what Paul described of Jesus, that there is no slave or free, Greek or Jew, as we are all one in Christ. Thus, this sense of community and relationship with God is what transforms, heals, and sustains us. It helps to decrease our anxieties and fears. It is what reduces the likelihood of domination, scapegoating, and violence.

We have experienced a number of wake-up calls, urging us to commit to the reestablishment of community. For example, the World Council of Churches has begun to address the need to build communities and has targeted Boston after an incident in which there was open gunfire at a funeral service for a gang member. The pastors, appalled at this violation, responded by gathering to formulate an active plan to recapture their community and to be present in it.

To rebuild the social fabric of their community, the pastors forged their Ten Point Plan to Mobilize Churches:

1. Foster church collaboration in sponsoring Adopt a Gang programs whereby organize and evangelize young people involved in groups.
2. Commission missionaries to accompany young African American and Hispanics in court, and to work with probation officers and school principals to develop tasks aimed at high-risk teens and their families.
3. Prepare street workers to help in the recovery of young drug addicts.
4. Establish economic development projects with community participation.
5. Establish mutual support links between suburban and downtown churches and ministries.
6. Initiate neighborhood crime watch programs in the areas around churches.
7. Establish relations between churches and health centers.
8. Promote the work of African American and Hispanic women and men on issues related to family responsibility and alternatives to gangs.
9. Establish crisis centers in the churches to help women victims of domestic violence or rape.
10. Develop identity programs in the churches to help African American and Hispanic people to value their own cultures and to appreciate the struggle of women, men, and the poor for dignity and freedom of their peoples.

A second poignant wake-up call occurred in East Los Angeles, in the midst of violent housing projects and numerous gangs, when a small group of mothers, from Dolores Mission Roman Catholic Church, who were praying the rosary at the funeral of one of their son's looked to their faith for an answer. They saw their plight as similar to that of the disciples in the stormy Sea of Galilee whom Jesus asked to leave their boat, walk on the water, and join him. The disciples were afraid but Jesus asked them to rely on their faith. As long as they believed, they could walk on water and overcome their fear. But, Peter, one of the disciples, demonstrated that when he began to doubt, he began to sink. Similarly, the mothers realized that this faith story was a metaphor for them. They were in a storm of violence and they too were afraid to step out of the boat and walk the walk of their savior, Jesus. They needed to overcome their fears, overcome their doubts, and believe that they too could walk out into the treacherous waters of their neighborhood. Through their initiation of "Love Walks," they stepped out of the boat. As a group, they simply began walking through the neighborhoods and talking with youth gang members. These "Love Walks" evolved into barbecues, parties, and other activities such as an economic development program in which gang members make and sell "Home Boy Tortillas." These mothers were the prophets for their community and addressed the alienation and fear through faith.

This group of East Los Angeles mothers reclaimed their community through their faith in God and their own active presence. They personally connected with God and with the youth of their community. They served as mentors and role models. They listened to their children and began addressing their need to belong. Their solution to the violence was basic and simple. It did not require state legislation, nor funding, nor hiring of personnel. All it required was faith, presence, and belief in the community.

THE LOSS OF RITUALS

Part of the alienation of our children today is that they lack the presence of God. They lack the rituals that speak to them in meaningful ways. We know that those who engage in formalized, religious activity of their faith traditions are less likely to engage in violence. Although attendance at church, temple, or synagogue does not necessarily make one a better person, it does however make one's understanding of reality different. We live in a society in which approximately 50 percent of marriages dissolve. Even the private intimacy of sex is no longer sacred, no longer ours. Television and the media regularly portray sexuality openly and casually, whether in scenes of passionate, perfect lovemaking in bed or barely clad celebrities at the Grammy Awards. It is as if we have lost that ritual of intimacy and must perform to a standard which is unreal. As we lose this intimacy, we lose a private piece of ourselves. We lose our boundaries and our identities. Realistically, physical intimacy is an extremely private affair in which there is no clear right or wrong. Yet, we are measured by the media's portrayal of how we should execute sex. To be deprived of the privacy of our own intimacy speaks to the profound deprivation of the soul.

In addition to having lost the stability of marriage and the intimacy of our sexuality, our society has recently suffered a number of other losses. With busy schedules, it is much less common to share the ritual of the family meal. We are constantly rushing to activities and ultimately rushing away from ourselves. Our lives are robotic and we have become technological tools of the 21st Century. The mothers of East Los Angeles demonstrated the power of presence and communication with the youth of their community. We must learn to stop rushing away from our youth.

Perhaps we should commit to recapturing another lost ritual, most vital to the Christian-Judeo faith traditions: keeping the Sabbath holy. It is vital that we take at least one day to remember and reflect on all of creation, on our place in this creation, and on our Creator. We can honor God on that day by resting, being with each other, fostering fellowship, and recalling the stories of our faith traditions. Today, few of us have days like that. Most of our days are consumed by work. We forget that we are humans and that humans are social beings. Yet, we offer few places and times when we can enjoy our humanness by being social and communal. Even in our work week, there is no sacred place, as we are driven by our faxes, e-mail, and cell phones. The paradox is that we are in greater contact with each other, but in a more alienated state, not face to face. There is nothing inherently wrong with the new technologies. However, we must designate a sacred time and space to connect with each other and with God, as had been planned for the Sabbath. Youth see the lack of this sacred space, the lack of a Sabbath. Thus, for them there is no God. And if there is no God, no greater being, no greater spirit, then there is no organizing principle. Will our youth learn that anything is sacred? Will they learn that they are sacred? If we do not see the power greater than us, that makes us sacred, that makes humans viable, important components of this universe, then we possess no true meaning. The value or meaning of a person is then defined by her or his utility. That utility is commodified and marketed. No longer are we in charge, as we are at the whim of the market. Much of the market is dominated by power. Thus, youth learn that violence is a means of gaining power, and a means to establish a sense of being and identity.

THE MEANING OF EXISTENCE AND THE VALUE OF THE SELF

Such is the way of gangs. It is not uncommon for a gang member to proclaim that the life of the member of another gang has little meaning. This lack of meaning extends to the self: if I want to do drugs today, I'll do drugs today. If I want to have sex, I'll have sex. If I want to kill somebody, I'll kill somebody. It just doesn't make any difference. I'm going to die sometime anyway. It doesn't make a difference." With such an attitudinal posture, it indeed makes little difference whether or not a youth chooses violence as a response to the environment.

Violence takes many forms, whether it is the 10-year-old child in San Antonio who has been sexually violated and is now pregnant, or the newest inductee to a gang, a little girl who must undergo initiation via hard kicks to the body from booted gang members. This little girl, after enduring such initiation, hugs and thanks the abusers for the opportunity to become a female gang member whose role will be to perform on-call sexual favors for the male gang members. Her need to belong is so painfully unfulfilled that it comes at the expense of personal safety and with self-denigration. Her body is not considered sacred nor valued. Her life will be surrounded by violence for years to come. How can she possibly have hope?

Yet, there is hope if we as adults can begin to take responsibility to recapture our communities and our youth. Clearly, our experience with youth gang members is that they want to belong and yearn to participate in more healthy ways. They are unfortunately locked into a kind of fatalistic identity. They are trapped by their needs for security and to protect their turf. They lack a vehicle to express what they need. They do not see the way out of the maze of violence and destruction.

UTILITY VS. INHERENT VALUE OF THE SELF

We should not, however, be falsely lured into the myth that violence occurs predominantly in gangs or similar cultures. Alienation of youth can be found across the socioeconomic strata. Alienation occurs when youth are pressured to accept standards that are external to the self: my worth is defined by what college I get into, how expensive my car is, and where I vacation, rather than my inherent value as a person.

With all the focus on fixing kids, maybe we need to consider repairing ourselves. We, the adults, are the role models. We provide the guidance. We develop the community and foster the sense of belonging. Yet, we are the ones who treat our kids as trophies, whether it is the affluent parent who claims, "My kid got into Harvard," the middle class parent who proclaims, "My kid is making $600,000 a year," or the Mexican American farm worker who exclaims, "My kid had a baby!" (even though the baby is one of seven, is born into poverty, and has a father in prison). We unknowingly treat our youth as if they are valued for their utility, and in turn their value of the self becomes tenuous. Valuing persons for their utility is pervasive in our society. As we search for contemporary heroes, there are few if any who are presently identified as the contemporary Martin Luther King, Jrs. Rather, individuals are designated as our heroes through their utility. Take for instance many sports figures who are valued and become present-day heroes because of their athletic ability or because of how much money they earn rather than for their strength of character. We present these heroes and role models to our youth in seductive, provocative ways. The media glamorizes the celebrity. In contrast, there is little glamour for the person of character and integrity. After whom will our children choose to pattern their behavior, their careers, and their lifestyles?

THE SPIRIT OF THE PEOPLE

Yet, youth are not entirely powerless. With guidance, they are capable of becoming active, vital, inspirited participants in their communities. It is important to listen to their voices, for it is through the opportunity to express their voices, and to be listened to, that youth are validated and view themselves as integral parts of the greater community. We have seen the youth of each generation actively respond to a variety of causes, whether serving in the Peace Corps, planting trees, or building homes for the underprivileged. We listen to their concerns and provide the structure for them to participate in the preservation of their communities, both locally and globally. We can assist youth in their vision by modeling the importance of preserving our communities for generations to come.

This forward-looking approach to the community, the culture, and the environment is what our country was based on. Our American forefathers designed our Declaration of Independence and Constitution with the future of our country in mind. The authors of *The Federalist* papers offered their impassioned writings in an effort to protect the future of the American government. Our forefathers attempted to be the voices of citizens to come. They designed a country not only for the needs of "today" but for the anticipated needs of the future. Their plans were derived from the spirit of the people, from passionate belief, and from a sense of fairness and just, moral order.

But how far does the fairness and just, moral order go in today's world? When we view the way in which countries express violence through controlled, technological battle, we see how removed we are from the spirit of the people. We selectively and methodically drop bombs, killing both enemy and innocent. The targets are objects. We see no faces, we see no people, we become unaware of the human suffering, and we do not experience the killing of the human spirit.

Indeed, the vicious spiral of violence that many young people see as bedrock reality provides no sense of future. In the midst of scandalous affluence, most young people, of all social classes, know of the pandemic violence of poverty that exists in cities, rural areas, and increasingly, even in suburban areas. To break from this violence, many young people mimic the violence that envelopes them by shooting or beating others, abusing or raping young women, or abusing themselves. In reaction to their violence, there is either more violence in the form of revenge killing, or child abuse, or unproductive encounters with the legal system. Law enforcement personnel are sucked into this vicious cycle as their paranoia increases with time spent within such circles. Rodney King, Amadou Diallo, and Abner Louima are expressions of the reaction of police officers to the fears of our society. What the young people, the scapegoats, then see is greater violence within the state of poverty. As the cycle turns more and more violent, society's compassion and care wane. "Those people" become the problem. We are in denial of our common humanity as created by God.

As a culture, we are sorely in need of recapturing our humanness, of recapturing the sense of awe and wonder of life. This awe and wonder can be found in the powerful simplicity of the barbecues in East Los Angeles. It can be found in the powerful simplicity of nature: experiencing towering mountains, vast canyons, and overwhelming oceans. Ultimately, we can experience our human spirit by connecting with our surroundings, and in doing so we connect with God. Introducing an inner city, underprivileged child to the secrets of a forest, through an Outward Bound type of program that introduces youth to the challenges of living in nature, fostering self-confidence and independence. Such a program is both empowering and reorganizing for that child. It opens that child to the possibility of the human spirit, to options never imagined. Such experiences place our humanness in perspective, so that we can understand that we fit into a higher order which is greater and more powerful than ourselves. These experiences teach us humility and respect, as well as trust in the human spirit and in God. The lack of humility, respect, and trust sets the stage for the expression of violence. Clearly, the perpetrators at Columbine responded to their years of victimization in a grandiose, distrusting way, with little respect for themselves or their victims. They lost their trust in humanity and in God.

FORGIVENESS

As humans we are born imperfect. We are destined to err and to hurt others. Although we may try to live our lives in ways that best express kindness, respect, and goodness, we can never be perfect. We must accept our fallibility, for not to do so would be irrational and unrealistic. We are social beings and thus we ultimately will be hurt, or violated by, our fellow imperfect humans. Given this state of affairs, we would benefit from a process that would address our fallibility and mend our wounds. This process is called forgiveness.

In South Africa, the Truth and Reconciliation Commission dealt with the horrors of apartheid, torture, intimidation, murder, and state-run terrorism. Nelson Mandela and Desmond Tutu, faithful Christians, realized that they could never move forward with their new South Africa unless they could at least acknowledge the atrocities that had occurred. They needed to provide an opportunity for the people of South Africa to process the pain and suffering they had endured. The Truth and Reconciliation Commission was an attempt at acknowledgment and moving forward. It exposed the atrocities and placed them in full view. This was an exceptionally painful experience. Its primary purpose was not to punish but to heal the wounds of the people. Some of the violent perpetrators were forgiven and granted amnesty as a result of this process. More importantly, fully cognizant of its past, South Africa is able to patiently rebuild trusting relationships that will serve as the foundation of its new country. Biblical healing begins with coming back into a right relationship with God. It is the generative source of true forgiveness.

We need to revisit the act of forgiveness. In many ways, we have forgotten how to forgive others as well as ourselves. Rather than forgive, we are too quick to respond with retaliation. As adults, we have forgotten how to teach our children how to forgive and more often than not we are poor role models of forgiveness. For the most part, what we teach our children, either knowingly or unknowingly, is revenge. Our slogans include, "Look out for Number One" or "Don't Get Mad, Get Even." Our youth learn that if "they" play tough, you need to play tougher. Violence in sports is in full view on wide-screen TV. Acts of forgiveness are rarely portrayed in the media. How often do we hear or say, "I'm sorry," in important, not trivial, matters? Perhaps we erroneously believe that forgiveness is weakness or that it condones the violation. In reality, it requires strength of character and tremendous self-confidence. Furthermore, forgiveness is not about saying it was OK that a person was murdered or raped, or OK that someone was abusive. It is about acknowledgment of the violation, acknowledgment of the human imperfection, reconciliation of the violator, and healing of the wounded—both the victim and the community.

The way in which we deal with criminals is indicative of our lack of forgiveness and the lack of a reconciliation process. There is no doubt that crimes should have strong and effective consequences. However, we are quick to put to death and punish without including the possibility of restorative justice, a way in which the community can be healed when a violation has occurred. In restorative justice, criminals are asked to face their crime as well as their victims. This is a process by which criminals are confronted with the pain that they have inflicted on another person, a family, or the network of people affected by the crime. Jointly, they all participate in developing a plan of restitution, some of which, but not all, may be financial. The concept of restorative justice is derived from the perspective that a crime or violation may be between two individuals, but that it is also a rendering of the fabric of the community. Through restorative justice, we can reknit and heal the community. For example, in the case of a rape, we may imprison the criminal, but do we feel any safer? That person may be released in five years. Do we then live in terror again? Or can the issues of domination and control be addressed both for the victim and the criminal. Will the victim have an opportunity to express her anger at the rapist? Will the rapist undergo the counseling process that may allow him to understand his fears and misplaced need to dominate and control? Restorative justice focuses on the criminal's responsibility to the community: as a criminal, how can I help make that community feel safe again? It is a healing of souls for the victim, the criminal, and the community.

THE POWER OF THE COMMUNITY

We are bound together inextricably by the nature of our humanity which in our faith tradition is a gift from God. God will help to heal, but we too are a part of that healing process. Forgiveness and restorative justice are ways that we can communicate to our children that there are alternatives to revenge and violence. An innovative program being conducted in a number of schools appoints peer mediators who are on call to prevent the escalation of conflict. These students intervene, employing communication skills to encourage the verbal expression of each party's viewpoint and the understanding of each perspective. This program reinforces the reality that the school is a community and that whenever there is a fight it affects the fabric of the school community. Each student's safety and security is impacted by the event: Can I walk down that hallway if those two will be there? Must I walk home a different way, avoiding that gang's turf? Peer mediators are vehicles for the school community to take responsibility for its members.

The power of community cannot be underestimated, whether the Beloved Community of Martin Luther King, Jr., a community in East Los Angeles, the community of South Africa, a local school community, or a community that has been violated. In all of these communities, the power of God, the power of human beings, and the power of nature is at work. Communities offer us our most valuable resource and our most direct solution to the problem of violence. As adults, we have the opportunity to develop our communities in ways that will prevent violence, discourage alienation, and will offer our youth a sense of hope, value, and trust in humanity. Communities cannot be bought or paid for. Instead, we will need to commit our time and our presence. Our faith and confidence in ourselves and in a higher power and spirit, in whatever positive way we define God, will determine our success in addressing the phenomenon of youth violence.

Chapter Eight

DEVELOPMENTAL MODELS FOR INTERVENTIONS TO PREVENT CONDUCT PROBLEMS

CELENE E. DOMITROVICH AND JANET A. WELSH

RECENT, HIGH-PROFILE crimes by youth have resulted in renewed interest in children's mental health and the social and developmental challenges facing young people. Epidemiological data suggest that between 12 percent and 22 percent of America's youth under age eighteen are in need of mental health services (National Advisory Mental Health Council, 1990), and an estimated 7.5 million children and adolescents suffer from one or more mental disorders (Office of Technology Assessment, 1986). Of particular concern are disruptive behavior disorders, which are often pervasive, highly stable and resistant to intervention. It is estimated that between 4 and 10 percent of children in America display clinical levels of externalizing behavior problems, which include noncompliance, aggression, truancy, substance use, and delinquency (Costello, 1990; Kazdin, 1995). In addition to the personal suffering experienced by these highly problematic children and their families, these disorders also have a tremendous cost to society. Children with conduct problems represent over one-third of all child mental health referrals (Kazdin, 1995), and many of the most serious and costly adult mental health and societal problems, including antisocial personality, substance abuse, and chronic crime, have their origins in early conduct problems.

Three diagnoses currently comprise the disruptive or externalizing behavior disorders of childhood: Oppositional Defiant Disorder (ODD), Conduct Disorder (CD), and Attention Deficit & Hyperactivity Disorder (ADHD) (DSM-IV; American Psychiatric Association, 1994). Although there are some similarities among these disorders, they are considered independent and unique diagnoses. Children with ADHD exhibit elevated levels of inattention and hyperactivity-impulsivity. ODD is characterized by a consistent pattern of defiant and disruptive behavior. Although ADHD children can be disruptive, they generally lack the negative quality that is the primary feature of ODD. However, about 40 percent of children with ADHD will go on to develop significant conduct problems (Offord et al., 1992). CD includes all of the features of ODD but it is a more severe and persistent problem: the primary diagnostic criteria include aggression or cruelty towards people or animals, destruction of property, deceitfulness or theft, and school or home rule violations. CD includes delinquent behaviors that are violations against individuals or property but it is not the same as *delinquency*, which is a legal (rather than psychological) term referring to crime committed by juveniles. This distinction is important when defining psychopathology. Many children and adolescents who engage in delinquent activity will also be conduct disordered (prevalence estimates vary but are generally between 50 percent and 90 percent) but there are some juvenile delinquents who do not have the diagnosis (Otto, Greenstein, Johnson, & Friedman, 1992). The constellation of problem behaviors included in these different diagnoses can be referred to more generally as *conduct problems.*

While some types of childhood mental health disorders are fairly amenable to treatment, conduct problems are particularly intractable and resistant to intervention efforts, even those efforts that are intensive and long term (Costello, 1990; Kazdin, 1985, 1987). There are several possible explanations for the poor treatment outcomes related to conduct problems. First, these difficulties are multifaceted, and are related to individual dispositional and genetic characteristics, maladaptive family interaction processes, poor school adjustment, deviant peer group dynamics, and negative socioeconomic and community factors such as poverty and exposure to violence. Second, by the time most treatment efforts commence, conduct problems have often been manifest in multiple, mutually reinforcing contexts. Finally, for many children conduct problems interfere with critical developmental adaptations, including forming secure attachments to caregivers, transitioning to school, and forming good relationships with nondeviant peers. Thus conduct problems may persist throughout childhood and adolescence. Given the difficulty of changing patterns of conduct problems once they have been established, prevention-oriented programs that are comprehensive, long term, and developmentally based seem particularly desirable.

The content of this chapter is organized into two major sections. The first section discusses the origins and theoretical foundations of prevention science, which provides the underpinnings for best practices in preventive interventions with conduct problem children. The second section provides examples of effective preventive interventions that have been conducted with preschoolers, grade school children, and adolescents. Examples will be provided to illustrate the ways that knowledge gleaned from earlier studies has influenced the development of later programs. In addition, we discuss how current state of the art programs attempt to prevent disruptive behavior problems with developmentally appropriate, long-term, multicomponent efforts.

THE PREVENTION SCIENCE APPROACH

The primary goal of prevention is to reduce the incidence and prevalence of disorders and increase the likelihood of positive outcomes in an identified group of individuals (Kellam, Koretz, & Moscicki, 1999). Preventive interventions are, by definition, conducted with individuals who do not have diagnosable disorders. For example, programs designed to prevent delinquency target youth who have not yet begun delinquent careers, while measles prevention programs administer vaccinations to people before they develop symptoms of the disease. Nonetheless, within the realm of prevention there is recognition that the actual risk for developing a particular disorder varies from group to group. Therefore, the Institute of Medicine (IOM) (1994) proposed a multilevel system to classify interventions depending upon the degree of risk associated with a targeted group. *Universal* programs are the broadest forms of preventive interventions. They target the general population and are unrelated to risk. Routine childhood vaccination programs, mandatory seat belt laws, and fluoridation of public water supplies are all examples of universal prevention programs. *Selected* programs target individuals or subgroups whose risk for developing a disorder is greater than average. Interventions for children of depressed mothers or children who have experienced the death of a parent would be considered selected. *Indicated* programs are conducted with individuals who are identified as having early signs or symptoms related to a particular disorder. Because juvenile delinquency in adolescence is related to aggression and poor social skills in childhood, a social skills-training program that targets aggressive children would be an example of an indicated delinquency prevention.

Prevention science has emerged from the integration of developmental theory with models from public health, epidemiology, sociology, and developmental psychopathology (Cicchetti, 1984; Cicchetti & Cohen, 1995; Kellam & Rebok, 1992; Kellam et al., 1999; Lorion, 1990; Sameroff, 1991; Sroufe & Rutter, 1984). It involves identifying precursor risk and protective factors in the individual and the environment, understanding the role of developmental processes in mental health, and explaining how multiple factors combine to maintain or change developmental trajectories (National Institute of Mental Health, 1993). Developmental theory and research provide a foundation for understanding the factors influencing growth and adaptation under normal circumstances. The field of developmental psychopathology extends this work by focusing on the relationship between typical and atypical developmental processes. This includes identifying risk and protective factors that contribute to resiliency or psychopathology, and understanding how patterns of adaptation and maladaptation emerge and function over time. The field of epidemiology is also interested in understanding disorders by examining them at the population level. Illnesses that occur in large groups are understood by examining variations in risk factors across individuals and their environment. Nonrandom distributions provide information on mediating or moderating factors that may contribute to the causal process involved in the development of disorders and other negative outcomes (Kellam & Rebok, 1992; Kellam, et al., 1999). These three important and complementary perspectives can be used to further understand conduct problems.

The Role of Risk and Protective Factors

The concept of risk and protective factors is central to both epidemiology and developmental psychopathology. Risk factors are variables that increase vulnerability for negative outcomes and protective factors reduce the likelihood of maladaptive outcomes under conditions of risk. A number of factors have been identified that place children at increased risk for psychopathology. Coie et al. (1993) grouped empirically derived, generic risk factors into seven individual and environmental domains: constitutional handicaps, skill development delays, emotional difficulties, family circumstances, interpersonal problems, school problems, and ecological risks. Although less is known about protective factors and their operation (Rutter, 1985; Kazdin, 1991; Luther, 1993), at least three broad domains of protective factors have been identified. The first domain includes characteristics of the individual such as cognitive skills, social-cognitive skills, temperamental characteristics, and social skills (Luther & Zigler, 1992). The second domain has to do with the quality of the child's interactions with the environment. These interactions include secure attachments to parents (Morissett, Barnard, Greenberg, Booth, & Spieker, 1990) and attachments to peers or other adults with prosocial values and behaviors. A third protective domain involves aspects of the larger social system, such as positive school-home relations or high-quality schools.

As stated previously, understanding the ways that risk and protective factors contribute to targeted outcomes is a critical step in the prevention research process. A strong etiological theory is what drives the specification of intervention goals and the overall design of the intervention. Intervention goals typically include the prevention of deleterious outcomes (e.g., absence of psychopathology, abstention from substance use) and the promotion of healthy development (Pittman & Cahill, 1992). In order to reach these goals, the program must modify (enhance or remove) the malleable risk factors (e.g. association with deviant peers) and enhance protective factors (e.g., effective social problem-solving, supportive adult relationship) that have been identified as the presumed proximal mediators in the etiological model. Discussed below are several developmental theories that assist in the identification and prioritization of risk and protective factors, and the design of preventive interventions.

The Role of Developmental Theory

Many development theorists conceptualize development as a progression through universal stages that are characterized by critical issues that must be negotiated or resolved (e.g., Erikson, 1963; Piaget, 1983). For example, around age two, toddlers enter a stage commonly referred to as the "terrible twos". During this stage, children are trying to exert their own autonomy, which is appropriate and adaptive. Caretakers must allow the child sufficient independence while providing the support that his or her young age requires. In developmental psychopathology, an individual's adaptation to critical events or specific developmental tasks is pivotal and where the effects of risk and protective factors are most evident. A child who is unable to successfully resolve one developmental task is at risk for subsequent developmental failures. Developmental stages and tasks provide guidelines for the potential timing and content of preventive interventions. For example, difficult temperament in infancy characterized by poor self-regulation, irritability, and difficulty being soothed, is an early risk factor that may exert a continued influence at later points in development. Young children with difficult temperaments are more likely to experience problems with critical developmental tasks such as entering school and establishing peer relations. Therefore, children identified as *difficult* in infancy are likely to be prime candidates for prevention programs that focus on these areas, particularly if the children already display other high-risk behaviors, such as aggression or impulsivity.

A second developmental concept central to both developmental psychopathology and prevention is the transactional model of development. When developmental models first attempted to account for the importance of environmental influences on child development (e.g. behaviorism, information processing), it was assumed that the individual was a somewhat passive recipient of environmental input and reactive to externally generated events. Transactional theory, on the other hand, regards the child as an active participant in his or her environment. Developmental outcomes are considered the result of dynamic transactions in which a child and the environment reciprocally influence one another over time (Sameroff & Chandler, 1975). Returning to the example of difficult temperament, transactional theory helps account for the variety of outcomes observed in children who appeared equally at risk as infants. Those children whose caretaking environments are compatible with their behavioral styles (e.g., a more sensitive, tolerant, nonreactive parenting style) tend to elicit less negative and coercive parenting, and thus facilitate the creation of more positive interactions for themselves over time. This awareness of the importance of a good fit between the infant and caregiver, and the contributions of both individuals to this fit, has significant implications for the development of preventive interventions. If a transactional model were applied to our example of difficult temperament, then temperamentally difficult infants would only be candidates for intervention if the fit with their environments (i.e., negative interactions with caregivers) seemed potentially detrimental.

Sources that shape developmental trajectories are not limited to individuals or families but may be found at all levels of the social ecology (Kellam, 1990). Indeed, most etiological models of disorders emphasize the interaction among genetic, biomedical, and psychosocial risk and protective factors (Coie et al., 1993). Developmental-ecological models of development, often used in sociology, developmental psychology, and developmental psychopathology, attempt to understand multiple influences on behavior over time. The principal underlying this model is that developing organisms are strongly influenced by their surrounding contexts. Bronfenbrenner's model of the nature and levels of context is one example of a developmental-ecological model that has contributed significantly to the field of prevention (Bronfenbrenner, 1979, 1995; Bronfenbrenner & Crouter, 1983). The model proposes that there are four levels for classifying context. The first level, the *microsystem,* involves the child's immediate social contexts such as the family, school, peer group, and neighborhood. The *mesosystem* encompasses the relationships between the various microsystems (e.g., the family-school connection or between the parents and the child's peer group). Interactions within both the microsystem and mesosystem are often affected by circumstances that do not directly involve the child. For example, children and youth may be significantly affected by changes in the social welfare system (e.g., welfare reforms, boundary changes for categorical services), or other social structures that set policies and practices that alter microsystem and mesosystem interactions. The *exosystem* is comprised of those contexts and actions that indirectly impact the child's development. Finally, the *macrosystem* represents the widest level of systems influence, consisting of the broad ideological and institutional patterns and events that define a culture or subculture, and including such things as societal attitudes toward corporal punishment or youthful offenders.

Developmental-ecological models can be used both to understand layers of influence on behavior, and also to identify potential targets and mediators of intervention. Within this model, some interventions may focus primarily on one or more aspects of the microsystem. These would include programs that target parenting practices or social skills in at-risk children. Alternatively, interventions could be directed toward the mesosystem. An example of this would be a program designed to strengthen home-school partnerships or improve parents' marital quality. Preventive efforts that target the exosystem might include the development of a new model of service delivery or reforming policies and regulations that impact children and families. Media campaigns that are designed to change widely held beliefs and attitudes (i.e., regarding drug use or corporal punishment) are preventive interventions that attempt to alter the macrosystem.

To summarize, ideas from developmental theory and developmental psychopathology can assist in the conceptualization and implementation of preventive interventions. Understanding the fit between characteristics of the child and characteristics of the environment and the active role that children play in shaping their world can help to identify which children may benefit from prevention programs. Ecological models underscore the different levels of social factors influencing child outcomes, and the need to consider these multiple levels when developing intervention programs. Although these theoretical models are relevant to many areas of prevention science, they may also be applied specifically to the risk factors associated with disruptive behavior problems.

A DEVELOPMENTAL MODEL OF DISRUPTIVE
BEHAVIOR DISORDERS

Compared to other mental health disorders, a substantial amount of basic research has been conducted in the last twenty years on the disruptive behavior disorders. We now have sophisticated developmental models of how these problems develop (Conduct Problems Prevention Research Group, 1992; Loeber & Dishion, 1983; McMahon & Estes, 1997; Patterson, DeBaryshe, & Ramsey, 1989; Reid & Eddy, 1997) and an awareness of the risk and protective factors involved in their initiation and maintenance. There is still substantial work to be done, however, in understanding the mechanisms that link these proximal and distal factors, and how the mechanisms operate over time to increase the likelihood of disorder (Institute of

Medicine, 1994). Developmental models of early-onset disruptive behavior disorders have incorporated a set of key factors in the child, family, and peer context that contribute to the emergence and maintenance of these problems. Causal factors and correlates in the broader social system (i.e., school or neighborhood) have also been included in these models. The model that will be presented in this section is best suited to describe the development of oppositional defiant disorder and the early-onset subtype of conduct disorder. For a more detailed review of this model see Conduct Problem Prevention Research Group (1992), McMahon and Estes (1997), Prinz and Connell (1997), or Reid and Eddy (1997).

Low birthweight, prenatal exposure to toxins, perinatal difficulties, and premature birth are some of the child-factors occurring early in life that have been linked to social-adaptational difficulties later in development (Olds, 1997; Sanson, Oberklaid, Pedlow, & Prior, 1991; Streissguth, Sampson, Barr, Bookstein, & Olson, 1994; Wakschlag et al., 1997). Another child-related factor that has already been mentioned as contributing to increased risk for conduct problems is difficult temperament. Children with dispositional tendencies toward high reactivity and poor self-regulation are at increased risk for disruptive behavior problems in the preschool period and later childhood (Bates, Bayles, Bennett, Ridge, & Brown, 1991; Eisenberg et al., 1996; Webster-Stratton & Eyberg, 1982). This appears to be particularly true when difficult temperament or hyperactivity is combined with environmental risk factors such as poverty or poor parenting (Sanson et al., 1991; Bates et al., 1991). When these factors combine, children may have difficulty with one of infancy's most critical tasks: the formation of a secure attachment relationship (Greenberg, Speltz, & DeKlyen, 1993). Research has shown that early insecure attachment is related to lower levels of competence with peers and higher levels of behavior problems in preschool children (Erikson, Sroufe, & Egeland, 1985; LaFreniere & Sroufe, 1985).

Family risk factors that have been related to child conduct problems include parental psychopathology, low social support, high levels of parental antisocial behavior and substance use, and family conflict (Cummings & Davies, 1994, Dodge, Pettit & Bates, 1994; Jennings, Stagg, & Connors, 1991; Robins, 1991; Wahler & Dumas, 1984). There are several ways in which these family factors may contribute to behavioral difficulties in children. First, children may directly model aggressive, antisocial interpersonal behavior that they observe at home and generalize it to other contexts (Putallaz & Heflin, 1990). Alternatively, children may be affected by family stressors that interfere with effective parenting. Although indirect, this appears to be one of the strongest mechanisms for transmission of risk factors from the parent to the child. For example, Larzelere and Patterson (1990) found that inconsistent and ineffective parenting mediated the relationship between early economic disadvantage and later delinquency in youth.

In general, research has shown that parents of children with disruptive behavior disorders tend to be less effective in managing their children's behavior and often engage in practices that actually contribute to and sustain their children's maladaptive behavior (McMahon & Wells, 1989; Patterson, 1982). These factors become particularly salient for children experiencing any of the biological risk factors outlined above. High levels of coercive and punitive discipline, the use of frequent reprimands, and low levels of warmth are parental behaviors that have been linked to elevated levels of child aggression and delinquency (Dishion, 1990; Eron, Huesmann, & Zelli, 1991; Loeber & Dishion, 1983, Pettit, Bates, & Dodge, 1993).

While some of the risk factors for conduct problems appear to reside in the child and others reflect problematic interaction patterns within the family, both types of risk factors are affected by conditions in the broader community context. Community variables associated with problematic behaviors in children include impoverished, unsafe or decaying neighborhoods, a lack of resources or strong social institutions such as churches or civic groups, and schools with significant numbers of high-risk students. Children in such communities may face social isolation from neighbors, physical danger or violence, and a lack of support or nurturing at school as teachers struggle to cope with many high needs students, often resorting to punitive, coercive classroom management strategies (Rutter, Maughan, Mortimore, Ouston, & Smith, 1979; Strain, Lambert, Kerr, Stagg, & Lenkner, 1983).

Coercive and negative behaviors that begin in the family context are often transferred to the school context (Reid, 1993). Children with a history of aggressive and disruptive behavior typically enter school without the skills necessary to regulate negative emotion in appropriate ways, to sustain attention to tasks, and to follow school rules. As a result, they have both academic and social problems in the school setting. Conduct problem children pose difficult management problems for teachers, who often become trapped in negativistic, coercive interaction patterns with them. Frequently, disruptive behavior in the classroom prevents children from engaging effectively in the learning process, and eventually these children may spend a great deal of time removed from school altogether for disciplinary reasons.

Compared to other youngsters, children with conduct problems have poorer social skills, higher rates of cognitive distortions (e.g., hostile attribution bias), and cognitive deficits (e.g., poor problem solving). In addition, children who are disruptive have more difficulty initiating and maintaining normative peer interactions. Over time, most children who continue to display significant amounts of aggression and socially inappropriate behavior are rejected by their peers, and their negative reputations reinforce their status (Dodge & Somberg, 1987). By the time these children enter middle school, the rejection and failure that they have experienced prevents them from developing a strong social bond to the adults and peers in the school setting (Hawkins & Weis, 1985; Hirschi, 1969). Deprived of the opportunities to develop socially skilled behaviors and form healthy friendships with normative peers, rejected and aggressive children are often drawn towards others like themselves, and in adolescence they may form deviant alliances that promote and reinforce antisocial behavior. They do not identify with the norms and values of the educational institution. Throughout adolescence, parental monitoring becomes increasingly important and one of the strongest family-level predictors of child antisocial behavior. Unsupervised youth who are involved in deviant peer groups are at great risk for truancy, dropout, unhealthy sexual behavior, delinquency, and substance use (Dishion & Loeber, 1985; Elliot, Huizinga, & Ageton, 1985; Eliott, Huizinga, & Menard, 1989).

To summarize, conduct problems often have their origins in early childhood, when child dispositional factors combine with ineffective parenting and result in poor parent-child attachment and escalating, coercive patterns of family interaction. Maladaptive behaviors and cognitions learned within the family can be generalized to the school and to peer contexts at school entry, persisting throughout childhood. These problem behaviors lead to social and academic maladjustment, rejection by mainstream social groups, and a failure to identify with normative institutions. In adolescence, antisocial behavior is further trained and supported in the deviant peer system, which may provide a gateway to delinquent activity.

Because disruptive behavior problems are often present throughout development, there are a number of points where preventive efforts might be beneficial. For example, parent education or consultation around management of a difficult infant or preschool child that results in the formation of a secure attachment and responsive parenting could conceivably prevent the development of coercive parent-child interactions. For children who are not identified until later in childhood, social skill and self-regulation training at school entry might allow for the development of positive peer relations, thus avoiding the negative trajectory associated with peer rejection. In fact, past early prevention efforts often targeted one or more of these skill domains or critical developmental tasks, but typically in isolation. Although these programs varied in their effectiveness, all yielded important information about the nature of risk with conduct problem children, and provided direction for subsequent, more comprehensive prevention efforts.

EFFECTIVE PREVENTION EFFORTS
FOR CONDUCT PROBLEMS

Past early intervention efforts directed at children with disruptive behavior disorders typically demonstrated modest effectiveness, but these improvements were not always maintained over time. Several conceptual and procedural problems with these early efforts probably contributed to these findings. First, these early prevention programs were usually short term and unidimensional in their focus, addressing a specific mediator of conduct problems for a brief period of time (e.g., Lochman, Burch, Curry, & Lampron, 1984). Second, many were conducted with small samples and focused exclusively on boys. Third, much of the previous work lacked a comprehensive developmental theory with a focus on specific adaptational challenges (e.g., adjusting to school entry, adjusting to middle school, etc.) facing children at various stages throughout childhood and adolescence. Or, some were models of how complex systems contribute to and maintain problem behaviors. Nonetheless, these studies have been extremely valuable for guiding subsequent intervention efforts. For example, early prevention programs targeting problem children often resulted in some degree of improvement in the specific behaviors targeted, but were ineffective at changing children's overall risk status. Peer-rejected children who participated in social skill training groups employing a coaching model sometimes showed positive changes in their social behavior, but these rarely translated into long-lasting improvements in their peer status or reputation (Putallaz & Wasserman, 1990). These failures highlight the limitations of an approach that considered the target child in isolation rather than as part of a dynamic social system encompassing both the classroom and the larger school climate. One modification of the coaching method, the *peer pairing* approach, pairs low and high status classmates together for cooperative and skill-building activities. The benefit of this approach is that the rejected child has the opportunity to model new skills and access other social networks within the classroom, while peers are given the chance to revise their opinions and expectations regarding the target child (Bierman & Furman, 1984; Oden & Asher, 1977).

While the majority of child-focused programs has yielded generally positive results, a few programs targeting high-risk adolescents have had harmful effects, with youth in the targeted groups exhibiting higher rates of problematic behavior following the intervention than control-group children (Dishion & Andrews, 1995; McCord, 1992). It appears that for adolescents in particular, the negative consequences associated with modeling and reinforcement of antisocial behavior by a deviant peer network outweigh any potential benefits of group-oriented interventions. Put more simply, high-risk youth who become acquainted with one another via group prevention programs apparently find more opportunities to engage in delinquent or troublesome behavior than those who receive no intervention at all. These studies were extremely useful in highlighting the developmental significance of the deviant peer network in adolescence, and indicate the need for different approaches to prevention for high-risk youth.

In the past decade, there have been tremendous advances in the field of prevention science, particularly in the theory, design, and evaluation of prevention programs. A substantial number of studies have documented the beneficial impact that programs can have on changing developmental trajectories and reducing negative outcomes. This research has influenced public policy and service delivery to the point where government agencies and consumers are rejecting interventions that have not been evaluated with high quality research designs, and calling instead for the use of empirically validated programs. Very few of these prevention programs have the specific goal of reducing diagnoses of conduct disorder, but rather attempt to change levels of symptomatology or mediating mechanisms (proximal risk factors) theoretically linked to the disorder. Interventions can be categorized by their focus (child, parent, both) and level (universal, selected, or indicated). The studies described below were selected because they were rigorously designed and evaluated. However, space constraints prohibits a comprehensive listing of all exemplary programs.

Single-Component Programs

Universal preventive interventions that attempt to reduce children's risk for conduct problems can be organized into those that promote nonviolent values and belief systems, those that promote the development of protective social-cognitive skills, and those that change the school ecology to be more supportive and less punitive. The Second Step program is an example of an effective curriculum-based model that focuses specifically on skills to understand and prevent violence (Grossman et al., 1997). The program has reduced observer-rated physical aggression and increased observer-rated prosocial behavior in classrooms.

Several effective universal prevention programs are designed to teach social-cognitive skills (e.g., emotion knowledge, self-control, problem-solving, refusal skills) with the hope that these skills will serve a protective function. The pioneers in this area are Shure and Spivak (1982) who designed the Interpersonal Cognitive Problem Solving (ICPS) program to teach children fundamental skills related to language, thinking, and listening skills involved in social problem solving. The program has significantly improved cognitive skills and reduced inhibition and impulsivity in both preschool- and elementary-age children. Another example of a school-based program that focuses on building the skills of students is Promoting Alternative Thinking Strategies (PATHS). PATHS has a different approach to building student social competence in that it teaches self-regulation and emotion knowledge skills in addition to social problem solving. PATHS has been evaluated in several trials with elementary-age children. In addition to significantly improved social-cognitive skills, children who received the program exhibited more adaptive behavior and fewer conduct problems two years after the program compared to those who did not receive it (Greenberg & Kusche, 1997; Greenberg, Kusche, Cook, & Quamma, 1995).

Finally, several universal programs are ecologically-focused and attempt to address contextual variables in the child's home or school as a means of reducing negative outcomes, rather than focusing exclusively in the individual child. One example is the School Transitional Environmental Project (STEP), a program that focuses on changing the school ecology by reducing school complexity, increasing teacher support, and creating student support systems so that school is less threatening to students during transitions (i.e., elementary to middle, middle to high school). Felner and colleagues (Felner & Adan, 1988; Felner, Ginter, & Primavera, 1982; Felner et al., 1993) found that STEP produced significantly lower levels of internalizing symptoms and delinquent behavior in students compared to controls.

There are also a number of single-component preventive interventions that have been effective with children who are already showing early signs of disorder. Child-focused selected and indicated programs typically target self-regulation, anger management skills, or peer relations. Lochman has developed and refined a cognitive-behavioral school-based intervention that focuses on developing anger-management skills in aggressive elementary and middle school-age boys (Lochman et al., 1984). The Anger Coping Program has been shown to lower boys aggressive and disruptive behavior in the classroom, and in some cases, improves parent ratings of aggressive behavior in the home (Lochman, 1985; Lochman et al., 1984; Lochman & Curry, 1986; Lochman, Lampron, Gemmer, Harris, & Wyckoff, 1989). As stated previously, Lochman's program and other child-focused interventions with at-risk populations tend to show positive results but are typically short-lived. For this reason, many of the larger-scale projects have incorporated these components as part of more comprehensive programs (e.g., Conduct Problems Prevention Research Group, 1992; Tremblay, Masse, Pagani, & Vitaro, 1996).

Parent-focused interventions with families of children who are at high risk for developing disruptive behavior disorders have primarily emphasized the role of discipline practices. Over the past twenty-five years there have been numerous demonstrations of the short-term effectiveness of social learning–based, parent-training and education intervention for families whose children displayed clinical levels of disruptive behavior problems. Examples of these are parenting programs that have emphasized the use of de-escalating, nonpunitive discipline strategies, parent anger management, educating parents about general developmental principles, and effective parent-child communication (Forehand & McMahon, 1981; Patterson, 1982; Patterson, Chamberlain, & Reid, 1982; Patterson, Reid, Jones, & Conger, 1975; Webster-Stratton, 1990; Webster-Stratton, Hollinsworth, & Kolpacoff, 1989; Webster-Stratton, Kolpacoff, & Hollinsworth, 1988). Recently, Webster-Stratton adapted her videotape series to a younger, Head Start population and applied this work in a preventive intervention (Webster-Stratton, 1998). Results of the evaluation of this intervention indicated that parents who received the intervention reported more effective discipline practices. According to observations and teacher ratings, children who received the program also exhibited significantly fewer conduct problems compared to controls at posttest and one-year follow-up.

Although there is some evidence of the effectiveness of parent education and training for promoting more positive parenting, there is little evidence at this time that parenting intervention alone has led to significantly reduced levels of symptomatology in school-aged populations over extended periods of time. One reason for the modest effects of parent training approaches may be the failure of this approach to address the multiple problems facing families of high-risk children. For example, parent training classes are unlikely to be effective in families experiencing significant poverty, marital conflict, social isolation, parent psychopathology, or vocational instability. Yet many of these problems co-occur with parenting deficits and maladaptive behaviors in children (Patterson, 1983; Webster-Stratton, 1990). In addition, the parent training approach fails to consider the significant independence of the family and peer environments; improvements in parental discipline and parent-child interaction may or may not promote changes in children's behavior and status with peers.

Recent findings by Webster-Stratton using parent training, and the combination of parent training and child skills training, replicate and bolster these early efforts and demonstrate longer-term effects (Webster-Stratton & Hammond, 1997). Similarly, Lochman has recently added a parent group component to his anger coping program, now referred to as the Coping Power Program. Initial results for this program are promising but the program is still undergoing evaluation (Lochman, 1998). These findings highlight the importance of using multi-component interventions that simultaneously target the multiple systems that contribute to the emergence and maintenance of conduct problems.

Multi-Component Programs

Although child-focused and parent-focused prevention models have shown some effectiveness, a new generation of multi-component models provides the promise of greater impact. Following from developmental models of risk and protection, interventions that target multiple environments (child, school, family, neighborhood) and multiple socialization agents (parent, teachers, peers) over extended developmental periods are probably necessary to alter the developmental trajectories of high-risk children who are already showing early signs of CD (Conduct Problems Prevention Research Group, 1992; Reid & Eddy, 1997). Multi-component programs have targeted early childhood, school-age children, and adolescents at the universal, selected, and indicated levels.

One example of an effective, multi-component program that has been conducted with preschool children is the High/Scope Perry Preschool Program (Berrueta-Clement, Schweinhart, Barnett, Epstein, & Weikart, 1984; Schweinhart & Weikart, 1980; Schweinhart, Weikart, & Larner, 1986; Weikart & Schweinhart, 1992). The program targets low-income children so it can be considered a selected program. High/Scope is a two-year intervention for preschool children that involves the combination of a classroom-based program (daily sessions that last 2.5 hours) and weekly home visits with caregivers by teachers. The classroom program is based on an extensive developmentally appropriate, structured curriculum based on principles of active learning and Piaget's models of child development. Teachers receive extensive training in the curriculum and the ratio of teachers to students is high. Home visits are designed to help caregivers provide educational support to their children and to problem solve challenging problems that occur during the sessions.

The program was evaluated on a sample of 123 African-American low-income children who were at risk of failing in school. A number of evaluation studies have documented the long-term effects for the programs (Berrueta-Clement et al., 1984; Weikart & Schweinhart, 1992). At age nineteen, youth who participated in the High/Scope Perry Program had higher educational achievement (i.e., graduated from high school, attended college), were more self-sufficient (i.e., were self-supporting, holding a job, less likely to be receiving public assistance) and less involved in delinquent activity (i.e., had fewer arrests, fewer teen pregnancies) than youth who had not received the program (Berrueta-Clement et al., 1984). Eight years later similar results were found. Program group members were more socially responsible, economically independent, and achieved higher educational levels (Weikart & Schweinhart, 1992).

Another multi-component program that combines parent and child-focused interventions is the First Steps Program (Walker, Kavanagh, Stiller,

Golly, Severson, & Feil, 1998; Walker, Stiller, Severson, Feil, & Golly, 1998). This indicated program intervenes with children and teaches them more adaptive behavior that is likely to foster social and academic success. The initial phase consists of a comprehensive screening process (Early Screening Project) which identifies kindergarten children exhibiting elevated levels of antisocial behavior. Families with an at-risk child receive a six-week home intervention in which program consultants help them develop ways of supporting their child's adaptive behavior. In school, target children participate in a classroom-based, skill-building and reinforcement program that lasts two months. The program was evaluated with forty-two subjects (two cohorts) using a randomized, experimental design. Teachers in this study reported significantly less aggressive and maladaptive behavior for intervention students compared to those in the control group. Observations indicated that program students showed more time engaged in academic activity. There were no group differences on teacher ratings of withdrawn behavior.

The majority of the multi-component programs are conducted with children during the elementary and middle school years. Linking the Interests of Families and Teachers (LIFT) is a multi-component, universal program that attempts to decrease risk and increase protective factors related to future violence and delinquency. LIFT focuses on the home, the individual student, the classroom and the peer group. In the home, LIFT works to teach parents effective forms of discipline and supervision, including consistent limit-setting and parental involvement. At school, a twenty-session program is taught to increase students' social and problem solving skills and to help students resist negative peer groups. Finally, LIFT uses a version of the intervention, the Good Behavior Game, to reduce inappropriate physical aggression on the playground.

Reid, Eddy, Fetrow & Stoolmiller (in press) conducted a randomized controlled trial with 671 children and their families from twelve public elementary schools in high-risk neighborhoods in Eugene, Oregon. At posttest, Reid and colleagues reported reductions in playground aggression, with the largest effect size among the most aggressive children, as well as improvements in family problem solving. At thirty months posttest, children from the treatment group were also significantly less likely to have been arrested.

The Seattle Social Development Project (SSDP) (Hawkins, Catalano, Morrison, O'Donnell, Abbott, & Day, 1992) is another example of a comprehensive universal prevention program that addresses multiple risk and protective factors across both individual and ecological domains (individual, school, and family). With a strong emphasis on creating and maintaining strong school and family bonds, the program combines modified teacher practices and parent training across a six-year intervention period. Classroom teachers were trained in SSDP instructional methods with three major components: proactive classroom management, interactive teaching, and cooperative learning. These teaching approaches were used in combination with (a) classroom-based cognitive and social skills training in first and sixth grades (refusal and life skills); and (b) parent training that emphasized child behavior management in first or second grade, academic support in second or third grade, and preventing drug use and antisocial behavior in fifth or sixth grade.

To assess the effects of full intervention and late intervention, a nonrandomized controlled trial with three conditions was created. The full intervention group received the intervention package from first through sixth grade. The late intervention group received the intervention package in grades five and six only, and the control group received no special intervention. Five hundred ninty-eight students were involved in the follow-up at age eighteen, six years after intervention. The findings indicated that students in the full intervention group reported significantly stronger attachment to school, improvement in self-reported achievement and less involvement in school misbehavior than did controls (Hawkins, Von Cleve, & Catalano, 1991; Hawkins, Catalano, Kosterman, Abbott, & Hill, in press). While no effects were shown for either the full or late intervention groups for lifetime prevalence of cigarettes, alcohol, marijuana or other illicit drug use at age eighteen, significantly fewer subjects in the full intervention group than in the control group had committed violent acts, reported heavy alcohol use in the past year, or engaged in sexual intercourse. There were no differences between the late intervention and control conditions; this provides a strong argument for beginning social competence programs early in the elementary years and continuing them across different developmental phases.

Tremblay and his colleagues (McCord, Tremblay, Vitaro, & Desmarais-Gervais, 1994; Tremblay, Masse, Pagani, & Vitaro, 1996; Tremblay, Masse et al., 1992; Tremblay, Vitaro et al., 1992; Vitaro & Tremblay, 1994) combined parent training and child social skill training in the Montreal Prevention Experiment. The program targeted 166 elementary school-age boys rated above the 70th percentile on a measure of aggressive and disruptive behavior. The subjects were randomly assigned to an intervention or a placebo control condition that lasted two years. The child component consisted of group skill training sessions in which children worked with normative peers to develop more prosocial and adaptive social behavior. Parents worked with family consultants approximately twice a month for two years to learn positive discipline techniques and how to support their child's positive behavior. Initial results did not reveal many group differences although at posttest intervention students were less likely (though not significantly) to be classified as seriously maladjusted. One counterintuitive finding was that intervention subjects were rated by their parents as significantly more disruptive (p < .02) and inattentive at posttest. The authors attributed this finding to changes in the mother's monitoring and ability to report accurately.

Group differences began to emerge on the follow-up assessments. Intervention students were significantly more likely to be on grade level at one-year follow-up (fourth grade) compared to controls. At the three-year follow-up when the boys were age twelve, treatment subjects were significantly less likely than control boys to engage in fighting according to teacher report or to be classified as having serious adjustment difficulties. According to self-report data from age ten to age twelve, treatment boys were also significantly less likely to engage in delinquent activity compared to controls. At age twelve, peer nominations of aggression from the best friends of boys in the treatment group were significantly lower than those made by best friends of controls. Effects of the treatment on other forms of antisocial behavior (e.g., self-reported stealing) and substance use continued into early adolescence (age eleven to fifteen). The results of the Montreal Prevention Experiment reflect the importance of extending assessments beyond the posttest point particularly when the behaviors being targeted by the intervention are more likely to occur later in development (e.g., delinquency). In this program, group differences between the intervention and control groups were apparent in multiple domains (i.e., academic, social, behavioral), emerged over time, and became increasingly significant.

Recently a consortium of prevention researchers have developed FAST Track, a schoolwide program that integrates universal, selective, and indicated models of prevention. It is intended to provide a comprehensive longitudinal model for the prevention of conduct disorders and associated adolescent problem behaviors (Conduct Problems Prevention Research Group, 1992). This randomized clinical trial involves fifty elementary schools in four U.S. urban and rural locations. The universal intervention includes teacher consultation in the use of the PATHS Curriculum (Kusche & Greenberg, 1994) throughout the elementary years. The targeted intervention package includes a series of interventions that involve the family (e.g., home visiting, parenting skills, case management), the child (e.g., academic tutoring, social skills training), the school, the peer group, and the community. Targeted children and families consist of those who are identified by a multi-stage screening for externalizing behavior problems during kindergarten. They consist of the ten percent of children with the most extreme behavior problems in schools in neighborhoods with high crime and poverty rates.

Results of the first three years indicate that there are significant reductions in special education referrals and aggression both at home and at school for the targeted children (Conduct Problems Prevention Research Group, 1998, 1999a, 1999b). FAST Track is predicated on a long-term model (i.e., the intervention will continue through middle school) that assumes that prevention of antisocial behavior will be achieved by building competencies and protective factors in the child, family, school, and community. The initial results provide evidence for improved social and academic development. Results of the universal component (i.e., PATHS) at the end of grade one show lower students' sociometric report peer aggression, and improved observers' ratings of the classroom atmosphere in the intervention sample (Conduct Problems Prevention Research Group, 1999b).

A final example of a multi-component intervention that targets older students is the Adolescent Transitions Program (ATP) (Andrews, Soberman, & Dishion, 1995; Dishion, Andrews, Kavanagh, & Soberman, 1996; Dishion & Andrews, 1995). This program is an indicated preventive intervention for behavior-problem adolescents and their parents. It is designed to improve the self-regulation of youth by teaching them problem solving skills. The parent component of the program attempts to improve parent management skills. In the original ATP evaluation, observations of parent-child dyads suggested that the program was successful at improving the quality of interaction in families. As noted previously, the impact on adolescents' behavior in school was only marginal, and for one treatment condition the adolescents' behavior actually worsened over time. Based on this research, Irvine and his colleagues (Irvine, Biglan, Smolkowski, Metzler, & Ary, in press) replicated ATP using only the parent component of the program. In this study, parent ratings of adolescents' behavior indicated significant treatment effects.

Summary

Over time, program developers and researchers have developed a more realistic perspective on the necessary intensity and comprehensiveness of programming to prevent psychopathology and promote positive development, especially with children and adolescents growing up in high-risk environments (Panel on High-Risk Youth, National Research Council, 1993). The success of prevention programs with conduct problem children and youth is enhanced by focusing not only on child behavior, but also the teacher's and family's behavior, the relationship between the home and school, and the needs of the schools and neighborhoods to support healthy norms and competent behavior.

CONCLUSION

Important and meaningful progress has been made in the prevention of conduct problems with children, families and schools during the last two decades. Developmental models that map the origins of these problems and the factors that maintain them, have become increasingly sophisticated. Further, more developers are utilizing this empirical knowledge to design developmentally sensitive programs that are comprehensive and that are sustained over longer periods of time. Many of the multi-component programs reviewed in this chapter include long-term follow-up assessments that not only document beneficial impact but provide convincing evidence for the cost-effectiveness of these interventions. This research has influenced public policy and service delivery to the point where government agencies and consumers are now calling for the utilization of empirically validated, effective models of intervention to address antisocial behavior in children and youth.

Although the programs outlined above represent *best practices* in prevention science applications, a number of serious limitations remain. First, most programs, even those that are comprehensive and multi-modal, continue to show somewhat modest effects. This is particularly true of programs targeting children and adolescents who present with multiple, severe risk factors. For example, early data from the FAST Track project revealed significant differences between control and intervention children with regard to a variety of problematic behaviors, yet one-third of the intervention children nonetheless continued to display high levels of behavior problems (Conduct Problems Prevention Research Group, 1998). Current models are still inadequate to change the social trajectories of the highest-risk groups, and many of these young people continue to experience negative outcomes despite high levels of intervention.

Second, while some programs demonstrate excellent effectiveness when implemented properly, poor-quality implementation can render them utterly ineffective. Many prevention researchers (Domitrovich & Greenberg, in press; Durlak, 1998; Scanlon, Horst, Nay, Schmidt, & Waller, 1977; Scheirer, 1987) have discussed the importance of monitoring implementation quality. Durlak (1998) notes that implementation information is important for determining what actually took place during an intervention, whether the critical program components were delivered, the quality of the delivery, and whether the target audience was reached. The majority of effective prevention programs do not measure implementation or only measure narrow dimensions. This implementation information is also rarely related to program outcomes which is unfortunate because measures of implementation quality can establish the internal validity of a program and, if related to outcomes, may explain any lack of program effects. Prevention science as a field is only beginning to address the formidable problem of implementation quality and the maintenance of program fidelity over time.

While implementation remains a challenge even for scientifically conducted demonstration trials, prevention scientists face another challenge of moving programs beyond the demonstration level and diffusing them into naturalistic settings. Because of these difficulties, many effective programs are not widely utilized with the groups in greatest need. Instead, schools, mental health providers and other professionals working with youth often lack a prevention science orientation, and may opt for programming with intuitive appeal but without empirical documentation of its effectiveness. Not surprisingly, many of the prevention programs actually utilized with children and youth lack any type of evaluation confirming their effectiveness, and are essentially "wisdom" based.

In order to address the needs of the most at-risk children and families, and sustain prevention efforts, communities need to develop collaborations across the major governing, social service, and law enforcement agencies. No one provider can afford the package of strategies and programs that are required at each level of need in each community. Local government officials, school personnel, mental health directors, and police officers do not traditionally communicate or work together. These individuals need to find ways to break down traditional barriers to collaboration with proactive and creative efforts. Communities should develop and share common conceptual models, language, and procedures. The long-term benefits of reducing antisocial behavior and its related problems (e.g., substance use, crime) will only be experienced after communities collaborate to identify the risks in their community, commit to comprehensive, empirically based, preventive interventions, and share the responsibility and financial burden of these programs.

REFERENCES

American Psychiatric Association. (1994). *Diagnostic and statistical manual of mental disorders* (4th ed.). Washington, D.C.: Author.

Andrews, D. W., Soberman, L. H., & Dishion, T. J. (1995). The Adolescent Transition Program: A school-based program for high-risk teens and their parents. *Education & Treatment of Children, 18*, 478-498.

Bates, J. E., Bayles, K., Bennett, D. S., Ridge, B., & Brown, M. M. (1991). Origins of externalizing behavior problems at eight years of age. In D. J. Pepler & K. H. Rubin (Eds.), *The development and treatment of childhood aggression* (pp. 93-119). Hillsdate, N.J.: Erlbaum.

Berrueta-Clement, J. R., Schweinhart, L. J., Barnett, W. S., Epstein, A. S., & Weikart, D. P. (1984). *Changed lives: The effects of the Perry Preschool Program on youths through age 19.* Ypsilanti, Mich.: The High/Scope Press.

Bierman, K. L., & Furman, W. (1984). The effects of social skills training and peer involvement on the social adjustment of preadolescents. *Child Development, 55*, 151-162.

Bronfenbrenner, U. (1979). *The ecology of human development: Experiments by nature and design.* Cambridge, Mass.: Harvard University Press.

Bronfenbrenner, U. (1995). Developmental ecology through space and time: A future perspective. In P. Moen, G. H. Elder, Jr., & K. Luscher (Eds.), *Examining lives in context: Perspectives in the ecology of human development.* (pp. 619-647). Washington, D.C.: American Psychological Association.

Bronfenbrenner, U., & Crouter, A. C. (1983). The evolution of environmental models in developmental research. In P. H. Mussen (Series Ed.) & W. Kessen (Vol. Ed.), *Handbook of child psychology: Vol. 1. History, theory, and methods* (4th ed., pp. 357-413). New York: Wiley.

Cicchetti, D. (1984). The emergence of developmental psychopathology. *Child Development, 55,* 1-7.

Cicchetti, D., & Cohen, D. J. (1995). *Developmental psychopathology: Vol. 2. Risk, disorder and adaptation.* New York: Wiley.

Coie, J. D., Watt, N. F., West. S. G, Hawkins, J. D., Asarnow, J. R., Markman, H. J., Ramey, S. L., Shure, M .B., & Long, B. (1993). The science of prevention: A conceptual framework and some directions for a national research program. *American Psychologist, 48,* 1013-1022.

Conduct Problems Prevention Research Group. (1992). A developmental and clinical model for the prevention of conduct disorders: The FAST Track Program. *Development and Psychopathology, 4,* 509-527.

Conduct Problems Prevention Research Group. (1998, August). *Results of theFast Track Prevention Project: Grade 3 Outcomes.* Paper presented at the American Psychological Association, San Francisco.

Conduct Problems Prevention Research Group. (1999a). Initial impact of the Fast Track Prevention trial for conduct problems: I. The high-risk sample. *Journal of Consulting and Clinical Psychology, 67,* 631-647.

Conduct Problems Prevention Research Group. (1999b). Initial impact of the Fast Track Prevention trial for conduct problems: II. Classroom effect. *Journal of Consulting and Clinical Psychology, 67,* 648-657.

Costello, E. J. (1990). Child psychiatric epidemiology: Implications for clinical research and practice. In B. B. Lahey & A. E. Kazdin (Eds.), *Advances in clinical child psychology.* Vol. 13 (pp. 53-90). New York: Plenum Press.

Cummings, E. M., & Davies, P. (1994). Maternal depression and child development. *Journal of Child Psychology and Psychiatry, 35,* 73-112.

Dishion, T. J. (1990). The family ecology of boys' peer relations in middle childhood. *Child Development, 61,* 874-892.

Dishion, T. J., & Andrews, D. W. (1995). Preventing escalation in problem behaviors with high-risk young adolescents: Immediate and 1-year outcomes. *Journal of Consulting and Clinical Psychology, 63,* 538-548.

Dishion, T. J., & Andrews, D. W., Kavanagh, K., & Soberman, L. H. (1996). Preventive interventions for high-risk youth: The adolescent transitions program. In. R. DeV. Peters & R. J. McMahon (Eds.). *Preventing childhood disorders, substance abuse and delinquency* (pp. 184-214). Thousand Oaks, Calif.: Sage.

Dishion, T. J., & Loeber, R. (1985). Male adolescent marijuana and alcohol use: The role of parents and peers revisited. *American Journal of Drug and Alcohol Abuse*, 11, 11-25.

Dodge, K. A., Pettit, G. S., & Bates, J. E. (1994). Socialization mediators of the relation between socioeconomic status and child conduct problems. *Child Development, 65*, 649-665.

Dodge, K. A., & Somberg, D. R. (1987). Hostile attributional biases among aggressive boys are exacerbated under conditions of threats to the self. *Child Development, 58*, 213-224.

Domitrovich, C. E., & Greenberg, M. T. (2000). The study of implementation: Current findings from effective programs that prevent mental disorder in school-aged children. *Journal of Educational and Psychological Consultation, 11*, 193-221

Durlak, J. A. (1998). Why program implementation is important. *Journal of Revention and Intervention in the Community, 17*, 5-18.

Eisenberg, N., Fabes, R. A., Guthrie, I. K., Murphy, B. C., Maszk, P., Holmgren, R., & Suh, K. (1996). The relations of regulation and emotionality to problem behavior in elementary school children. *Development and Psychopathology, 8*, 141-162.

Elliot, D. S., Huizinga, D., & Ageton, S. S. (1985). *Explaining delinquency and drug use.* Beverly Hills: Sage Publications.

Elliott, D.S., Huizinga, D., & Menard, S. (1989). *Multiple problem youth: Delinquency, substance use, and mental health problems.* New York: Springer-Verlag.

Erikson, E. (1963). *Childhood and society* (2nd ed.). New York: Norton.

Erikson, M. F., Sroufe, L. A., & Egeland, B. (1985). The relationship between quality of attachment and behavior problems in preschool in a high-risk sample. In I. Bretherton & E. Waters (Eds.), Growing points in attachment theory and research. *Monographs of the Society for Research in Child Development, 50* (1-2, Serial No. 209).

Eron, L. D., Huesmann, L. R., & Zelli, A. (1991). The role of parental variables in the learning of aggression. In D. J. Pepler & K. H. Rubin (Eds.), *The development and treatment of childhood aggression* (pp. 169-188). Hillsdale, N.J.: Erlbaum.

Felner, R. D., & Adan, A. M. (1988). The school transitional project: An ecological intervention and evaluation. In R. H. Price, E. L. Cowen, R. P. Lorion, & J. Ramos-McKay (Eds.), *14 ounces of prevention: A casebook for practitioners* (pp. 111-122). Washington, DC: American Psychological Association.

Felner, R. D., Brand, S., Adan, A. M., Mulhall, P. F., Flowers, N., Sartain, B, & DuBois, D. L. (1993). Restructuring the ecology of the school as an approach to prevention during school transitions: Longitudinal follow-ups and extensions of the school transitional environment project (STEP). *Prevention in Human Services, 10*, 103-136.

Felner, R. D., Ginter, M., & Primavera, J. (1982). Primary prevention during school transitions: Social support and environmental structure. *American Journal of Community Psychology, 10*, 277-290.

Forehand, R., & McMahon, R. J. (1981). *Helping the noncompliant child: A clinician's guide to effective parent training.* New York: Guilford.

Greenberg, M. T. & Kusche, C. A. (1997). *Improving Children's Emotion Regulation and Social Competence: The effects of the PATHS curriculum.* Paper presented at meeting of Society for Research in Child Development, Washington, D.C.

Greenberg, M. T. & Kusche, C. A. (1998). *Promoting social competence and preventing maladjustment in school-aged children: The effects of the PATHS curriculum.* Manuscript submitted for publication.

Greenberg, M. T., Kusche, C. A., Cook, E. T., & Quamma, J. P. (1995). Promoting emotional competence in school-aged deaf children: The effects of the PATHS curriculum. *Development and Psychopathology, 7,* 117-136.

Greenberg, M. T., Speltz, M. L., & DeKlyen, M. (1993). The role of attachment in the early development of disruptive behavior problems. *Development and Psychopathology, 5,* 191-213.

Grossman, D. C., Neckerman, H. J., Koepsell, T. D., Liu, P., Asher, K. N., Beland, K., Frey, K., & Rivera, F. P. (1997). Effectiveness of a violence prevention curriculum among children in elementary school. *Journal of the American Medical Association, 277,* 1605-1611.

Hawkins, J. D., Catalano, R. F., Kosterman, R., Abbott, R., & Hill, K. (In press). Preventing adolescent health-risk behaviors by strengthening protection during childhood. *Archives of Pediatrics and Adolescent Medicine.*

Hawkins J., Catalano R., Morrison D., O'Donnell J., Abbott R., & Day L. (1992). The

Seattle Social Development Project: Effects of the first four years on protective factors and problem behaviors. In J. McCord & R. Tremblay (Eds.), *The prevention of antisocial behavior in children* (pp. 139-161). New York: Guilford.

Hawkins, J. D., Von Cleve, E., & Catalano, R. F. (1991). Reducing early childhood aggression: Results of a primary prevention program. *Journal of the American Academy of Child and Adolescent Psychiatry, 30,* 208-217.

Hawkins, J. D. & Weis, J. G. (1985). The social development model: An integrated approach to delinquency prevention. *Journal of Primary Prevention, 6,* 73-97.

Hirschi, T. (1969). *Causes of delinquency.* Berkeley: University of California Press.

Institute of Medicine. (1994). *Reducing risks for mental disorders: Frontiers for preventive intervention research.* Washington, D.C.: National Academy Press.

Irvine, A. B., Biglan, A., Smolkowski, K., Metzler, C. W., & Ary, D. V. (In press). The Effectiveness of a Parenting Skills Program for Parents of Middle School Students in Small Communities. *Journal of Consulting and Clinical Psychology.*

Jennings, K. D., Stagg, V., & Connors, R. E. (1991). Social networks and mothers' interactions with their preschool children. *Child Development, 62,* 966-978.

Kazdin, A. E. (1985). *Treatment of antisocial behavior in children and adolescents.* Homewood, Ill.: Dorsey Press.

Kazdin, A. E. (1987). Treatment of antisocial behavior in children: Current status and uture directions. *Psychological Bulletin, 102,* 187-203.

Kazdin, A. E. (1991). Prevention of conduct disorder. *In the prevention of mental disorders: Progress, problems, and prospects.* Washington, D.C.: National Institute of Mental Health.

Kazdin, A. E. (1995). *Conduct disorders in childhood and adolescence* (2nd ed.). Thousand Oaks, Calif.: Sage.

Kellam, S. G. (1990). Developmental epidemiological framework for family research on depression and aggression. In G. R. Patterson (Ed.), *Depression and aggression in family interaction* (pp. 11-48). Hillsdale, N.J.: Erlbaum.

Kellam, S. G., Koretz, D., & Moscicki, E. K. (1999). Core elements of developmental epidemiologically based prevention research. *American Journal of Community Psychology, 27*, 463-482.

Kellam, S. G., & Rebok, G. W. (1992). Building developmental and etiological theory through epidemiologically based preventive intervention trials. In J. McCord & R. E. Tremblay (Eds.), *Preventing antisocial behavior: Interventions from birth through adolescence* (pp. 162-194). New York: Guilford Press.

Kusche, C. A., & Greenberg, M. T. (1994). *The PATHS curriculum: Promoting alternative thinking strategies.* Seattle: Developmental Research Programs.

Larzelere, R. E., & Patterson, G. R. (1990). Parental management: mediators of the effect of socioeconomic status on early delinquency. *Criminology, 28*, 301-323.

LaFreniere, P. J., & Sroufe, L. A. (1985). Profiles of peer competence in the preschool: Interrelations between measures, influence of social ecology, and relation to attachment history. *Developmental Psychology, 21*, 56-69.

Lochman, J. E. (1985). Effects of different treatment lengths in cognitive-behavioral interventions with aggressive boys. *Child Psychiatry and Human Development, 16*, 45-56.

Lochman, J. E. (1998). *Indicated prevention of substance use in high risk boys.* Unpublished grant proposal submitted to the National Institute of Drug Abuse.

Lochman, J. E., Burch, P. R., Curry, J. F., & Lampron, L. B. (1984). Treatment and generalization effects of cognitive-behavioral and goal-setting interventions with aggressive boys. *Journal of Consulting and Clinical Psychology, 52*, 915-916.

Lochman, J. E., & Curry, J. F. (1986). Effects of social problem-solving training and self-instruction training with aggressive boys. *Journal of Clinical Child Psychology, 15*, 159-164.

Lochman, J. E., Lampron, L. B., Gemmer, T. C., Harris, S. R., & Wyckoff, G. M. (1989). Teacher consultation and cognitive-behavioral intervention with aggressive boys. *Psychology in the Schools, 26*, 179-188.

Loeber, R., & Dishion, T. (1983). Early predictors of male delinquency: A review. *Psychological Bulletin, 93*, 68-99.

Lorion, R. P. (1990). Developmental analyses of community phenomena. In P. Toluene, C. Keys, F. Cheroot, & L. Jason (Eds.) *Researching community psychology: Issues of theories and methods* (pp. 32-41). Washington, D.C.: American Psychological Association.

Luther, S. S. (1993). Annotation: Methodological and conceptual issues in research on childhood resilience. *Journal of Child Psychology and Psychiatry & Allied Disciplines, 34*, 441-452.

Luther, S. S., & Zigler, E. (1992). Intelligence and social competence among high-risk adolescents. *Development and Psychopathology, 4*, 287-299.

McCord, J. (1992). The Cambridge-Sommerville Study: A pioneering longitudinal-experimental study of delinquency prevention. In J. McCord & R. Tremblay (Eds.). *Preventing antisocial behavior: Interventions from birth to adolescence* (pp. 196-209). New York: Guilford.

McCord, J., Tremblay, R. E., Vitaro, F., & Desmarais-Gervais, L. (1994). Boys' disruptive behavior, school adjustment, and delinquency: The Montreal prevention experiment. *International Journal of Behavioural Development, 17*, 739-752.

McMahon, R. J., & Estes, A. (1997). Conduct problems. In E. J. Mash & L. G. Terdal (Eds.), *Assessment of childhood disorders* (3rd ed.). New York: Guilford.

McMahon, R. J., & Wells, K. C. (1989). Conduct disorders. In E. J. Mash & R. A. Barkley (Eds.), *Treatment of childhood disorders* (pp. 73-134). New York: Guilford.

Morissett, C. E., Barnard, K. E., Greenberg, M. T., Booth, C. L., & Spieker, S. J. (1990). Environmental influences on early language development: The context of social risk. *Development and Psychopathology, 2*, 127-149.

National Advisory Mental Health Council. (1990). *National plan for research on child and adolescent mental disorders.* Rockville, Md: DHHS Publication No. 90-1683.

National Institute of Mental Health (1993). *The prevention of mental disorders: A national research agenda.* Bethesda, Md.: NMHA.

Oden, S., & Asher, S. R. (1977). Coaching children in social skills. *Child Development, 48*, 495-506.

Office of Technology Assessment, United States Congress. (1986). *Children's mental health: Problems and services-A background paper.* Washington, D.C.: Government Printing Office.

Offord, D., Boyle, M. H. Racine, Y. A., Fleming, J. E. Cadman, D. T., Blum, H. M., Byrne, C., Links, P. S., Lipman, E. L., MacMillan, H. L., Rae Grant, N. I., Sanford, M. N., Szatmari, P., Thomas, H., & Woodward, C. A. (1992). Outcome, prognosis, and risk in a longitudinal follow-up study. *Journal of the American Academy of Child and Adolescent Psychiatry, 31*, 916-923.

Olds, D. L. (1997). Tobacco exposure and impaired development: A review of the evidence. *Mental Retardation and Developmental Disabilities Research Reviews, 3*, 257-269.

Otto, R. K., Greenstein, J. J., Johnson, M. K., Friedman, R. M. (1992). Prevalence of mental disorders among youth in the juvenile justice system. In J. J. Cocozza (Ed.), *Responding to the mental health needs of youth in the juvenile justice system.* (pp. 7-48). Seattle: National Coalition for Mentally Ill in the Criminal Justice System.

Panel on High-Risk Youth, National Research Council. (1993). Losing generations: *Adolescents in high-risk settings.* Washington, D.C.: National Academy Press.

Patterson, G. R. (1982). *Coercive family process.* Eugene, Ore.: Castalia.

Patterson, G. R. (1983). Stress: A change agent for family process. In N. Garmezy & M. Rutter (Eds.), *Stress, coping and development in children* (pp. 235-264). New York: McGraw-Hill.

Patterson, G. R., Chamberlain, P., Reid, J. B. (1982). A comparative evaluation of a parent-training program. *Behavior Therapy, 13*, 638-650.

Patterson, G. R., DeBaryshe, B. D., & Ramsey, E. (1989). A developmental perspective on antisocial behavior. *American Psychologist, 44*, 329-335.

Patterson, G. R., Reid, J. B., Jones, R. R., & Conger, R. E. (1975). *A social learning approach to family intervention (Vol. 1): Families with aggressive children.* Eugene, Ore.: Castalia.

Pettit, G. S., Bates, J. E., & Dodge, K. A. (1993). Family interaction patterns and children's conduct problems at home and school: A longitudinal perspective. *School Psychology Review, 22*, 403-420.

Piaget, J. (1983). Piaget's theory. In P. Mussen (Ed.), *Handbook of child psychology: Vol. 1.* (pp. 102-128) New York: Wiley.

Pittman, K. J., & Cahill, M. (1992). *Pushing the boundaries of education: The implications of a youth development approach to education policies, structures, and collaborations.* Washington, D.C.: Council of Chief State School Officers.

Prinz, R. J., & Connell, C. M. (1997). Conduct disorders and antisocial behavior. In R. T. Ammerman & M. Hersen (Eds.), *Handbook of prevention and treatment with children and adolescents: Intervention in the real world context.* New York: John Wiley & Sons.

Putallaz, M., & Heflin, A. H. (1990). Parent-child interaction. In S. R. Asher & J. D. Coie (Eds.), *Peer rejection in childhood* (pp. 189-216). Cambridge, Mass.: Cambridge University Press.

Putallaz, M., & Wasserman, A. (1990). Children's entry behaviors. In S. R. Asher & J. D. Coie (Eds.), *Peer rejection in childhood.* (pp. 60-89) New York: Cambridge University Press.

Reid, J. B. (1993). Prevention of conduct disorder before and after school entry: Relating interventions to developmental findings. *Development and Psychopathology, 5,* 243-262.

Reid, J. B., and Eddy, M. J. (1997). The prevention of antisocial behavior: Some considerations in the search for effective interventions. In D. Staff , J. Breiling, & J. D. Maser (Eds.), *Handbook of antisocial behavior.* (pp. 343-356) New York: John Wiley & Sons.

Reid, J. B., Eddy, J. M., Fetrow, R. A., & Stoolmiller, M. (In press). Description and immediate impacts of a preventive intervention for conduct problems. *American Journal of Community Psychology.*

Robins, L.N. (1991). Conduct disorder. *Journal of Child Psychology and Psychiatry, 32,* 193-209.

Rutter, M. (1985). Resilience in the face of adversity: Protective factors and resistance to psychiatric disorder. *British Journal of Psychiatry, 147,* 598-611.

Rutter, M., Maughan, B., Mortimore, P., Ouston, J., & Smith, A. (1979). *Fifteen thousand hours: Secondary schools and their effects on children.* Cambridge, Mass.: Harvard University Press.

Sameroff, A. J. (1991). Prevention of developmental psychopathology using the transactional model: Perspectives on host, risk agent and environmental interactions. In *The prevention of mental disorders: Progress, problems, and prospects.* Washington, D.C.: National Institute of Mental Health.

Sameroff, A. J., & Chandler, M. J. (1975). Reproductive risk and the continuum of caretaker casualty. In F. D. Horowitz (Ed.), *Review of child development research* Vol. 4 (pp. 187-244). Chicago: University of Chicago Press.

Sanson, A., Oberklaid, F., Pedlow, R., & Prior, M. (1991). Risk indicators: Assessment of infancy predictors of pre-school behavioral adjustment. *Journal of Child Psychology and Psychiatry, 32,* 609-626.

Scanlon, J. W., Horst, P., Nay, J., Schmidt, R. E., & Waller, A. E. (1977). Evaluability assessment: Avoiding type III and IV errors. In G. R. Gilbert & P. J. Conklin (Eds.), *Evaluation management: A source book of readings* (pp. 71-90). Charlottesville, Va.: U.S. Civil Service Commission.

Scheirer, M. A. (1987). Program theory and implementation theory: Implications for evaluators. In L. Bickman (Ed.), *Using program theory in evaluation* (pp. 40-67). San Francisco: Jossey-Bass.

Schweinhart, L. J., & Weikart, D. P. (1980). *Young children group up: The effects of the Perry Preschool Program on youths through age 15.* Ypsilanti, Mich.; The High/Scope Press.

Schweinhart, L. J., Weikart, D. P., & Larner, M. B. (1986). A report on the High/Scope preschool curriculum comparison study: Consequences of three preschool curriculum models through age 15. *Early Childhood Research Quarterly, 1,* 15-45.

Shure, M. B., & Spivack, G. (1982). Interpersonal problem solving in young children: A cognitive approach to prevention. *American Journal of Community Psychology, 10,* 341-356.

Sroufe, L. A., & Rutter, M. (1984). The domain of developmental psychopathology. *Child Development, 83,* 173-189.

Strain, P. S., Lambert, D. L., Kerr, M. M., Stagg, V., & Lenkner, D. A. (1983). Naturalistic assessment of children's compliance to teacher's requests and consequences for compliance. *Journal of Applied Behavior Analysis, 16,* 243-249.

Streissguth, A. P., Sampson, P. D., Barr, H. M., Bookstein, F. L., & Olson, H. C. (1994). The effects of prenatal exposure to alcohol and tobacco: Contributions from the Seattle longitudinal prospective study and implications for public policy. In H. L. Needleman & D. Bellinger (Eds.), *Prenatal exposure to toxins* (pp. 148-183). Baltimore: The Johns Hopkins University Press.

Tremblay, R. E., Masse, L. C., Pagani, L., & Vitaro, F. (1996). From childhood aggression to adolescent maladjustment: The Montreal prevention experiment. In. R. DeV. Peters & R. J. McMahon (Eds.), *Preventing childhood disorders, substance abuse and delinquency* (pp. 268-298). Thousand Oaks, Calif.: Sage.

Tremblay, R. E., Masse, B., Perron, D., LeBlanc, M., Schwartzman, A. E., & Ledingham, J. E. (1992). Early disruptive behavior, poor school achievement, delinquent behavior, and delinquent personality: Longitudinal analyses. *Journal of Consulting and Clinical Psychology, 60,* 64-72.

Tremblay, R. E., Vitaro, F., Bertrand, L., LeBlanc, M., Beauchesne, H., Boileau, H., David, L. (1992). Parent and child training to prevent early onset of delinquency: The Montreal longitudinal-experimental study. In J. McCord & R. E. Tremblay (Eds.), *Preventing antisocial behavior: Interventions from birth through adolescence* (pp. 117-138). New York: Guilford.

Vitaro, F., & Tremblay, R. E. (1994). Impact of a prevention program on aggressive children's friendships and social adjustment. *Journal of Abnormal Child Psychology, 22,* 457-475.

Wahler, R. G., & Dumas, J. E. (1984). Changing the observational coding styles of insular and noninsular mothers: A step toward maintenance of parent training effects. In R. F. Dangel & R. A. Polster (Eds.), *Parent training: Foundations of research and practice* (pp. 379-416). New York: Guilford Press.

Wakschlag, L. S., Lahey, B. B., Loeber, R., Green, S. M., Gordon, R. A., & Leventhal, B. L. (1997). Maternal smoking during pregnancy and the risk of conduct disorder in boys. *Archives of General Psychiatry, 54,* 670-680.

Walker, H.M., Kavanagh, K., Stiller, B., Golly, A., Severson, H.H., & Feil, E.G. (1998). First step to success: An early intervention approach for preventing school antisocial behavior. *Journal of Emotional and Behavioral Disorders, 6,* 66-80.

Walker, H., Stiller, B., Severson, H. H., Feil, E. G., & Golly, A. (1998). First step to success: Intervening at the point of school entry to prevent antisocial behavior patterns. *Psychology in the Schools, 35,* 259-269.

Webster-Stratton, C. (1990). Long-term follow-up of families with young conduct problem children: From preschool to grade school. *Journal of Clinical Child Psychology, 19,* 144-149.

Webster-Stratton, C. (1998). Preventing conduct problems in Head Start children: Strengthening parenting competencies. *Journal of Consulting and Clinical Psychology, 66,* 715-730.

Webster-Stratton, C., & Eyberg, S. M. (1982). Child temperament: Relationship with child behavior problems and parent-child interactions. *Journal of Clinical Child Psychology, 11,* 123-129.

Webster-Stratton, C. & Hammond, M. (1997). Treating children with early-onset conduct problems: A comparison of child and parent training interventions. *Journal of Consulting and Clinical Psychology, 65,* 93-109.

Webster-Stratton, C., Hollinsworth, T., & Kolpacoff, M. (1989). The long-term effectiveness and clinical significance of three cost-effective training programs for families with conduct-problem children. *Journal of Consulting and Clinical Psychology, 57,* 550-553.

Webster-Stratton, C., Kolpacoff, M., & Hollinsworth, T. (1988). Self-administered videotape therapy for families with conduct-problem children: Comparison with two cost-effective treatments and a control group. *Journal of Consulting and Clinical Psychology, 56,* 558-566.

Weikart, D. P., & Schweinhart, L. J. (1992). High/Scope Perry Preschool Program. In J. McCord and R. E. Tremblay (Eds.), *Preventing antisocial behavior* (pp. 146-166). New York: Guilford Press.

Chapter Nine

RESPONDING TO TRAUMATIC DEATH IN THE SCHOOL: THE NEW JERSEY MODEL

MAUREEN M. UNDERWOOD AND KAREN DUNNE-MAXIM

BACKGROUND

WHEN A SCHOOL COMMUNITY experiences the sudden traumatic death of a student or faculty member, it is important to the life of the school as a whole and to those who are personally affected by the death to acknowledge the event. This acknowledgment is appropriately directed at providing opportunities for the entire school population to deal with the death in a format that provides support, control, and structure. Its focus is not on the deceased but on the needs of the living, and intervention, which is termed *postvention*, is designed to facilitate resolution of the loss and a return to the normal routine of the school as quickly as possible. Postvention strategies play an intrinsic role in containing both suicide contagion and the other potentially destructive coping responses that often occur among young people subsequent to the violent death of one of their peers or role models (Dunne-Maxim & Underwood, 1991).

The New Jersey Adolescent Suicide Prevention Project at the University of Medicine and Dentistry of New Jersey–University Behavioral HealthCare was established through legislation in 1985. Early project goals, which focused on the development of postvention techniques, were initiated after multiple suicides in a northern New Jersey community in the late 1980s focused international attention on the state's response plan for addressing management and containment of the tragedy. The postvention model initiated in the aftermath of this tragedy was the basis for recommendations subsequently disseminated nationally by the Centers for Disease Control and Prevention (CDC). The New Jersey Project has, in fact, collaborated with CDC in several other areas of suicide prevention, including recommendations for media coverage that minimize contagion. This information is included in a document which has also received national distribution (CDC, 1994).

154

While the project's initial postvention activities were primarily directed to recovery following high school suicides, requests were received with increasing frequency for postvention following other sudden violent deaths, e.g., the murders of elementary and middle school students, the deaths of multiple students in car crashes, and sudden faculty deaths. To meet these needs for postvention which were not restricted to deaths by suicide and encompassed all phases of the life cycle, the project expanded its initial focus. Resource materials were adapted to cover the continuum from elementary and middle school through high school and specific training material was added to address recovery from homicide and other types of traumatic losses.

COMMUNITY CONTEXT

One of the significant features of the New Jersey postvention model is that it emphasizes the involvement of the entire community in the resolution of grief after the death of one of its members, rather than delegating the entire responsibility to the school. This is particularly important after a suicide, where the dynamics of grief include blaming and scapegoating that are often primarily targeted at the school. Additionally, this postvention design reflects the fact that sharing responsibility also increases and broadens the resource base, augmenting the school's response capacity with that of the community at large. This facilitates provision of support to students at times when school is not in session such as weekends or school vacations, or at funeral-related activities that take place off school property. Finally, broadening the response base provides access to those affected by the loss in a context other than the school, such as church groups, community clubs, or sports teams.

To operationalize this model, the resources and expertise that existed at the state level had to be decentralized and similar response capabilities created in counties and municipalities statewide. In the early stages of the project, a series of training seminars, coordinated through the State Departments of Education and Human Services, were offered to educators and mental health professionals at regional levels throughout the state to introduce both the postvention model and the concept of community responsibility. Additional workshops were provided for individual school districts upon request as long as representatives from the community were also involved. More recently, county forums have been held that are sponsored by the County Office of Emergency Management. These forums bring together community leaders and decision makers and outline the postvention paradigm as part of each county's legislatively mandated mental health emergency plan.

Concurrently, dissemination of the program model to diverse communities and populations has been addressed through publication of a manual that contains specific techniques and guidelines for postvention implementation. *Managing Sudden Traumatic Loss in the Schools* is now in its fourth printing, with mor than 20,000 copies having been distributed nationwide (Underwood & Dunne-Maxim, 1997). The manual suggests practical strategies for loss management based on both theory and the actual experiences of more than 400 schools where the New Jersey project has intervened. A series of videotapes drawn from the content of the manual have also been produced. These videos have been designed to offer support and direction from experts during the crisis per se to specific segments of the school community.

POSTVENTION DESIGN

The theoretical foundation of the postvention plan is based on crisis intervention strategies, grief theory, and suicide prevention techniques. The plan's goals are realistically simple: to minimize contagion and to facilitate the grief process. Emphasis is placed on the provision of support, control, and structure to all those affected by the loss and these three concepts are echoed throughout the program content. Educators are urged to evaluate all decisions during the crisis in light of these framing principles. This provides them with a simple and effective tool for measuring their adherence to the goals of crisis intervention.

Grief theory is incorporated in the program's recognition that the ability of children and youth to deal with loss is related to their emotional and cognitive development (Nagy, 1948). There is also an understanding that certain types of losses, especially those that are violent and sudden, complicate the grieving process (Worden, 1992). The program emphasizes, however, that with education and direction, members of the school community can understand these complications and respond appropriately to the issues they generate. Finally, the organization of the grieving process around specific tasks that provide support, control, and structure provides a useful and simple paradigm that brings together grief theory and crisis intervention theory in a practical rather than theoretical way (Underwood & Dunne-Maxim, 1997).

The incorporation of suicide prevention techniques is critical regardless of the circumstances of the death. Because youth are so susceptible to contagion and copycat behavior, there is a delicate balance between doing too much, which may glamorize a death, and doing too little, which may stigmatize it (Gould, Wallerstein & Davidson, 1989; Lamb, Dunne-Maxim, Underwood, & Sutton, 1991). Walking this delicate line is sometimes complicated by the fact that schools should follow the same policies and procedures, regardless of the circumstances of the death. While a school may understand the need for a cautious response in the aftermath of a suicide, this same approach may not characterize its response to a death under other circumstances, such as life-threatening illness. The need for consistency of response underscores the critical need for schools to consider establishing policy before they are faced with a crisis that may make objectivity difficult.

The systems perspective that emphasizes the need for the involvement of the larger community as part of the crisis management plan is echoed within the school community itself. Specific tasks for school superintendents, building administrators, and crisis team members, as well as ancillary staff such as office personnel and bus drivers are outlined. With lines of responsibility clearly delineated, some of the chaos that often accompanies a crisis is minimized and a more organized, efficient response can be anticipated. Schools find this organizational structure to be particularly reassuring since it clearly indicates administrative involvement and support for line staff, who may feel isolated and overwhelmed in meeting student needs. This delineation of responsibility also extends to community resources, whose roles in providing ancillary support to the school are clearly spelled out.

POSTVENTION IMPLEMENTATION

Because the timing of interventions is an essential element in effective crisis response, it may be helpful to review some of the key components of the postvention model in relation to when they occur during the process. An assumption is made, however, that the most effective postvention response is one that has been proactively addressed in advance of a crisis and that all members of the school community are familiar with their roles in the plan's operation

First Stage

Learning About the Death

Dissemination of accurate information about the death is where the postvention process ideally begins. The community agency that is first informed of the death, which is generally the police or sheriff's department, begins the communication chain. The school superintendent is usually the first school official who is informed and is responsible for informing other administrators within the district. It's important to inform not only the principal of the school directly affected by the death but the principals of all other schools in the district since they, too, may have students or staff directly impacted by the loss. Notification of the president of the school board of the affected school is another critical task usually delegated to the superintendent.

If the death has occurred during hours when school is not in session or over the weekend and it receives any type of public attention, there is a good chance students may already be aware of it and talking about it via e-mail. With the rapidity at which misinformation can be communicated in this manner, school officials may want to consider posting some official notification, with limited but accurate details on the school's web site. In a recent situation, three middle school students and a parent were involved in a traffic accident. While one student and the adult were killed instantly, misinformation circulated by friends over the Internet stated that all three students had perished. This exacerbated the trauma until the next day when more accurate information was released.

Initiating the Crisis Team

A meeting of the school's crisis team as quickly as possible is crucial. When a death takes place during a regular school week, the team should schedule an early morning meeting to review its plans. Organization of a response for deaths that occur during school vacations or holidays is facilitated by an established plan that clearly outlines a response strategy and delineates responsibilities during those periods of time. In any case, crisis team members should keep a copy of both the plan and the contact numbers for team members at home to be available in case of an emergency outside of school hours. Community crisis team members should also be alerted. The community team, which can include clergy, mental health professionals, emergency medical service representatives, and juvenile officers should be on-call to supplement school resources as needed.

Informing Faculty

Contacting all faculty and staff is also a priority. Most schools use their already established "snow-chain" as a way to communicate information about what has transpired. It is important to remember to include all school staff–bus drivers, cafeteria and maintenance workers, and administrative staff–because they, too, have relationships with the students and may be affected by the death. Bus drivers, in particular, should be helped to anticipate the reactions of students who will board their buses. Drivers can set the tone for the school's response by validating the reactions of the students, avoiding the gossip and rumors that are inevitable after a traumatic death, and noticing the students who may need extra support once they arrive at school.

Informing Parents

When the circumstances of the death are extremely traumatic, many schools use their Parent Teacher Organization (PTO) to call all school families to inform them of both the death and the school's planned response. A PTO volunteer reads a scripted message written by school administrators that includes a contact number for additional information or questions. Following a script assures that everyone receives accurate information that reflects the school's current understanding of the situation. This may be the same information that is posted on the school's web site.

Contacting the Family of Affected Students

Personal contact with the family of the deceased may be accomplished over the phone or in a visit. While the principal is usually the most appropriate person to do this, it is supportive to both the school administrator and the family if a crisis team member accompanies the principal on this visit. Offering condolences and getting information about funeral plans are two key reasons for this visit.

When the trauma revolves around a circumstance in which students other than the deceased have been involved, it is important that the school administrator contact these families as well to offer support and assistance. This may be difficult when one student is implicated in the murder of another, but it is important for administrators to recognize that for recovery and healing after trauma to be effective, all the victims in the school community must be acknowledged and supported. The procedure for referring these students and their families to crisis counselors and/or community resources should also be spelled out.

Removing Locker Contents

Another immediate task for the crisis team to consider is dealing with the contents of the deceased student's locker or desk. Even if the contents are not returned to the family for some time, peers may go through the belongings of the deceased and take mementos that are more appropriately disposed of by the family. The school might also anticipate that students may create a memorial at the locker or the parking spot of the deceased student. Putting up a notice to indicate that the items and notes will be collected and given to the family after the funeral is a way to minimize the distress students sometimes exhibit when they find these mementos have been removed.

Although it is not as critical to perform during the initial phase of the crisis, another important task is to remove the name of the deceased student from the school's mailing list. It is often a source of great pain for parents to continue to receive mailings from the school after their child's death, so taking care of this as soon as possible after the death eliminates both the pain and embarrassment that often result when it is overlooked.

Dealing with the Media

The school administrator must be prepared to deal with the media. To reduce the risk of misinformation, the school should appoint only one media spokesperson. This individual's sole responsibility during the crisis will be to supply press briefing material to the media. This material should be written, whenever possible, to ensure the accuracy of its content and to attempt to give the school some control over the direction the stories may take. For example, information about what the school and community are doing to address the needs of the survivors can shift the focus of attention from the tragedy itself to the recovery process. The media may need to be reminded quite often that it is the prerogative of the family, not the school, to provide information about the victim. The school is within its legal rights to limit media access to school grounds; the presence of reporters and camera crews can contribute to the students' emotional distress and continue an inappropriate focus on the school as the center of activity. With this in mind, it can also be helpful to schedule press briefings away from the affected school, for instance, in the mayor's office or public library.

Responding to the Community

Since the school can expect to receive phone calls from parents and community members, prepare the staff responsible for answering the phone with written information to assist them in responding to inquiries for information. In many schools, it is the principal who returns calls requiring additional information in order to reinforce the perception that the school administration is in control of the crisis response plan. It is helpful to have a list of community resources to facilitate referrals to those families who may require or request additional support.

Second Stage: Interventions

Day One

FACULTY MEETING. The structured response of the crisis team to the school community begins as the team reaches out to faculty and staff at a meeting held early in the morning on the first day after the crisis. It is important to begin the meeting by letting staff members talk about their reactions to the event since they will not be able to help and support students if they have not been helped themselves. Many schools have found that counselors from the community team are more helpful than school crisis counselors in helping faculty members express their grief since school staff members are sometimes uncomfortable in expressing feelings to a colleague. Students, on the other hand, tend to resist talking to outsiders so they are best helped by school staff with whom they are familiar.

A written memo should be distributed to faculty summarizing the information the school has received about the death as well as the information that is to be communicated to students. Reminders not to engage in speculation or rumors are helpful and sometimes faculty feel better prepared if a specific response is suggested, for example, "I know there are a lot of stories going around about what happened last night, but all I know is what I heard at the faculty meeting. And I guess I feel that in the long run, it may not matter so much how those students died but that they're no longer here with us." It is always useful to reinforce that the circumstances of the death are less important than the fact that the school community has lost valuable members.

Faculty should also be informed about the location of crisis counseling stations and the procedures for dismissing students from class in order to use them. Since there are some students who will be more affected by the death than others, the faculty should be reminded that they are the front-line staff making these referrals as they are in the best position to observe and evaluate a child's behavior. Students who may be at more risk than others will include:
- close friends of the deceased
- students on teams, in clubs, or in activities with the deceased
- friends of siblings of the deceased
- students who may have witnessed the death
- students with recent losses
- vulnerable students

Vulnerable students who may be at elevated risk can include youth with experiences that are not necessarily common knowledge in the larger school community, e.g., students who have made previous suicide attempts or are in recovery from drug or alcohol addictions. The school nurse is usually aware of this type of confidential information about students so her input in identification and assessment of these higher risk students is imperative.

Helping faculty anticipate the reactions of students is another objective of the initial faculty meeting. The *Managing Sudden Traumatic Loss* manual contains handouts that can be duplicated and distributed to staff to help them understand the ways in which youth react to particular types of deaths. It also offers helpful ways for faculty to respond (Underwood & Dunne-Maxim, 1997). In addition, faculty might benefit from some guidance about the scheduling of classroom activities. In general, it is a good idea to try to stick as closely to scheduled activities as possible to reinforce the structure and control of the normal school routine. Activities that should be carefully screened include those that deal with topics related to the trauma, i.e., suicide, homicide, etc., which may exacerbate the distress of affected students. It is also beneficial to establish a rumor control center, where faculty can report the unofficial, unvalidated information that may be circulated after a trauma. Many schools have identified the office of the assistant principal as the place where gossip about suicide pacts, bomb threats, and the like can be referred for investigation.

The school's procedures for dealing with the media should also be reviewed and distributed in writing at this meeting. It is critical that all staff members understand who has been identified as the media spokesperson for the school district and that no comments, even those that are off the record, are to be made by any staff member. Research studies have documented that certain types of media coverage of traumatic deaths can contribute to contagion or copycat behavior in vulnerable youth who may have had no personal relationship with the deceased (Davidson & Gould, 1989). In addition, media coverage may not always present an accurate representation of the facts and can contribute to the misinformation that complicates resolution of trauma.

Faculty members who had the deceased student in their classes are usually reassured if a crisis team member follows the daily schedule of the deceased. It is often difficult to be faced with the empty seat in the classroom, which is a concrete reminder of the loss. These classes usually benefit from an extended discussion of students' feelings and reactions which is facilitated by a crisis team member who may be less affected by the death than the classroom teacher.

Lastly, the faculty should be provided with a list of community resources for themselves. Just as there will be some students who are more affected by the death than others, so, too, will there be some faculty members who are more vulnerable. It is important to anticipate the needs of staff and faculty members by providing referral resources for support in the community, thus empowering them to seek assistance.

STUDENT SUPPORT. The nature of the trauma will determine how many crisis stations should be set up to provide support for students. Students can be dismissed from regular classroom activities to share their feelings with a group of ten to twelve of their peers. While these small groups are the ideal way to validate and support students' reactions to the death, crisis team members should be prepared to intervene with students who may congregate in school hallways or off school grounds. In particular, students often take solace at the home of the deceased which can be comforting but overwhelming for the family and many schools dispatch a crisis counselor to the scene to provide support and control at that location.

An additional group of students that requires outreach are those students who are absent. It is important that each of these students be contacted to determine if their absence is in any way related to the trauma. This procedure should be repeated with absentees on subsequent days as well.

ADDITIONAL MEETINGS. At the end of the day, some schools schedule an optional faculty meeting to discuss the events of the day and review school plans for upcoming days. A debriefing for the crisis team, however, should be mandatory. This meeting provides the crisis staff with the opportunity to discuss their own reactions to the day, with team members providing support and validation for each other. Other agenda items include evaluation of the crisis plan, with discussion on what parts of the plan may need modification on subsequent days. The functioning of crisis stations should also be reviewed, and rotation of crisis team responsibilities for subsequent days should be considered. Faculty and staff needs should be discussed as well as contacts with the family of the deceased. All crisis contacts with students should be summarized and plans articulated for follow up as appropriate.

Day Two

MEDIA INTERACTION. The level of the crisis should diminish after the first day, although pressure from the media may increase in attempts to find new angles for news stories. The school's media spokesperson can turn these media requests into opportunities to review prevention strategies, with focus on the proactive strategies being taken by the school and community to contain the impact of the tragedy.

FUNERAL PLANNING. Planning the school's strategy for funeral activities is usually considered on Day Two if this information is available from the family. Community resources may be employed to supplement crisis team members at all funeral activities, especially if a large student turnout is expected. It is also important to arrange classroom coverage for faculty members who wish to attend funeral services. Both students and staff may be anxious about the funeral since they may not know what to expect. Crisis staff should make opportunities to hold discussions about the type of services the family may be having and review the protocol for participation. Often, community crisis team members like clergy or funeral directors are exceptionally helpful in this regard.

COMMUNITY MEETING. Depending on the circumstances of the death, there may be pressure from members of the community to hold a meeting to provide parents and other community members with an opportunity to express their feelings about the death. These requests should be approached with great concern and care because these types of venues challenge adherence to the principles of crisis intervention. Providing structure and control can be extremely difficult, if not impossible, with a large group of people at a time of high emotionality. Because blame, scapegoating, and anger are common grief reactions in the aftermath of a traumatic death, especially when the deceased is a child, large groups of people often feed on these emotions and the school is commonly the first target.

Especially in situations that receive extensive press coverage, the presence of the media can inflame the crowd and make focused discussion and the provision of support extremely problematic. Despite the best intentions and preparation of school administrators, these meetings often deteriorate into painful and angry expressions of the community's helplessness over the death. What is recommended, instead, is that the school wait to schedule a parent or community meeting until at least a week after the death when the intensity of feelings has had an opportunity to diminish. As parents arrive at the school for the meeting, they can be subdivided into smaller groups of ten to twelve members and led to individual classrooms by crisis counselors who will facilitate these small groups. Each group is also given the opportunity to decide whether it chooses to include a media representative. In this way, control and structure are maximized and parents actually receive more support than they would in a larger session. If the school is placed in the position of having no input into the scheduling of a large community meeting, religious settings like churches or temples seem to provide atmospheres that are more conducive to crowd control than are school auditoriums.

Day of the Funeral

Many schools report that crisis levels on the day of the funeral approximate those of the first day of the trauma. Advance planning, however, can address the administrative concerns related to issues like funeral attendance, transportation to the funeral, and classroom coverage. If students return to school after the funeral, it may be necessary to provide support groups to help them deal with their reactions to the services. As with the crisis stations that were utilized in the earlier days of the crisis, these support groups are best located in areas other than the classroom so that students who did not attend the services can continue with normal class activities.

A SPECIAL ISSUE: CONTAGION CONCERNS

An issue of particular concern to the school administration is handling requests for remembering or memorializing the deceased. These requests may be generated by the parents of the deceased or by the students themselves, and while they are always well-intentioned, they sometimes can present problems in implementation that are related to the public health issue of contagion after a traumatic loss event, particularly suicide.

The Concept of Contagion

One of the first times the concept of contagion came to the attention of the general public was following the death of Marilyn Monroe when there were reports of an unexpectedly large number of suicides shortly after her death. As defined by the Centers for Disease Control and Prevention, contagion is a process by which exposure to the suicide or suicidal behavior of one or more persons influences others to commit or attempt suicide (Brook, 1990). In particular, deaths that are sensationalized and receive a great deal of attention may lead to other violent deaths (CDC, 1988). While several studies have detailed cases of contagion following a youth suicide, educators who have personally experienced this phenomenon in their schools affirm its existence and impact (Dunne-Maxim et al., 1992). As one principal whose New Jersey high school experienced two suicides six months apart to the day said, "We thought the worst had happened when we lost one student to suicide and we worried that there might have been something we could have done to prevent the death. But after the second suicide—I wonder if we will ever recover."

While media coverage of a traumatic death has been implicated in contagion behavior, so too are memorial activities that sensationalize or glamorize the deceased (Dunne-Maxim & Underwood, 1991). While parent and student desires to remember the deceased are certainly understandable, they often call attention not just to the deceased student but also to the circumstances of the death. Even before the funeral, administrators may be pressured to plant trees, dedicate yearbooks, or name scholarships after the deceased. Murals or special plaques to adorn school walls may be requested and it is a fact that these types of memorials often keep the death "alive" and serve as grim reminders of the tragic loss. Thus, the school community must balance between commemorating the life and not glamorizing the death, especially if it is a result of self-destructive behavior, such as suicide, drug overdose, or a drunk-driving accident.

Avoiding Contagion

The challenge, then, is how to commemorate a death in a way that does not encourage contagion. While this may sound simple and straightforward, many schools have found themselves embroiled in controversy following their attempts to minimize contagion after a traumatic death. Without policy or procedures to guide them, they have made decisions that inadvertently stigmatized a student who died by suicide by treating the death differently than a death due to other circumstances. In some cases the death was not acknowledged at all, and became a destructive focus of community energy, keeping the circumstances of the death alive for a lengthy period of time and directing divisive attention to both school administrators and the board.

Memorialization Guidelines: What To Do

Memorials in general reflect a desire to commemorate the lives of those who are deceased in personal and meaningful ways. No one who requests a memorial activity has any intention of creating an atmosphere that puts another young person at risk and, often, a simple explanation of the concept of contagion can positively alter the direction of a memorial request. For example, in one school, a group of students wanted the yearbook to include a collage of pictures of the deceased with the quotation, "Friends are Forever." After discussion with the yearbook advisor about contagion issues, the students changed the collage to include their pictures as well and amended the quotation to "Friends Can Be Bridges Over Troubled Waters."

Another yearbook concern involves how to acknowledge deceased students in a manner that reflects their lives rather than their deaths. Instead of black-framing yearbook photos, several schools include a page that mentions all the students who would have graduated with a particular class, regardless of the reason for their absence. So students who have moved are included with those who are deceased in recognition that "these are all students whom we miss."

The graduation ceremony provides an opportunity for a thoughtful remembrance of the deceased senior. Mentioning the name of the deceased at the beginning of the student roll call, and perhaps also including a moment of silence in her or his memory, acknowledges the student in a manner that does not detract from the presentation of diplomas. This keeps the remembrance in perspective with the focus on graduation, which is to celebrate the senior class's accomplishments. It also reflects the reality that not everyone in the school may have been affected by the death, no matter how popular the deceased seemed to be and thus, the extended acknowledgment of the deceased student may be inappropriate.

Concerns about memorials, however, are not restricted to graduation activities; they often begin as soon as the school learns of the death and as administrators begin to struggle with how to inform the student body. Inviting the students to observe a moment of silence in memory of the deceased is an accepted way to respectfully acknowledge the death without being sensational or overreactive. It also provides students with the opportunity for private reflection about the personal meaning of the death. Planning for the memorial should, of course, include a structured crisis plan that provides additional support for the students who are most affected by the loss.

Students often create rather dramatic memorials themselves at the locker or parking space of the deceased, with flowers, personal messages, and mementos. Most school administrators respect the need of students for these displays but have controlled them by indicating that the remembrances will be removed after the funeral and given to the family of the deceased as a reflection of the students' sympathy. The family of the deceased should be consulted about the placement of these tributes, especially if their home is involved. The family of a young boy who had been murdered responded to an amassing of flowers and mementos on their front lawn with the following sign: "We appreciate your show of sympathy in the death of our son, but we ask that you leave your tributes at the cemetery and respect the privacy of our grief. Thank you."

Remembering that the family of the deceased is the appropriate recipient of expressions of sympathy and loss may be helpful in the selection of other memorial activities for students. Several schools keep scrapbooks to be used by students as memory books where they can record their feelings and remembrances. Other schools assist students in creating videotaped recollections; both of these tributes are presented to the family.

More activity-focused memorials have included organizing a day of community service, sponsoring mental health awareness programs, supporting peer counseling programs, or fund-raising for research and prevention groups related to the cause of the death such as the American Cancer Society, the American Foundation for Suicide Prevention, or SADD (Students Against Destructive Decisions). Purchasing library books that address educational topics pertaining to how young people can cope with loss deal with emotional problems such as depression are also examples of life-affirming ways to remember the deceased.

A frequent and sometimes controversial memorial request made by the family is for the establishment of a scholarship fund in the name of the deceased. Keep in mind that if a school has a scholarship named in the memory of one child who dies, other such requests will need to be honored. If the death is from a self-destructive cause scholarship requests may be problematic. Is announcing the scholarship year after year at graduation sending the appropriate message to the students? One school solved this dilemma by having a general scholarship fund honoring all members of the school community who died and individuals were therefore not mentioned. In another case, the family of the deceased provided a music scholarship for a needy child from a school in another geographic location.

Memorialization Guidelines: What Not To Do

Activities that call attention not only to the death but also set a difficult precedent for the manner in which all future deaths are to be handled should be avoided. These include actions such as flying the flag at half staff, or acknowledging the death on the school's outdoor sign board, which publicly draws dramatic attention to the death, or dismissing the school early, or cancelling school on the day of the funeral, which can make the death seem like an occasion for a school holiday. Even having the funeral procession drive slowly by the school may appear to give more status to the deceased in death than in life.

While living memorials like the planting of trees are natural, life-affirming responses to death, they can also be problematic. Several schools have reported that the collection of trees planted over the years in response to student deaths by suicide are now referred to as "the suicide garden" or "the death arbor". One school recalled the consternation of a family when the tree that had been ceremoniously planted in honor of their deceased child had been accidentally destroyed by another youngster's dirt bike. Another school remembered the public relations crisis that occurred when the expansion of the physical plant of the school included an area in which a "cemetery of trees" had been planted.

Hanging plaques that commemorate the deceased on school property bring another set of problems. Creating a permanent part of the environment that is a constant reminder of death contradicts the life-affirming mission of the school. It also draws special attention to students who have died, which may feed contagion. In the suicide note of a fourteen-year-old, he wrote, "My name will vanish when I die and maybe if I am lucky the school will have a plaque for me." His school has several plaques in its foyer for students who have died from a variety of causes, including suicide. Many schools have related their concerns about existing plaques, planning to remove them once all those who have known the deceased students are no longer at the school.

Holding memorial services in the school must also be approached carefully. Because many students have limited exposure to the death of a peer, they may have a great deal of anxiety that affects their response to the death. Large groups of students are not easy to control under the best of circumstances, but the potential for a memorial service to get out of hand increases exponentially with increases in student emotion. On the other hand, schools report that memorial services that have been held in religious settings seem to remain orderly, which may be related to the general societal expectations for quiet, controlled behavior in places of worship. These may, therefore, serve as appropriate substitutes for families who request memorial services on school property.

Prohibiting or preventing any expression of remembrance for a deceased student can also create problems. Public outcry has often greeted administrators who omitted the name of a deceased senior in a graduation ceremony or had the student's picture deleted from the yearbook. There is a delicate balance between doing too little and doing too much which requires serious consideration by administrators and board members before an action takes place.

Policy Guidelines

Although a policy on memorialization is not required by either law or code, a wise school board will consider this issue in a proactive manner when it can be guided by the critical thinking and objective judgment that a climate of crisis often precludes. Not only will administrative decisions benefit from thoughtful input from the board, but a well-articulated and disseminated policy may avert the public relations nightmares that are often synonymous with a perceived crisis in the school.

While there may be recognition by administrators about the need for caution in approving memorial activities after a suicide, a more difficult challenge involves implementing a uniform policy to be followed regardless of the circumstances of the death. Unless such a policy is established and followed, the district leaves itself open to criticism that it is stigmatizing a death by suicide when memorialization activities for deaths under other circumstances are allowed.

The intent of the board guidelines on memorialization should be to minimize the potential for putting other students at risk, to respond to all deaths in a uniform manner, and to facilitate support for the process of grieving. Educators developing comprehensive guidelines on memorialization should consider the following:

1. Be educated about the issues related to the impact of memorialization on suicide contagion and educate administrators about the need for caution in the selection of memorialization activities. Remember the developmental issues that make imitative behavior a particular concern for youth.

2. Establish a districtwide committee to generate a list of memorialization activities that meet board guidelines. Make sure this committee includes both parent and student representation. It may also be helpful to include a survivor of suicide, who can provide her or his own perspective in the decision making. Require all requests for memorialization activities to be reviewed by this committee, then submitted to building administrators for final approval.

3. Establish a districtwide decision-making process that provides clear guidelines for selection of all memorialization activities.

4. Disseminate these guidelines for memorials to all district schools and parent organizations. Parent organizations can be exceptionally helpful in providing community support for board policy if they understand the rationale behind policy decisions. Since decisions about memorialization can be controversial, it is helpful to have as much educated support as possible from a variety of community sectors in advance of a situation that requires difficult decision making.

CONCLUSION

Recovery following a traumatic death is a process that takes time. While it may appear that the school has returned to business as usual following the funeral, the altered perspective and healing that accompany the resolution of mourning cannot be hurried. Each school will move through the process at its own pace, which will be as unique as each loss.

A clear focus on the needs of the living, the survivors, will help a school anticipate some of the difficult decisions that will need to be made in the aftermath of a tragic death. While no school district wants to predict a student death, most districts that have confronted tragic loss will acknowledge that proactive planning provided the structure and support to contain the impact of the crisis, to facilitate the management of grief, and to return the school community to normal functioning as quickly as possible.

REFERENCES

Brook, J. (1990). The state of injury in New Jersey. *Injury and Surveillance Program.* Trenton, N.J.: New Jersey Department of Health.

Centers for Disease Control. (1988, August). CDC recommendations for the prevention and containment of suicide clusters. *Morbidity and Mortality Weekly Report, 37,* 5-6.

Centers for Disease Control. (1994, April). Suicide contagion and the reporting of suicide: Recommendations from a national workshop. *Morbidity and Mortality Weekly Report, 43,* (No. RR-6).

Davidson, L. E., & Gould, M. S. (1989). Contagion as a risk factor for youth suicide. In *Alcohol, drug abuse, and mental health administration. Report of the Secretary's Task Force on Youth Suicide, 2* (pp. 88-109). Washington, D.C.: U.S. Department of Health and Human Services, Public Health Service, (Publication no. ADM 89-1622).

Dunne-Maxim, K., Godin, S., Lamb, F., Sutton, C., & Underwood, M. (1992). The aftermath of youth suicide-providing postvention services to the school and the community. *Crisis, 13* (1), 32-38.

Dunne-Maxim, K., & Underwood, M. (1991). Keeping afloat on suicide's wake. *The School Administrator,* 76-81.

Gould, M., Wallerstein, S., & Davidson, L. (1989). Suicide clusters: A critical review. *Suicide and Life-Threatening Behavior, 19* (1), 17-27.

Lamb, F., Dunne-Maxim, K., Underwood, M., & Sutton, C. (1991). The role of the postvention consultant. In A. A. Leenars & S. Wenckstern (Eds.), *Suicide intervention in schools.* Washington, D.C.: Hemisphere.

Nagy, M. (1948). The child's theories concerning death. *Journal of Genetic Psychology, 73,* 3-27.

Underwood, M., & Dunne-Maxim, K. (1997). *Managing sudden traumatic loss in the schools.* New Brunswick, N.J.: University of Medicine and Dentistry of New Jersey-University Behavioral HealthCare.

Worden, W. (1992). *Grief counseling and grief therapy.* New York: Springer Publishing Co.

Chapter Ten

VIOLENCE IN THE SCHOOLS: LEGAL ISSUES OF CONFIDENTIALITY, SECURITY, AND CIVIL RIGHTS[1]

NATHANYA G. SIMON

CURRENT AND PROPOSED SCHOOL SECURITY MEASURES

THERE IS NO AREA of the country, and no facet of our population, that is exempt from the growing spread of violence and drug use. As acts of senseless brutality invade our community and workplace, we are forced to confront the reality of violence in our schools. Within the past two years, we have witnessed a series of violent incidents across the country, most notably the shootings at Columbine High School in April, 1999. With this in mind, school districts can no longer sit idle while our youth continue to proceed toward a path of violent behavior. The maintenance of a safe environment in our nation's public schools must be a critical part of any school agenda.

Student Search

The national precedent for school searches comes from the New Jersey courts. In *N.J. v. T.L.O.* (1985), a Piscataway Township High School student was suspended from school and prosecuted for drug-related activity based on evidence seized from her handbag by an administrator. At the time the evidence was seized from the student, the administrator suspected the student was in possession of only cigarettes. The State brought delinquency charges against T.L.O. in the Juvenile and Domestic Relations Court of Middlesex County. T.L.O. moved to suppress the evidence found in her purse based upon a violation of the Fourth Amendment. Under the Fourth Amendment

1. Paula Mercurio, Esq., an associate with Schwartz Simon Edelstein Celso & Kessler LLP, is acknowledged for her assistance in the preparation of this chapter.

of the United States Constitution, citizens have the right to be "secure in their persons, houses, papers, and effects, against unreasonable searches and seizures . . ." by the federal government (U.S. Constitution, Amendment IV).

In denying T.L.O.'s motion to suppress the evidence, the Juvenile Court found that the search conducted by school officials was a reasonable one. On appeal, the Appellate Division affirmed the trial court's finding that there had been no Fourth Amendment violation. The Supreme Court of New Jersey disagreed with the Juvenile Court's conclusion that the search of the purse was reasonable. According to the majority, the fact that T.L.O. may have possessed cigarettes in her purse had no bearing on the accusation against T.L.O. for smoking in the lavatory. The school official did not receive any information that cigarettes were in T.L.O.'s purse. Thus, the search of T.L.O.'s purse was not justified. Thereafter, the United States Supreme Court granted the State of New Jersey's petition for *certiorari*, requesting a case review.

The United States Supreme Court held that the legality of a search of a student should depend upon the reasonableness of the search. To meet this reasonableness test, a search of a student by a teacher or other school official must be "justified at its inception." This means that school officials must have reasonable grounds for suspecting that the search will turn up evidence that the student is committing a criminal act or is violating school rules. The search must also be "reasonable in scope." In other words, the measures used to effect the search must be reasonable and related to the objectives of the search. Furthermore, the search must not be excessively intrusive, considering the seriousness of the alleged misconduct and the age and sex of the student. It is important to note that the decision in *T.L.O.* was based on a search conducted by school authorities acting alone, rather than searches conducted by school officials in conjunction with or at the behest of law enforcement agencies. By using a reasonableness standard as the touchstone for any student search, teachers and school administrators will be guided by common sense and reason. In *T.L.O.*, the United States Supreme Court found that the search of T.L.O.'s purse was reasonable under the circumstances.

In reviewing the validity of a search, the courts will also take into consideration the level of police involvement. As agents of the state, school officials are subject to the Fourth Amendment's protection against unreasonable searches and seizures (see also *In re D.E.M.*, 1999). It is important to analyze whether school officials are acting as agents of the state, or whether the school officials are acting as agents of the police. This inquiry is critical because the legality of a search conducted by school officials is measured by a lower standard than a search conducted by law enforcement officers.

In the recently published case of *In re D.E.M.* (1999), a student was charged with possession of a weapon on school property, carrying a firearm without a license, possession of a firearm by a minor, and altering or obliterating marks of identification. D.E.M. filed an omnibus pre-trial motion to suppress the physical evidence obtained following the school official's investigation. The suppression court found that the principal and assistant principal acted as *agents* of the police during the investigation. The suppression court found that the police supplied the school officials with information with the intent of instigating an investigation. The suppression court held that the school officials lacked the necessary reasonable suspicion to support the investigation.

The Superior Court of Pennsylvania disagreed with the suppression court's analysis. The record contained no evidence that the police coerced, dominated, or directed the actions of the school officials. Significantly, the police did not request or in any way participate in the school official's investigation. Thus, the Court also found it significant that the police were not present when the school officials conducted the investigation of D.E.M. Thus, the Court held that the principal and assistant principal did not act as agents of the police.

In conducting a search of a student's person, school officials should be well-versed in the legal requirements which comprise a constitutionally permissible search. School officials should be aware of critical factors that may impact a court's determination of reasonableness. Some of the factors which should be taken into consideration in determining the manner in which searches may be conducted include:
- the age and sex of the student;
- the behavior record of the student;
- the need for the search;
- the purpose of the search;
- the type of search that will be conducted;
- the reliability of the information used to conduct the search;
- the relative importance of making the search without delay; and
- the nature and severity of the problem in the overall school environment.

In New Jersey, members of the teaching staff, principals, or other educational personnel are statutorily prohibited from conducting a strip search or body cavity search of a pupil (see N.J.S.A. 18A:37-6.1).

Any search of a student's person should be conducted privately by a teacher, administrator, or security guard of the same sex as the student. Prior to initiating the search, it is important to inform the student of the reasons for the search. It is also beneficial for the school to maintain a detailed documentation of all searches conducted by school officials. Although school officials are not required to notify parents or legal guardians prior to conducting a lawful search, parents or legal guardians should be notified as soon as possible after completion of the search.

School officials should be aware of the consequences of conducting an illegal search. First, evidence of the crime discovered during the search will likely be subject to the exclusionary rule (New Jersey Association of School Administrators, 1999). The exclusionary rule is a court-created doctrine that requires the suppression of evidence obtained illegally by law enforcement officers who perform a search without probable cause. Second, a school administrator who violates a student's constitutional rights may be liable under 42 U.S.C. 1983, which provides in pertinent part:

> Every person who, under color of any statute, ordinance, regulation, custom, or usage, of any State or Territory or the District of Columbia, subjects, or causes to be subjected, any citizen of the United States or other person within the jurisdiction thereof to the deprivation of any rights, privileges, or immunities secured by the Constitution and laws, shall be liable to the party injured in an action at law, suit in equity, or other proper proceeding for redress, except that in any action brought against a judicial officer for an act or omission taken in such officer's judicial capacity, injunctive relief shall not be granted unless a declaratory decree was violated or declaratory relief was unavailable.

If acting within the scope of their employment, and performing a search in good faith, school officials are provided with immunity from such claims. However, if the school official violates a clearly established rule of law, or knowingly conducts a search that is unlawful, good faith immunity will not protect a school official. The school official may be personally liable for compensatory and possibly punitive damages.

In summary, a *search* entails conduct by a school official which involves peeking, poking, or prying into a private area or closed, opaque container, such as a purse, knapsack, briefcase, or clothing (Kimmelman, 1997). Any search encompasses the balancing of the following competing interests: (1) the student's Fourth Amendment right of privacy and security; and (2) the interest of school officials in maintaining order, discipline and safety. It is important for teachers or school officials to be guided by the reasonableness standard promulgated in *T.L.O.*, as well as common sense. In order to survive constitutional scrutiny, a search must be reasonable not only at its inception, but also in its scope. Finally, any questions as to the appropriateness of a proposed search should ordinarily be resolved in favor of respecting the student's privacy interests.

Use of Drug-Detection Canines

The courts have generally agreed that the use of trained narcotics dogs to detect the presence of drugs on objects, as opposed to people, is not a search within the meaning of the Fourth Amendment. Of the few courts to consider the use of drug-detection canines on individual students, the majority has concluded that it is a search within the meaning of the Fourth Amendment. Therefore, the search may not be justified in the absence of reasonable suspicion.

Locker Inspection Program

Ordinarily, we think of lockers as a place for students to keep their personal items during the day. Students typically use their locker to safeguard their books, pens, clothing, and makeup, or perhaps to hang pictures of their family, friends, or celebrities. However, the reality is that lockers are also used in the course of completing drug transactions, or as a "safe" place to keep a weapon during the school day. As a result, more schools are implementing locker inspection programs to prevent the use of lockers as a means of criminal activity.

In the case of *State of New Jersey v. Engerud* (1983), a local police detective notified a vice principal regarding a telephone call from a person claiming to be the father of a student. The caller said that the student was selling drugs in the school, and that it was the school's responsibility to stop the student. The principal and the assistant vice principal decided to open the student's locker through the use of a passkey that could open any locker in the building. In conducting a search of the locker, the principal and the assistant vice principal discovered two plastic bags containing packets of a white substance. It was later determined that the substance was methamphetamine. In addition to the methamphetamine, a package of marijuana rolling paper was also discovered in the student's locker.

The student was charged with unlawful possession of a controlled dangerous substance, as well as unlawful possession of a controlled dangerous substance with intent to distribute. The Law Division denied a motion to suppress the evidence obtained from the locker search. Thereafter, the student appealed the decision, and the Supreme Court of New Jersey certified the student's appeal directly.

The Court recognized that the student had an expectation of privacy in the contents of his locker. As a "home away from home" for a student during the four years of high school, a locker serves as a student's personal domain. The Fourth Amendment should protect the personal effects that a student places in a locker. A student is justified in believing that a master key will only be employed by school officials in situations of request or convenience. Therefore, the Court found that the facts did not support a reasonable ground to believe that this student's locker contained evidence. The official action was not based on a reliable informer, nor independent corroboration. The principal and assistant vice-principal acted on an anonymous tip without taking any further action towards confirming the informant's reliability. The Court limited the breadth of its holding by stating, "[h]ad the school carried out a policy of regularly inspecting students' lockers, an expectation of privacy might not have arisen" (*State of New Jersey v. Engerud*, 94 N.J. 331, 349, 1983).

In response to the Court's decision, the Legislature adopted N.J.S.A. 18A: 36-19.2. The statute provided that "[t]he principal or other official designated by the local board of education may inspect lockers or other storage facilities provided for use by students so long as students are informed in writing at the beginning of each school year that inspections may occur."

Vehicle Searches

Although there is limited case law discussing the constitutionality of vehicle searches in the school setting, it is generally permissible to search a vehicle owned and operated by a student and parked on school grounds. In *People in the Interest of P.E.A.* (1988), the search of a student's vehicle was upheld due to school officials' reasonable belief that the vehicle was the means of transporting drugs to school and concealing drugs during school hours. A vehicle search was also upheld in *State of Florida v. D.T.W.* (1983). However, in *Jones v. Latexo Independent School District, et al.* (1980), the court held that a sniff search of a student vehicle exceeded the bounds of reasonableness. The court found it significant that the students did not have access to their vehicles while school was in session. Therefore, the school's legitimate interest in what students had left in their vehicles was minimal at best.

School officials may search a student's vehicle that is left in a school parking lot when they have reasonable grounds for suspecting that the search will disclose evidence that the student has violated or is violating either the law or the rules of the school. While it is generally permissible for school officials to search a student's vehicle on school property, a different situation arises in the case of vehicles parked on roads or streets surrounding the school property. It is important to distinguish between student vehicles parked in parking areas maintained by the school district, and student vehicles parked on public streets surrounding the school property. School officials should notify the police if there is any suspicion that students are using their vehicles in furtherance of any criminal activity.

Under certain circumstances, school officials may be able to conduct random, suspicionless weapon and/or drug searches of student vehicles on school grounds. To justify such a policy, school districts should demonstrate that there is a history of weapon and/or drug problems in the school, and that a vehicle search policy represents a reasonably effective means of combating that problem. For example, school districts may want to demonstrate that students have access to their vehicles during the school day. Consequently, it is possible that students are bringing either weapons and/or drugs from their vehicles into the schools. Alternatively, the school may show that weapons and/or drugs are used or exchanged within the immediate area of the student parking lot. The searches should be conducted in a manner that is only as intrusive as necessary to further the interests of the school in preventing the presence of weapons and/or drugs.

The vehicle searches must be conducted in a manner that curtails undue discretion on the part of the school officials. In conducting suspicionless searches, school officials should use either a uniform method of selection or a random system, such as every fourth vehicle. School districts should implement a policy that alerts students that vehicles brought on school property may be subjected to a search where there is particularized reason to believe that evidence of a crime or violation is present in the vehicle.

The Use of Metal Detectors in the Schools

The use of metal detectors in schools is a relatively recent phenomenon. Although very few jurisdictions have addressed the use of metal detectors in schools, those jurisdictions that have considered the issue have ruled that the use of metal detectors in public schools does not violate students' Fourth Amendment rights.

In *People v. Dukes* (1992), a New York Court held that the search of a public high school student did not violate the Fourth Amendment, even though individualized suspicion was absent. In *Dukes*, special police officers from the school safety task force set up metal detector scanning posts one morning in the lobby of the school. The students had been informed at the beginning of the school year that searches would take place.

The procedure essentially called for handheld devices to be used, and all students entering the building were to be searched. If the lines became too long, the officers were permitted to limit the search using a random formula for searching the students. Further, the officers were prohibited from singling out individual students unless they had reasonable suspicion to believe that a student had a weapon. If the student's bag activated the device, the officer was to request the bag for a weapon search. If the student's body activated the device, the officer was to request that the student remove any metal objects, and conduct a second scan. If the device was set off a second time, the officer was to conduct a pat-down search in a private area. Once an object was found which appeared to have activated the device, the search was to terminate.

Dukes was subjected to the foregoing procedure and was found to have possessed a five-inch switchblade knife. At the student's trial for possession of the weapon, the student moved to have the evidence suppressed pursuant to the exclusionary rule. The Court denied the motion and held the search was constitutionally permissible even though the Board lacked individual suspicion before conducting the search. The Court explained that the type of search conducted was an administrative search, and thus individualized suspicion was not a component of the reasonableness factor. The Court noted that an administrative search absent of individualized suspicion, is reasonable where the intrusion involved is minimal compared to the government's interest in conducting the search in the first place.

The constitutionality of school metal detector searches was also upheld in the Pennsylvania courts in the case of *In Re: F. B.* (1995). *F. B.* involved a Philadelphia city high school that allowed city police officers to conduct metal detector scans and bag searches. Upon entering the building, the officers led the students to the gymnasium where they formed lines. One by one the students were asked to step up to a table and empty the contents of their pockets onto the table. The students' jackets and bags were handed over to the officers. While one officer scanned the students' belongings, a second officer would scan the students with a handheld metal detector. The searches were to be conducted in this manner until such time as the gymnasium became too crowded, at which point school administrators would randomly select students to be searched. As a result of a search, a student was found to be in possession of a Swiss Army knife and was placed under arrest for possession of a weapon on school grounds.

On appeal from a court order denying the student's motion to suppress the evidence seized, the student argued that the search was not reasonable in light of the *T.L.O.* factors. Specifically, the student argued that the search was not "justified at its inception," because there were no reasonable grounds to suspect that the student was carrying a weapon. The court rejected this argument and stated that the *T.L.O.* Court did not decide whether individualized suspicion was an essential element of the reasonableness standard for searches by school officials. However, the Court also noted that in *T.L.O.*, the Court had stated that "the Fourth Amendment imposes no irreducible requirement of individualized suspicion," and that there are exceptions to the requirement of individualized suspicion "where privacy interests implicated by a search are minimal, and where other safeguards are available to assure that the individual's reasonable expectation of privacy is not subject to the discretion of officials in the field" (In Re: F.B, 658 A.2d 1378, 1382, Pa. Super. 1995).

Finding that "the school's interest in ensuring security for its student far outweighs the juvenile's privacy interest," the Court rejected the student's argument that his privacy interest was not outweighed because the search in question was a search of his body. The Court also rejected the student's argument that his expectation of privacy had not been protected from the discretion of the officials in the field, as the *T.L.O.* Court seemed to require. The Court emphasized that:

> Although we believe written guidelines would be prudent, we find that there are other safeguards present in this case. Specifically, the officers who conducted the student searches followed a uniform procedure as they searched each student; after each student's personal belongings were searched, the student was scanned by a metal detector. This uniformity served to safeguard the students from the discretion of those conducting the search (In Re: F.B., 658 A.2d. 1378, 1382, Pa. Super. 1995).

Similarly in *Thompson v. Carthage* (1996) the court upheld a metal detector search where a school district found knife cuts on the seats of a school bus.

In sum, the bulk of the reported cases that have considered metal detector searches in the schools have uniformly upheld the searches because of the special needs that exist in a school setting; that is, to protect the safety of students. According to these decisions, the need to protect students from weapons overrides the individual student's right to privacy, and searches under such circumstances do not constitutionally require that there be individualized suspicion. This is particularly true when there is a history of school violence and/or weapons possession at the particular school in question.

While the New Jersey courts have not yet considered the constitutionality of metal detector searches in the schools, it is probable that the courts would likely uphold such a search so long as the students are given advance notice that such searches will be conducted. Further, if every student is not going to be searched as they enter the school building, it is important to ensure that the searches be conducted using some random formula (such as searching every third or fourth student) so that the students cannot claim that they are being singled-out for no apparent reason. In addition, if there is the need to pat-down a student as a result of the metal detector being activated, the pat-down should be conducted by an authorized individual of the same sex as the student.

It is advisable for a school district to formulate a metal-detector search policy, that should be distributed to every student, prior to implementing such searches. The policy should explain the search process and detail where and when the searches will be conducted.

Use of Surveillance Equipment

We are exposed to the use of surveillance cameras in banks, shopping malls, and dressing rooms. However, many school districts are now using or considering the installation of surveillance cameras to monitor student activity on school buses and throughout the public schools (Dumenigo, 2000). It is felt that surveillance cameras would limit the presence of unauthorized people on school property and allow staff to investigate vandalism to cars (Grey, 1996). Following the lead of such states as Delaware, Virginia, and Washington, some New Jersey public school districts have installed video surveillance cameras on their school buses (Fisher, 1994). While cameras and other security measures have been used in urban districts, the use of surveillance equipment is a relatively new phenomenon in suburban schools. Among the suburban schools considering the use of surveillance equipment in New Jersey are South Brunswick, Sayreville, Carteret in Middlesex County, and Franklin Township High School in Somerset County.

In the past several years, an increasing number of New Jersey's urban school districts have implemented the use of surveillance cameras. As the largest high school in the state, Elizabeth High School has had cameras monitoring its students in four buildings since 1977. With the spread of violence permeating through all types of high schools, New Jersey's suburbs and rural areas are considering implementing surveillance cameras as a means of controlling increasing violence and drug use. For example, Carteret is installing a 17-camera system throughout Carteret High School that will cost the school district approximately $10,000. In Sayreville, the school board is reviewing bids for a 16-camera surveillance network that would monitor and record activity in the hallways, entrances, and other areas during the hours the high school is in use.

Vandalism, monitoring trespassers, and checking inappropriate student behavior are the most commonly cited reasons for installing surveillance equipment. However, with the prevalence of violence across the country, most notably the shootings at Columbine High School, prevention measures are even more important. Clearly, school districts are taking a proactive stance towards protecting the welfare of students and faculty.

Recently, the U.S. Department of Justice issued a report outlining appropriate uses for security technologies for schools and law enforcement agencies. According to the report, acceptable areas for surveillance would include hallways, parking lots, lobbies, gymnasiums, auditoriums, cafeterias, supply rooms, and classrooms.

In order to maintain discipline on school buses, school districts may choose to install surveillance cameras in their vehicles. There are no cases that directly address the validity of video cameras on school buses. However, in *Desilets v. Clearview Regional Board of Education* (1993), the Appellate Division upheld a general search of student hand luggage prior to a school field trip. In upholding this blanket search policy without any individualized suspicion of wrongdoing, the Court stated:

> Our memories are not so short that we cannot recall the rich opportunity for mischief which the field trip provides to some students. The need for close supervision in the schoolhouse is intensified on field trips where the opportunities abound to elude the watchful eyes of chaperones. Administrators and teachers have a duty to protect students from the misbehavior of other students. . . . We also observe that a teacher confronted with a serious problem of misbehavior or injury in the schoolhouse readily has available to him or to her substantial resources to deal with the problem, such as other teachers and administrators, a school nurse, and quick access to police and ambulance services, if necessary. On the other hand, chaperones on a field trip are relatively isolated. See *Webb v. McCullough* (1987) in which the court recognized that 'there are many more ways for a student to be injured or to transgress school rules or laws during a non-curricular field trip than during relatively orderly school hours." In *Webb*, the Court of Appeals held that a school administrator's search of a student's hotel room while on an extended field trip to Hawaii from Tennessee did not violate the Fourth Amendment (*Desilets v. Clearview Regional Board of Education*, 1993).

The concerns that teachers and administrators have while students travel on field trips are extremely similar to the problems that exist on a school bus every day. Each of these activities provides numerous additional opportunities for a student to be "injured or to transgress school rules or laws." Therefore, if the court upheld a blanket search policy without any individualized suspicion prior to a student field trip in *Desilets*, it appears that a court would likely uphold a board of education's decision to place video cameras on its school buses, with the sole intent to reduce and/or prevent disciplinary problems. Furthermore, since the courts have given latitude to school districts in searching areas where students might allege to have an expectation of privacy, such as school lockers, it appears that students would have an even lesser expectation of privacy about a public school bus.

If a school district decides to install video cameras on its school buses, it should first notify all of the pupils involved and their parents. Generally, school personnel have a duty to exercise reasonable supervisory care to ensure the safety of students entrusted to them. Their accountability for injuries resulting from failure to discharge that duty is firmly established (see *Jackson v. Hankinson*, 1968). Where school authorities have provided transportation to and from school in a school bus, this obligation continues during the course of the transportation. If a board negligently fails to discharge its duty and consequential injury results to a child, the board can be held accountable.

Secondly, the school board should adopt a policy, setting forth some of these basic determinations: which individual(s) will have access to the video tapes; under what circumstances will the tapes be released; whether the tapes are to be reviewed daily/weekly/monthly or whether they will only be reviewed when an incident is reported; which individual(s) will review the tapes; and finally, how long each tape is to be maintained.

The use of surveillance equipment in our schools is not universally accepted by all individual rights' groups. Some public interest groups, including the American Civil Liberties Union in New Jersey, do not believe that surveillance cameras are the answer to protecting students in our schools. There is a contention that surveillance cameras in schools can not only make children feel untrustworthy and vulnerable in their environment, but may have a chilling effect upon the exercise of individual rights. However, in response, school officials and their advocates contend that the minimal intrusion is outweighed by the necessity to ensure the safety and well-being of the students and faculty in all school-related settings.

Early Prevention Programs and Community Initiatives

A comprehensive plan towards school safety and security requires that school administrators include appropriate violence prevention programs. This may include the following early prevention programs: providing counseling and social services to students; designing an effective discipline policy; training school staff in all aspects of violence prevention; providing crisis response services; providing all students access to school psychologists or counselors; preparing an annual report on school crime and safety; and implementing schoolwide education and training on avoiding and preventing violence.

We must also keep in mind the strength of our community, including local businesses, religious organizations, law enforcement personnel, and libraries. We cannot ignore the value in creating an effective support system for our youth through community initiatives. It is important to make our youth feel safe at all times, including during the time period spent away from home and school. School personnel should cooperatively work with local businesses and other community partners to create a safe environment outside of the school. If students feel safe in their community, these feelings will likely be transported into the school setting.

NEEDS OF SECURITY VS. CIVIL LIBERTIES IN THE SCHOOL ENVIRONMENT

Fourth Amendment Issues

The Fourth Amendment guarantees the privacy of persons against certain arbitrary and invasive acts by officers of the government or those acting at their direction (*Camara v. Municipal Court of San Francisco*, 1967). This constitutional guarantee is extended to the states through the Fourteenth Amendment of the United States Constitution which states:

> No states shall make or enforce any law which shall abridge the privileges or immunities of citizens of the United States; nor shall any State deprive any person of life, liberty, or property, without due process of law; nor deny to any person within its jurisdiction the equal protection of the laws (U.S. Constitution, Amendment XIV).

It is a general principal of law that students' constitutional rights are not lost in the school environment. The United States Supreme Court has stated "it can hardly be argued that either students or teachers shed their constitutional rights...at the schoolhouse gate" (*Tinker v. Des Moines Independent Community School District*, 393 U.S. 503, 509, 1969)." Also, in *Goss v. Lopez* (1975) it was established that whenever students face loss of an important substantive right, they share with every person protected by the Constitution the right to procedural due process. Furthermore, the "Fourteenth Amendment, as now applied to the States, protects the citizen against the state itself and all of its creatures—Boards of Education not excepted" (*West Virginia State Board of Education v. Barnette*, 319 U.S. 624, 1943). Therefore, school officials must respect a student's legitimate and reasonable expectation of privacy.

In comparison, it is a well-accepted point of law that not all individuals enjoy the same degree of privacy protection (see *N.J. v. T.L.O.*, 1985). For example, in *Hazelwood School District v. Kuhlmeier* (1988) school officials were permitted to censor the school paper. The Supreme Court has held that unemancipated children do not have substantially the same rights to privacy as adults (see *Acton v. Vernonia School District 47J*, 1995). Since children are subject to a degree of supervision and control by school officials, a student has a lower expectation of privacy (see *Skinner v. Railway Labor Executive's Association*, 1989).

The Fourth Amendment protects the privacy interests of persons within the jurisdiction of the United States against unreasonable searches and seizures. In *T.L.O.*, the United States Supreme court has ruled that searches of students by school officials do not violate the Fourth Amendment if the searches are reasonable under all of the circumstances.

First Amendment Issues

The United States Supreme Court has limited First Amendment protections for certain student speech in the context of the schools (see *Hazelwood School District v. Kuhlmeier*, 1988; *Bethel School District No. 403 v. Fraser*, 1986). In *Tinker v. Des Moines Independent Community School District* (1969), the Supreme Court upheld the First Amendment right of students to wear black armbands as a gesture of political speech. The Court recognized that student speech could be restricted where it "materially and substantially interfered with the requirements of appropriate discipline in the operation of the school" (*Burnside v. Byars*, 363 F.2d 744, 749, 5th Cir., 1966). The school's interest in protecting others from harm may outweigh a student's rights of expression, especially if student speech impedes the ability of others to properly function within the school environment. In determining whether free speech protections may be limited in the school setting, school administrators may consider whether there will be a substantial likelihood of disruption to the learning process.

Although schools officials may be justified in disciplining students for threats against students and faculty, it is important for schools to consider the students' First Amendment speech rights. In the case of *Lovell v. Poway Unified School District* (1996), a student told her school guidance counselor that she would shoot her unless changes were made to her class schedule. The counselor filed a disciplinary report, and informed the principal that she felt threatened by the statement. The student denied threatening the counselor and claimed that she did not mean any harm towards the counselor. After meeting with both the counselor and the student, the school suspended the student for three days. The student filed a claim against the school in federal court, claiming a violation of her First Amendment speech rights. The lower court held that school officials violated the student's free speech rights because her statement did not contain "the requisite *threat* required by law . . . to allow infringement on her right of free speech." Accordingly, the lower court held that the school district's suspension was impermissible.

On appeal, the Ninth Circuit acknowledged the standard promulgated in Tinker and stated:

> . . . whether a reasonable person in [the student's] position would foresee that [the counselor] would interpret her statement as a serious expression of intent to harm or assault . . .

and further stated:

> Given the level of violence pervasive in public schools today, it is no wonder that (the counselor) felt threatened. Nonetheless, we do not mean to suggest that one need only assert that he or she felt threatened by another's conduct in order to justify overriding that person's right to free expression. While courts may consider the effect on the listener when determining whether a statement constitutes a true threat, the final result turns upon whether a reasonable person in these circumstances should have foreseen that his or her words would have this effect (*Lovell v. Poway Unified School District,* 90 F.3d 372, 9th Cir., 1996).

The Ninth Circuit then reversed the lower court and ruled that the student's statement was "unequivocal and specific enough to convey a true threat of physical violence." Since the student's statement was not protected by the First Amendment, the school district's disciplinary actions did not violate the student's right to free expression under either federal or state law. While it remains to be seen whether the Ninth Circuit's reasoning will be applied to similar situations involving student threats, it is likely that as long as violence in the schools is a reality, the court's reactions to advance verbal threats will be taken more seriously and will be curtailed in the public school setting.

It is inevitable that school administrators will be confronted with the difficult position of distinguishing between constitutionally protected speech and a true threat of violence. For example, *Watts v. United States* (1969) held that the statement, "If they ever make me carry a rifle the first man I want to get in my sights is L.B.J." was political hyperbole and not a true threat given its context. Thus, school administrators will be forced to determine whether a statement falls outside the parameters of the First Amendment. Under an objective standard, the school administrator must question "whether a reasonable person would foresee that the statement would be interpreted by those to whom the maker communicates the statement as a serious expression of intent to harm or assault" (see *United States v. Orozco-Santillan,* 903 F.2d 1262, 1265, 9th Cir., 1990)." However, it is critical that any alleged threats be evaluated in consideration of the overall factual circumstances, including the relationship between the speaker and audience, the social environment, and the reaction of the listener. Although school administrators must study the content of the language itself, it is equally important to consider the circumstances surrounding the alleged threat.

Issues Involving Special Education Students

The Individuals with Disabilities Education Act (IDEA) (20 U.S.C. §1401 *et seq.*) and Section 504 of the Rehabilitation Act of 1973 (20 U.S.C. §706(8), §794, & §794 (a)) have been interpreted as prohibiting the long-term suspension or expulsion of a disabled student when the misconduct is a manifestation of the student's disability, even if the activity involves dangerous or violent behavior. While both national and state policies mandate special protection for students with disabilities, other policies are enacted that impose stricter school discipline. Thus, there is an inherent conflict between the rights of disabled students, and the interests of other students and faculty members.

While school discipline often involves changing a student's educational placement, IDEA's *stay-put* provision limits a school district's ability to remove special education students from the school environment. The rationale of the stay-put provision in the disciplinary area is to "insure that a school cannot eject a child and change his educational placement without complying with due process requirements" (see IDEA, 20 U.S.C. §1415 (j) and Tennessee v.Department of Mental Health & Mental Retardation v. Paul B, 1966). Procedural due process for special education students is governed by the stay-put provision. Whenever a local educational agency proposes to initiate or change the educational placement of a special education student, the student must remain in the current placement until all proceedings to effect the change have been completed. This provision applies unless the parents and the educational agency agree otherwise. The procedural safeguards include strict notice requirements, opportunities for mediation, impartial due process hearings on the record, the right to appeal to state or federal courts without regard to jurisdictional amount, and reimbursement of certain costs and reasonable attorney fees. In the disciplinary setting, the stay-put provision emphasizes the competing interests between the district's mandate to provide a free and appropriate education in the least restrictive environment, and the schools' responsibility to maintain safety and order. Since the discipline of students, including suspension, expulsion, or referral to juvenile authorities, usually requires a change in educational placement when applied to disabled students, the strict requirements of the stay-put provision must be followed by school officials. In order to take a disciplinary action constituting a change in the student's educational placement, a manifestation determination must be made in order to determine whether the misconduct was a manifestation of the student's disability.

Generally, a student who brings weapons to school may be expelled from school for one year (see IDEA, 20 U.S.C. 8921 and N.J.S.A. 18A: 37-8). However, it is clear that school administrators must comply with IDEA before expelling a student under the statute. Thus, a full manifestation determination, along with all the attendant IDEA due process rights, must be afforded to the student prior to any expulsion. However, if the disciplinary action involves dangerous weapons, activities, or illegal drugs, the IDEA temporarily minimizes the impact of the stay-put provision. IDEA permits school districts to place special education students in appropriate interim alternative education settings for up to forty-five days without violating the provisions regarding change of placement.

The individualized education program (IEP) team must determine that the interim alternative education setting otherwise meets IDEA requirements. The setting must enable the student to continue to participate in the general curriculum, must meet the goals and provide services consistent with the current IEP, and must address the misconduct involving illegal drugs or weapons (see IDEA, 20 U.S.C. §1415 (k) (7) a). In this situation, the student may remain in the current placement, prior to the determination of misconduct. A district, may, however, request an expedited hearing if school personnel maintain it is dangerous for a student to remain in the current setting. A hearing officer may order a change in placement to an appropriate interim setting for not more than forty-five days if 1) the officer finds the current placement is substantially likely to result in injury, 2) the district has made reasonable efforts to minimize the risk of harm in the current placement, including the use of supplementary aids and services, and 3) interim placement will enable the student to continue in the general curriculum and continue to receive services to meet IEP goals.

Additionally, nothing in IDEA shall be construed to prohibit the reporting of a crime committed by a child with a disability to appropriate authorities, or to prohibit the authorities from proceeding with enforcement. "An agency reporting a crime committed by a child with a disability shall ensure that copies of the special education and disciplinary records of the child are transmitted for consideration by the appropriate authorities to whom it reports the crime" (IDEA, 20 U.S.C. § 1415 (k) (9)). Any such transmission is to the extent permitted by the Family Educational Rights and Privacy Act.

In situations where a student does not bring a weapon or illegal drugs to school, a school district must prove by substantial evidence that the student is likely to injure himself or others if maintained in his current placement. For example, the court in *Honig v. Doe* (1988) held that a plain reading of the Act did not allow for suspension longer than ten days unless the school system could show in court that leaving the student in the current setting was "substantially likely to result in injury either to himself or herself, or to others." Proof by substantial evidence is defined as "beyond a preponderance of the evidence" (IDEA, 20 U.S.C. §1415 (k) (10) C). In addition, if the school district believes it is dangerous for the child to remain in his current setting pending any proceedings, it may request an expedited hearing.

There is a question whether the protections under IDEA compromise safety in our schools and for staff. In affording special protection to disabled students who contribute to school disruption and violence, are we preventing the public schools from maintaining safety for all students and faculty? With the increasing number of violent incidents and drug-related crimes in our schools, are we creating a hurdle for school officials that will inevitably be felt by the entire public school community?

III. ROLES OF SCHOOL PERSONNEL IN THE RECOGNITION OF RISK AND CONFIDENTIALITY

A Uniform State Memorandum of Agreement Between Education and Law Enforcement Officials

In 1988, the Department of Law & Public Safety and the Department of Education (1999) issued a model agreement for use by local law enforcement and education officials. The Uniform State Memorandum of Agreement Between Education and Law Enforcement Officials ("Agreement") was designed to promote cooperation between local school districts and law enforcement agencies on a variety of common issues, including safe school environment.

All New Jersey school districts are required by rules and regulations issued by the State Board of Education to adopt and implement policies and procedures that are "consistent with and complementary to" the State Memorandum of Agreement approved by the Department of Law and Public Safety and the Department of Education. N.J.A.C. 6:29-10.1 provides in pertinent part:

> The purpose of this subchapter is to establish uniform Statewide policies and procedures for cooperating with law enforcement operations and activities on or nearer school grounds to ensure a safe school environment, and to identify the circumstances under which school officials shall refer violations to the police for handling...[s]uch policies and procedures shall be consistent with and complementary to the State Memorandum of Agreement approved by the Department of Law and Public Safety and the Department of Education.

Accordingly, all public school districts throughout New Jersey will be required to adopt and implement the revised uniform agreement. The Department of Law revised the Agreement in 1992 and 1999. The most recent revisions reaffirm the commitment between law enforcement and education officials to contain and account for problems associated with drug and alcohol abuse, as well as the ramifications of violence among school-age children. State administrative code requires all district boards of education to adopt and implement policies and procedures to ensure cooperation between school staff and law enforcement authorities. According to N.J.A.C. 6:29-10.2 district boards of education must include policies and procedures in all matters relating to: 1) unlawful possession, distribution and disposition of controlled dangerous substances, including anabolic steroids, drug paraphernalia, alcohol, firearms, and other deadly weapons; and 2) the planning and conduct of law enforcement activities and operations occurring on school property, including arrest procedures and undercover school operations.

In response to recent national tragedies involving youth violence, school officials are required to report to police incidents involving planned or threatened violence by students (Department of Law & Public Safety and Department of Education, 1999). The prompt reporting of suspected incidents of planned or threatened violence will permit appropriate intervention by law enforcement or judicial authorities, even where the threat technically does not rise to the level of criminal conduct. Prior to the 1999 revision, the agreement only required the reporting of suspected drug offenses and offenses involving the actual use or possession of firearms. There is also a requirement for police and prosecutors to respond promptly to any information provided by school officials concerning planned or threatened violence. After reporting, information from the law authorities may be shared with the school administration for implementation of an appropriate educational plan. Additional provisions encourage local education and law enforcement officials to discuss the need to develop a specific bomb threat plan to respond to bomb scares, as well as to develop procedures to respond to crises involving gunfire. All such provisions serve to compel or encourage an increased level of cooperation between school officials and law enforcement officials.

Applicable Statutes, Regulations, and Other Formal Policies

School officials must be aware of the applicable statutes that govern the responsibility of school officials to report acts of violence or vandalism. Generally, any school employee observing or having direct knowledge from a participant or victim of an act of violence must file a report describing the incident to the school principal (see N.J.S.A. 18A: 17-46). The principal must notify the district superintendent of schools of the action taken regarding the incident. It is also important to note that under N.J.S.A. 18A: 37-2.3, the principal is required to notify the appropriate law enforcement agency of a possible violation of the New Jersey Code of Criminal Justice. The board of education may not discharge or in any manner discriminate against a school employee as to his employment because the employee filed a report of violence. Any employee discriminated against shall be restored to his employment and shall be compensated by the board of education for any loss of wages arising out of the discrimination. However, if the employee ceases to be qualified to perform the duties of this employment he shall not be entitled to restoration and compensation.

Annually, at a public meeting, the superintendent of schools must report to the board of education all acts of violence and vandalism (N.J.S.A. 18A: 17-46). Similarly, the Commissioner of Education is required to submit an annual report to the education committees of the Senate and General Assembly detailing the extent of violence and vandalism in the public schools (N.J.S.A. 18A:17-48). The report must also include recommendations towards alleviating the problem of violence and vandalism in New Jersey schools. School boards should adopt written policies that address reporting violence and vandalism on school premises.

CONCLUSION

School boards are adopting effective policies and practices aimed at improving school safety. While there is no one solution towards preventing violence in our schools, as a community of educators, legislators, law enforcement personnel, parents, and neighbors, it is clear that there must be a cooperative joining together to educate our children and to provide them with the support and means to seriously address the issues.

REFERENCES

Acton v. Vernonia School District 47 J, 115 S. Ct. 2386, 2391 (1995) (citing 59 Am. Jur. 2d Parent and Child § 10 (1987).

Bethel School District No. 403 v. Fraser, 478 U.S. 675, 682, 683 (1986).

Burnside v. Byars, 363 F.2d 744, 749 (5th Cir., 1966).

Camara v. Municipal Court of San Francisco, 387 U.S. 523, 528 (1967).

Department of Law and Public Safety and the Department of Education, *Uniform State Memorandum of Agreement Between Education and Law Enforcement*, 4.6-4.13 (July 23, 1999).

Desilets v. Clearview Regional Board of Education, 265 N.J. Super 370, 373 (App. Div. 1993).

Dumenigo, A. (February 1, 2000). Coming soon to a school near you: Surveillance. *The Star-Ledger,* 29-31.

Fisher, R. G. (September 18, 1994). Videos on buses. *The Star-Ledger* (WL 788 9472)

Goss v. Lopez, 419 U.S. 565 (1975).

Grey, A. (July 23, 1996). Franklin ponders placing cameras in high school as a safety measure. *The Star-Ledger* (WL 795 2926).

Hazelwood School District v. Kuhlmeier, 484 U.S. 260, 266, 267 (1988).

Honig v. Doe, 484 U.S. 305 (1988).

Individuals with Disabilities Education Act, 20 U.S.C. § 1401, § 1415, § 8921 (1997). In re D.E.M., 727 A.2d 570, 572, 574 (Pa. 1999).

In re F.B., 658 A.2d 1378-1382 (1995).

Jackson v. Hankinson, 51 N.J. 230, 235, 236 (1968).

Jones v. Latexo Independent School District, et. al. 499 F. Supp. 223 (E.D.Tex. 1980).

Kimmelman, I. I. (October, 1977). *Attorney General's guidelines regarding school searches.*

Lovell v. Poway Unified School District, 90 F.3d 367, 369, 372 (9th Cir. 1996), *rev'g* 847 F. Supp. 780, 785 (S.D. Cal.1994).

New Jersey Association of School Administrators (February, 1999). Search and seizure of students in public schools. *Administrative Guide, 29* (2), 2.

N.J. v. T.L.O, 469 U.S. 325, 328-330, 333-334,341-342 (1985).

N.J.A.C. 6:29-10.1, 6:29-10.2.

N.J.S.A. 18A: 36-19.2, 37-2.3, 37-6.1, 37-8, 17-46, 17-48.

People v. Dukes, 580 N.Y.S.2d 850, 851, 852-853 (1992).

People in the Interest of P.E.A., 754 P.2d 382 (Colo., 1988).

Section 504, 1973 Rehabilitation Act, 20 U.S.C. § 706 (8), 794.

Skinner v. Railway Labor Executive's Association, 489 U.S. 602, 627 (1989).

State of Florida v. D.T.W, 425 So.2d 1383 (Fla. Dist. Ct. App. 1983).

State of New Jersey v. Engerud, 94 N.J. 49, 331, 338, 349 (1983).

Tennessee Department of Mental Health & Mental Retardation v. Paul B., 88 F.3d 1466, 1472 (6th Cir. 1966).

Tinker v. Des. Moines Independent Community School District, 393 U.S. 503, 509 (1969).

Thompson v. Carthage School District, 87 F. 3d 979 (8th Cir. 1996).

United States v. Orozco-Santillan, 903 F.2d 1262, 1265 (9th Cir. 1990).

U.S. Constitution, Amendment IV.

U.S. Constitution, Amendment XIV.

Watts v. United States, 394 U.S. 705 (1969).

Webb v. McCullough, 828 F.2d 1151, 1157 (6th Cir. 1987).

West Virginia State Board of Education v. Barnette, 319 U.S. 624 (1943).

Chapter Eleven

MENTAL HEALTH PROFESSIONALS AND VIOLENCE: ARE YOU READY?

CHRISTOPHER R. BARBRACK

The best lack all conviction while
the worst are full of passionate intensity.

W.B. Yeats, *The Second Coming.*

INTRODUCTION

I SPEND MUCH of my time as an attorney consulting with and advising mental health professionals (MHPs) and organizations before and after violent incidents perpetrated by their clients. I use the term MHP to describe the wide variety of individuals who offer mental health services, instead of the term *provider*, which I regard equivalent to *vendor* and not an appropriate term for professionals. Furthermore, I use the terms *client* and *patient* interchangeably to refer to those individuals who receive mental health services.

The focus of this chapter is to describe ways that MHPs can understand, analyze, and manage violent and violence-prone individuals in the course of treatment. Whether youth or adult, there are common concerns and factors that need to be addressed by MHPs, that will be addressed in this chapter. These include 1) the conflicting values of safety and freedom and the professional dilemma for the MPH; 2) the connection between violence and mental health, so that MHPs may understand why they are unwittingly drawn to the front line of dealing with violence and why they will find themselves having to deal with violence whether or not they intend to do so; 3) confidentiality and the so-called duty to warn; 4) the internal dialogue and decision making that occur when MHPs are confronted with violent and violence-prone clients, as one of my long-time interests has been in the decision-making processes of conflict-ridden professional situations (Barbrack, 1978); and briefly, 5) the historical and scientific contexts of the above issues.

The premise of this chapter is that the vast majority of MHPs is neither expecting to deal with nor prepared to deal with the violent or violence-prone patient. Certainly, if professionals are motivated by this book, *Shocking Violence*, to become more aware of and involved in the area of violence, they must do so in a manner that is consciously attuned to the needs of their clients and consistent with their professional ethics and state licensing/certification regulations.

It is axiomatic that both MHP and client experience a confidential relationship, meaning that the professional is expected not to divulge treatment-related revelations that occur in psychotherapy. This idea originated in the attorney-client relationship and has a long history in medicine. A confidential relationship is believed to encourage persons who need help to seek that help and to divulge whatever is necessary for professionals to properly do their jobs. It is deemed to be in the public interest that persons requiring the services of lawyers and doctors not be impeded in pursuing such services. Policies regarding confidentiality in mental health treatment are typically found in state laws and regulations. In a litigation context, privilege, that is the patient's right to prevent the professional from disclosing confidential information that is sought in a legal context (e.g., litigation), is the corollary of confidentiality.

When MHPs find themselves in relationships with violent and violence-prone individuals, they are forced to confront issues of confidentiality. When is it proper to divulge confidential information for the sake of preventing a violent act? In this regard it is important to note that patients may react very negatively to the prospect or fact of their confidences being broken (Barbrack, 1996; Barbrack, in preparation). Origins of problems between MHPs and patients can be traced back to the beginnings of relationships when professionals do not fully set forth the nature and limitation of the confidential relationship. Often, the therapeutic relationship continues without any breach of confidentiality, despite close calls and intermittent, risky patient behavior. Perhaps, on the basis of reactive reassurances from the patient, the MHP takes no action. But later, for reasons that may have nothing to do with what is contemporaneously occurring in therapy, the MHP makes a decision to breach the confidentiality, based on past behavior rather than on a thorough current evaluation of the patient's status. Unlike ordinary citizens, many MHPs are *obliged* to reveal confidential information for the sake of preventing serious harm. This scenario places the professional, who is accustomed to operating within the confines of a private and confidential relationship, on the horns of a dilemma.

The chapters in this text, *Shocking Violence*, graphically illustrate the prevalence of violence in American society. Contemporary mental health journals (see Winick & LaFond, 1998) devote considerable space every month or so to topics ranging from murder, assassinations, mutilation, bombings, kidnapping, and rape to road rage, sexual harassment in schools and workplaces, domestic violence, and bullying. The Internet is an excellent source of information regarding these topics, with websites such as that of the Violence Institute of New Jersey at the University of Medicine and Dentistry of New Jersey, www.umdnj.edu/vinjweb. Many courts and legislatures in Mercer County, New Jersey, where I practice, have mandated that MHPs play a primary role in identifying and otherwise managing violent and violence-prone individuals. This task is multidimensional and, at its root, involves an ability to strike a balance between the competing values of public safety and personal freedom (see *Portee v. Jaffee*, 1988).

FREEDOM AND SAFETY

Americans have the right to be safe and the right to be free. Circumstances sometimes drive these rights into fierce competition with one another. Achieving a balance between safety and freedom is a dynamic part of the ongoing experiment embodied by this country. Driven by current events, MHPs, who wish to contain and minimize violence for the sake of promoting safety, must also be mindful not to unduly compromise their clients' freedom to be and act in whatever ways their clients choose.

One of the most extreme curtailments of freedom is institutionalization. Most institutionalized populations fall into two categories: the patients who need treatment and the patients who need to be locked up to protect society (Turbheimer & Parry, 1992). MHPs, on the verge of breaching confidentiality for the sake of safety, must recognize the distinction between their clients' need for treatment and society's pressure for protection and safety (Bigelow, Bloom, Williams, & McFarland, 1999). If the primary allegiance of MHPs is to their clients, then knowing that curtailment of client freedom may not always be in the best interests of their clients is *de riguer*. This knowledge contributes to the professional's ethical dilemma but is a necessary burden. When it comes to violence, our society renders the professional's job even more difficult by virtue of society's apparent ambivalent attitude toward violence (see Rodlum, Farmer, Pearl, & Van Acker, 2000). Thus, proactive professionals may find themselves whipsawed by societal crosscurrents, political decision makers, and the courts.

MENTAL HEALTH AND VIOLENCE

Violence is of interest to MHPs because they are dedicated to trying to understand the human condition, and to treating both the victims and the perpetrators of violence. My experience as a clinical psychologist, trainer of clinical psychologists, and attorney has led me to repeatedly question the knowledge base, training, and experience that equip MHPs to function as experts in the area of violence. What happens in many instances is that the MHP becomes unwittingly involved with violence, yet sorely lacks expertise to handle violent and violence-prone clients. Managing such clients, MHPs often discover themselves, usually briefly, in very desperate situations. My experience has taught me that as long as MHPs are willing to present themselves as experts in their field, society may ardently rely upon them for their presumed ability to address violence. To their credit, some MHP professional organizations have fought long and hard to disclaim the ability to predict behaviors such as dangerousness (Weinstock, 1988). In contrast, there is another group of professionals that is comprised of individuals who claim expertise in this area (see Modlin, 1989), who specialize in violent behavior, and whose training and expertise effectively support this specialization. They are well-versed in the ethical and legal dilemmas alluded to here.

Even under the best circumstances, the decision making involved in working with violence is fraught with uncertainty. Therefore, professionals working in the field must be appropriately humble and circumspect and, at the same time, must be capable of facing danger and of making courageous decisions. This paradox is a significant challenge for the professional who is thrown inadvertently into the fray.

Why is it that many, if not most, MHPs become involved in violent situations without intending to do so? I believe there is a simple explanation. Violence tends to co-exist with various psychological problems. The literature on violence is vast. The diligent reader can benefit from unearthing the infinite number of nuggets of disconnected and often counterintuitive findings as well as those that are more routine and self-evident. I believe it is the task of the expert to locate, appreciate, and disseminate such findings, especially the counterintuitive ones. Similarly, in court an expert witness is not called upon to testify to that which is obvious to anyone with a modicum of common sense and experience but to illuminate factual situations in ways that are beyond common sense so that such situations are not misconstrued. For example, if a physician goes to Las Vegas, loses $250,000 and then, upon exiting a casino, sober, pushes a bystander into oncoming traffic, anyone can reach the conclusion that the physician is a bad gambler and not an actor. But, it would take an expert to show how these behaviors might be expressions of a bipolar illness. Judges and juries depend on the latter kind of information from experts. So too society relies on the MHP to illuminate therapeutic relationships with understanding that may be counterintuitive while in the purview of the knowledgeable professional.

There is an apparent relationship between some kinds of psychological problems (e.g., bipolar illness and psychosis) and violence but not other forms of psychological problems (e.g., depression and anxiety) and violence (Stueve & Link, 1997). Violent juveniles have been found to exhibit a relatively high degree of paranoia, loosening of associations, and hallucinations as well as psychomotor epilepsy, abnormal EEGs, and soft neurological signs (Scott, 1999). Upwards of 80 percent of violent males and females have been found to meet the DSM-IV criteria for a Conduct Disorder (Eppright, Kashani, & Robinson, 1995). There are indications in the literature of the comorbidity of violence with ADHD (Attention Deficit Hyperactivity Disorder) (Barkley, Fisher, and Ederbrock, 1990) and with depression (O'Shaugnessey, 1992). There seems to be a growing consensus in the literature that violence between parents has an adverse effect upon children (Holden, Geffner, & Jouriles, 1998). Considering the above information, it is easy to speculate that many inchoately, latently violent individuals are treated by MHPs because of their manifest psychological problems. Thus, MHPs are often unaware of the impending violent episodes that may occur during the course of a psychotherapeutic relationship. The foregoing is merely illustrative of how MHPs can become unwittingly involved with violent and violence-prone individuals.

Conversely, it is obvious that not all or even many persons who manifest psychological problems are prone to commit violent acts. In fact, there is some evidence that, with regard to known offenders, clinical or psychopathological variables are either not related to or are negatively correlated with repeated criminal acts (Bonta, Law, & Hanson, 1998; Swanson, 1994), meaning that many of these offenders do not exhibit mental disorders that can be diagnosed. This is precisely the kind of nonintuitive finding that MHPs can use to inform decision makers regarding the interplay between psychopathology and violence. In light of these factors, it is essential that MHPs work through issues of confidentiality, safety, and freedom at the outset of any therapeutic relationship. Furthermore, MHPs need to understand the place and context of confidentiality in psychotherapy.

CONFIDENTIALITY

Privacy, Truth, and Facts in Psychotherapy

Most would consider Sigmund Freud to be the founder of modern psychotherapy or at least a very important figure in the intellectual history of modern psychotherapy. Freud believed that the treatment relationship had to establish an alliance of trust so that the client's unconscious process might unfold in the form of transference. According to Guttmacher & Weilhofen (1952):

> The psychiatric patient confides more utterly than anyone else in the world. He exposes to the therapist not only what his words directly express; he lays bare his entire self, his dreams, his fantasies, his sins, and his shame. Most patients who undergo psychotherapy know that this is what will be expected of them, and that they cannot get help except on that condition . . . It would be too much to expect from them to do so if they knew that all they say—and all that the psychiatrist learns from what they say—may be revealed (p. 160).

This sentiment is as widely held today as it ever was. Confidentiality is the cornerstone of all psychotherapies. However, in *Jaffe v. Redmond* (1996), the plaintiffs wanted to obtain the notes of a social worker therapist. The plaintiff's attorneys prepared very comprehensive briefs in which they argued in part, citing many empirical studies, that confidentiality was not an essential part of the effective therapy relationship. The United States Supreme Court disagreed and ruled that therapeutic interactions between clients and social workers were protected by the Federal Rules of Evidence. This case revealed that historical and logical arguments in favor of confidentiality are compelling but may still be challenged by countervailing positions and evidence.

Freud and his followers used techniques such as analysis of dreams, slips of the tongue, and free association. The material produced by the patient was not investigated outside of the consulting room for the sake of establishing accuracy. In Freud's approach and in virtually every other ensuing approach to psychotherapy, except for the more recent behavioral in vivo approaches, the therapist accepts and works with what the client says and does within the four walls of the consultation room. Unlike Sherlock Holmes, Freud did not have to investigate in order to establish what *really happened* to the client (Friedman, 1999). In fact, in the late eighteenth century, Freud abandoned outside, nontreatment contact with his patients due to its interference with the transference relationship (Jones, 1955). Thus, what was actually occurring on a day-to-day basis in the patient's life was not important to know. Conversely, the legal system is only interested in what really happened.

When a client presents a risk of serious danger in the consultation room, the therapist cannot always rely exclusively upon questioning of the client as a means to determine that the risk does not reach a certain, critical threshold. Depending upon the situation, the therapist might have to contact the client's spouse, employer, teachers, roommate, or parents in order to establish the parameters of the risk. It is difficult to imagine such conversations not including some disclosures of confidential material by the therapist. In fact, the very act of reaching outside of the consultation room to make such contacts, regardless of what is said, threatens the therapeutic relationship.

The therapist is often in a position to process conflicting information from the foregoing contacts. The therapist is forced to establish the truthfulness of these various sources in order to make an informed decision regarding the probability of violence, even though some courts (see *State v. Michaels*, 1995) have stated emphatically that psychologists (i.e., MHPs) have no particular expertise in determining truthfulness.

Parenthetically, it is important to note that the legal system has a very different concept of truthfulness than the mental health system that tends to accept the patient's version of what really happened for the sake of promoting treatment (McNulty & Wardle, 1994). In psychotherapy, this relaxed and expansive acceptance of what really happened stems from the clinician's desire to avoid false negatives. The clinical approach will accept the working hypothesis that what a client says is true if that's what it takes to accurately identify and treat the client's actual problems. Conversely, the legal system abhors false positives, i.e., convicting an innocent person, and will readily accept false negatives, letting guilty parties go free. Thus, the legal system is very strict in its assessment of its truth (Rassin & Merckelback, 1999). These clashing views of the truth cannot be easily resolved and will continue to create confusion and misunderstandings between MHPs, courts, and attorneys. This is one of many good reasons why MHPs are advised to be very cautious in interacting with the police, courts, and attorneys (Barbrack, in press).

Confidentiality after the *Tarasoff* Decision

The integrity of the confidential psychotherapist-patient relationship remained more or less intact for one hundred plus years until a psychiatric patient killed a student and the California Courts determined that the psychiatrist had a duty to warn the victim of the risk the student faced from his patient. The victim's name was Tatiana Tarasoff and the principles of this case are commonly referred to simply as *Tarasoff.*

Many professionals and lay persons do not fully appreciate the profound change in psychotherapy wrought in some places by the so-called *Tarasoff* decisions. Consider this language from the court's opinion (*Tarasoff*, 1976):

When a psychotherapist determines, or pursuant to the standards of his profession should determine, that his patient presents a serious danger of violence to another, he incurs an obligation to use reasonable care to protect the intended victim against such danger. The discharge of such duty may require the therapist to take one or more various steps, depending upon the nature of the case, including warning the intended victim or others likely to apprise the victim of the danger, notifying the police or taking whatever steps are reasonably necessary under the circumstances (p. 431).

The foregoing opinion governs in the state of California. Many other states have also adopted this kind of language or variations of it. The *Tarasoff* obligation was introduced into New Jersey common law by *McIntosh v. Milano*, 168 NJ Super. 446 (1979). In New Jersey, the duty to warn is now incorporated in licensing regulations for psychologists, NJAC 13:42-8.5 (a)(1), and social workers, NJAC 13: 44G-12.3(a)(4). The particulars of state laws or regulations in the area of duty to warn vary across states in some very important ways and ought to be studied on a state-by-state basis. In fact, some MHPs may not be obliged to breach confidentiality. Likewise, states like Florida have no such duty to protect based upon the following reasoning: confidentiality should be preserved and MHPs are not particularly adept at predicting dangerousness (see *Boynton v. Burglass*, 1991). In states where a duty to warn and protect is imposed, the MHP must make a reasonable determination: 1) Is there a threat of serious danger? 2) Is this threat imminent? 3) Is there an identifiable victim? Pursuing these questions requires a factual inquiry that may go beyond what the client says and does in the consultation room. Hence, the *Tarasoff*-type duty has two main effects: 1) it undermines the confidentiality of the therapy relationship and 2) it requires that the therapist change roles so that investigation in and perhaps outside of the therapy relationship is required.

In any event, many mental health professionals in the country are grappling on a daily basis with the duty to warn and protect in situations where they treat violent and violence-prone individuals. The decision to disclose should be the product of a painstaking analysis. The clinician must evaluate the adverse effects of disclosure on the client, mindful that the clinician's primary duty is to avoid harming the client (Hook & Cleveland, 1999).

Breaching Confidentiality for Violence and for Managed Care

The absolute minimum of confidential information the MHP has to divulge, let's say to the police, in the course of trying to protect the client or the client's victim, is very little. Unfortunately, once the decision to breach is made, what often follows is a disinhibition wherein the MHP divulges much more than necessary. A similar phenomenon occurs in reporting incest. Many state statutes require that the incest reporter do just that – report and not "discuss at length." Although child protective workers would like more detail, the law requires that one reports only what is required and permitted to report. Likewise, in notifying the police regarding the potentially violent patient, a few details about the nature of the risk, as well as the client's whereabouts are all that are required. Implicit in this disclosure is that the person is in fact a client. In other words, excepting the client's violent proclivities, the client's privacy may be left largely intact.

Contrast this with the disclosures routinely required by managed care companies, especially those that are "ERISA qualified," falling under the federal, self-insured employer umbrella and exempt from state law. Some states such as New Jersey have a so-called "Peer Review Law" that prohibits the MHP from making detailed disclosures to managed care companies, even if the client consents. The intent is to protect the client from undue pressure to divulge unnecessary details of the therapy to the insurance company. Since not all MHPs are equally prohibited, those who are can be at a disadvantage in the contemporary marketplace when the insurer decides not to cover services because of nondisclosure by the MHP. The MHP is required by the insurer to reveal personal, clinical information, and the client is faced with the dilemma of noncertification for additional treatment unless the client authorizes the disclosures and the MHP complies.

Oddly, I find that MHPs tend to agonize much more over breaching confidentially in the context of a violent client than in regard to an insurer's or managed care company's request. This may be due to the fact that the former requires more independent initiative on the part of the MHP and the latter can be blamed on the managed care company, an instance of diffusion of responsibility.

DECISION MAKING IN DEALING WITH
THE VIOLENT CLIENT

When I receive a call from an MHP in desperate straits with a violent or violence-prone client, I spend much time listening and much time reassuring and reminding the professional that she or he did not commit or threaten to commit the violent act, and that she or he is wearing the "white hat" in this situation. Once the preliminary reassurances are complete, the colloquy goes something like this.

CRB: Yeah, it certainly sounds as if the client is dangerous [to an identifiable person] and it's imminent and serious.

Dr. X: I know but what do you think I should do?

At this point, there is an array of available options (Felthous, 1999) that has to be considered that can involve good clinical thinking/judgment and courageous actions, as well as dishonesty, naiveté, and discounting.

CRB: What about calling the police?

Dr. X: Do you think I should?

The proposed police call involves breaching confidentiality and betraying the client's trust. Confidentiality is so crucial in psychotherapy that a breach warrants very careful analysis, including a painstaking review of alternatives to a breach. Since the MHP is often overwrought in this situation, she or he tends to narrow, rather than expand, the possible options (Mann & Janis, 1985). Deciding to breach confidentiality may involve a decision scheme that might look something like this:

> *Is there a threat of serious harm?*
> *Is the threat imminent?*

Assuming for a moment that the average MHP is equipped to make these determinations, affirmative answers bring the analysis to a critical threshold:

> *Are there resources available to intervene?*
> *Will my intervening reduce the risk?*

For example, are there trained professionals and hospital beds available to treat the patient? If the MHP believes that these resources do not exist or that the resources appear to exist but are not effective, e.g., a hospital's decision-making apparatus is designed to almost never hospitalize the violent or violence-prone individual, then the MHP may decide to "go through the motions" and refer the client to the hospital or call the police to escort the client to the hospital in order to protect the MHP from liability. However, if resources do not exist, the MHP may be disinclined to take any action.

The dimension of this decision-making process that focuses on the MHP's personal protection and self-interest is rarely discussed in articles written by MHPs. Yet, I believe one or more personal considerations are likely included in every situation in which the MHP deliberates about breaching the confidence. Such considerations might include, "If I breach confidentiality, what is the risk that . . ."

> *I will be physically hurt?*
> *my family will be physically hurt?*
> *I will be sued?*
> *I will be reported to the licensing board?*
> *I will be involved in other time-consuming hassles?*

Conversely, "If I do not breach confidentiality, what is the risk that . . ."

> *The patient will seriously hurt herself or himself or others?*
> *I will be held liable to the patient and the third party?*
> *my malpractice coverage will not cover the damages?*

As this analysis continues, the MHP can become quite anxious and hyper-vigilant, thus suboptimizing problem-solving abilities. At this point, the MHP needs to engage in appropriate self-talk, seek support from colleagues and ad hoc supervisors, and acquire legal advice. Unfortunately, there is a common tendency at these times to turn inward and magically wish that the problem would just go away, a process of denial. The fact that the problem does often evaporate tends to reinforce this kind of magical thinking as well as what in some cases might be considered unethical, unprofessional behavior.

If by breaching confidentiality the MHP is worried about being seriously harmed either financially or physically, the MHP may approach this decisional process differently, perhaps by attributing different valences to the seriousness or imminence of the expected violence. It might be a more acceptable bargain to risk the client's violence toward another person than to risk serious personal financial or physical detriment. Ultimately, the decision to breach confidentiality appears to be a highly idiosyncratic one that involves the MHP's personal interest as much as anything else. This observation is supported by research and was studied in regard to the decision of whether or not to hospitalize. Engleman, Jobes, Berman, and Langbern (1998) investigated the question of what factors contribute to the decision to hospitalize a dangerous patient. The findings were counterintuitive since the best predictors of the hospitalization decision were 1) the clinician's tendency to make decisions in a particular direction, 2) whether or not the contact with the patient occurred in a hospital or mobile unit, and 3) bed availability. Dangerousness posed by the individual made no significant contribution to the decision to hospitalize. This situation closely parallels the difficult-to-predict decision to breach confidentiality.

The specific phenomenon of breaching confidentiality should also be studied. I would speculate that many of the identified factors in the above study interact in a complex fashion to predict whether or not the clinician will breach confidentiality. Further, the low probability of violent events may lead the MHP to conclude that she or he has much less at stake by not reporting than by reporting. This is not only wrongheaded but a dangerous assumption.

Acknowledgment of the role played by personal and subjective factors in the decision to breach confidentiality also has an important implication for professional training, i.e., to better understand one's fears and anxieties as they play a role in one's professional behavior. Insightful, professional training can expose the reality of the universality and acceptability of the fact that professionals become afraid and sometimes, or perhaps most of the time, act accordingly.

WHEN MHPS TACKLE VIOLENCE: A POSTSCRIPT

MHPs are usually certified or licensed by the state. They possess special privileges and special responsibilities. When acting in a professional role, they are not merely ordinary citizens and cannot undertake actions, however just and worthy, without considering the strictures of licensure and certification. Moreover, MHPs ought to have a scientifically informed perspective on dealing with social problems. Each of these awarenesses should help the MHP to avoid the pitfalls that lurk in every psychosocial intervention, including those interventions focused on violence.

Thirty plus years ago, Abraham Maslow was President of the American Psychological Association and Lyndon B. Johnson was President of the United States. The country was in the midst of the Vietnam War and the Great Society. In this contemporary context, experimental psychologist Donald T. Campbell wrote a landmark article (1969) that advised us to employ analytic approaches in the understanding of behavior and social phenomena. Some agree with Bertrand Russell's comment that the mark of a civilized human being is the ability to read a column of numbers and then weep! However, analytic approaches, relying on mathematics and logic, help make sense of reality. Campbell's earlier work (Campbell & Stanley, 1966) amounted to an extraordinary contribution to applied research in the social sciences and formed the basis of the idealism of the age (Campbell, 1969):

> The United States and other modern nations should be ready for an experimental approach to social reforms, an approach in which we try out new programs designed to cure specific social problems, in which we learn whether or not these programs are effective, and in which we retain, imitate, modify or discard them on the basis of apparent effectiveness on the multiple imperfect criteria available (p. 409).

In explaining the intricacies of field experiments, quasi-experimental designs and threats to experimental validity, Campbell analyzed various social reform programs. For example, in 1955, the governor of Connecticut instituted a very rigorous crackdown on speeding. After one year, the number of deaths due to automobile accidents decreased from 324 to 284 and the crackdown was hailed a success. However, Campbell's perceptive analysis revealed how various other factors, including statistical regression effects, could have accounted for most if not all of the observed reduction in traffic deaths. Professionals who work in the context of violence, particularly in a concerted fashion, should be guided by the wisdom of the likes of Donald Campbell, validating observed effects through careful consideration and healthy skepticism.

MHPs who aspire to intervene in violence must consider this scientific perspective and ask questions such as: Is the incidence or nature of violence worse now than in the past? Where are the most violent segments of this society and why? Would a social intervention against violence serve an implicit political agenda? What knowledge is there in the mental health literature, e.g., valid and reliable assessments and interventions, that can be brought to bear on the problem of violence? What effective interventions are now in place? What interventions have failed and why?

Working with violent clients, and the systems in which they function, requires acting or not acting decisively in the face of uncertainty. One must understand that violence and danger are dynamic and ever-changing. Being able to exercise good clinical judgment that simultaneously reflects an appreciation for the rights of the individual and of the commonweal are essential. If professionals are inspired to become involved in combating violence, they should avoid the pitfalls of what is referred to as the "3B" method. Social reformers sometimes *B*low into a situation, *B*low off about it, usually to people who know more about it and who are more greatly affected by it, and then *B*low out, never to be heard from again. Violence has been part of our existence since Cain and Abel, and dealing with it responsibly requires a thoughtful, broad-based, and sustained approach. Expectations for success should be modest and MHPs should remain first and foremost loyal to their clients.

Finally, I believe that it would be helpful if MHPs more fully appreciated their own power. The state license or certificate invests in the professional a social trust that includes the use of reasonable judgment. Courts tend to be loathe to second-guessing professionals who have exercised reasonable judgment and this includes the judgment to breach confidentiality for the sake of the violent patient and the potential victim. Conversely, this empowering message should not obscure the need for professional training in the management of the violent and violence-prone patient.

REFERENCES

Barbrack, C. R. (1978). Interdisciplinary decision making: A response to the challenge of PL 94-142. *School Psychology in New Jersey, 19*, 31-37.

Barbrack, C. R. (1996). *Confidentiality of mental health records.* Presented at Mental Health and the Law: New Jersey Legal Issues of Providing Mental Health Services by Medical Educational Services, Eau Claire, Wisconsin, August 26.

Barbrack, C. R. (In preparation). *Keeping secrets: Mental health careworkers and client privacy.*

Barbrack, C. R. (May, 2000). Transitional liability in marriage and family therapy: Risk management against Board of Examiners complaints and penalties. *Family Outlook.*

Barkley, R. A., Fisher, M., & Edelbrock, C. S. (1990). The adolescent outcome of hyperactive children diagnosed by research criteria: An 8 year prospective follow-up study. *Journal of the American Academy of Child and Adolescent Psychiatry, 29,* 546-47.

Bigelow, D. A., Bloom, M. D., Williams, M., & McFarland, B. H. (1999). An administrative model for close monitoring and management for high risk individuals. *Behavioral Sciences and the Law, 17,* 227-235.

Bonta, J., Law, M., & Hanson, K. (1998). The predictors of criminal and violent recidivism among mentally disordered offenders: A meta-analysis. *Psychological Bulletin, 123,* 123-142.

Boynton v. Burglass, 590 So. 2d 446 (Fla. App. 3 Dist. 1991).

Campbell, D. T. (1969). Reforms as experiments. *American Psychologist, 24,* 409-429.

Campbell, D. T. & Stanley, J. C. (1966). *Experimental and quasi-experimental designs for research.* New York: Rand McNally.

Guttmacher, M. S., & Weilhofen, H. (1952). Sex offenses. *Journal of Criminal Law and Criminology, 42,* 153-175.

Engleman, N. B., Jobes, D. A., Berman, A. L. & Langbern, L. I. (1998). Clinician's decision making about voluntary commitment. *Psychiatric Services, 49,* 941-945.

Eppright, T. D., Kashani, J. H., & Robinson, B. D. (1995). Co-morbidity of conduct disorder and personality disorder in an incarcerated juvenile population. *American Journal of Psychiatry, 150,* 1233-1236.

Felthous, A. R. (1999). The clinician's duty to protect third parties. *The Psychiatric Clinics of North America, 22,* 49-60.

Friedman, L. (1999). Why is reality a troubling concept? *Journal of the American Psychoanalytic Association, 47,* 401-425.

Holden, G. W., Geffner, R., & Jouriles, E. N. (1998). *Children exposed to marital violence: Theory, research and applied issues.* Washington, D.C.: American Psychological Association.

Hook, M. K. & Cleveland, J. L. (1999). To tell or not: Breaching confidentiality with clients with HIV or AIDS. *Ethics and Behavior, 9,* (4), 365-381.

Jaffe v. Redmond, 116 S.Ct. 1923 (1996).

Jones, E. (1955). *The life and work of Sigmund Freud,* Volume 2. New York: Basic Books.

Mann, L. & Janis, I. (1985). *Decision making: A psychological analysis of conflict, choice and commitment.* New York: Free Press.

McIntosh v. Milano, 168 NJ Super 446 (1979).

McNulty, C., & Wardle, J. (1994). Adult disclosure of sexual abuse: A primary cause of psychological distress. *Child Abuse & Neglect, 18,* 549-555.

Modlin, H. C. (1989). Forensic pitfalls. *American Academy of Psychiatry and the Law, 17,* 415-419.

Neilsen, W. J. (1996). Privileged communications: The psychologist-patient privilege. *Seton Hall Law Review, 27,* 1123.

O'Shaughnessy, R. J. (1992). Aspects of forensic assessment of juvenile offenders. *The Psychiatric Clinics of North America, 15,* 721-735.

Portee v. Jaffee, 84 NJ 88 (1988).

Rassin, E., & Merckelback, H. (1999). The potential conflict between clinical and judicial decision making heuristics. *Behavioral Sciences & the Law, 17,* 237-248.

Rodlum, P. C., Farmer, T. W., Pearl, R., & Van Acker, R. (2000). Heterogeneity of popular boys' antisocial and prosocial configuration. *Developmental Psychology, 36,* 14-24.

Scott, C. L. (1999). Juvenile violence. *Psychiatic Clinics of North America, 22,* 77-83.

State v. McBride, 213 NJ Super 255 (App. Div. 1886).

State v. Michaels, 136 NJ 299 (1995).

Stueve, A., & Link, B. (1997). Violence and psychiatric disorders: Results from an epidemiological study of young adults in Israel. *Psychiatric Quarterly, 68,* 327-342.

Swanson, J. W. (1994). Mental disorder, substance abuse and community violence: An epidemiological approach. In J. Monahan & H. Stedman (Eds.), *Violence and mental disorder: Developments in risk assessment* (pp. 101-136). Chicago: University of Chicago Press.

Tarasoff v. Regents of University of California, 17 Cal 3d 425, 551 P. 2d. 334, 131 Cal Rptr 14 (1976).

Turbheimer, E., & Parry, C.D.H. (1992). Why the gap? Practice and policy in civil commitment hearings. *American Psychologist, 47,* 646-655.

Weinstock, R. (1988). Confidentiality and the new duty to protect: The therapist's dilemma. *Hospital & Community Psychiatry, 39,* 607-609.

Winick, B. J., & LaFond, J. Q. (1998). Special themes: Sex offenders: Scientific, legal and policy perspectives. *Psychology, Public Policy and Law, 4.*

Charles C Thomas
PUBLISHER • LTD.

P.O. Box 19265
Springfield, IL 62794-9265

A Leader in Behavioral Sciemces Publications

- Dennison, Susan T.—**A MULTIPLE FAMILY GROUP THERAPY PROGRAM FOR AT RISK ADOLESCENTS AND THEIR FAMILIES.** '05, 242 pp. (8 1/2 x 11), 62 il., 4 tables, paper.

- Horovitz, Ellen G.—**ART THERAPY AS WITNESS: A Sacred Guide.** '05, 212 pp. (7 x 10), 85 il., spiral (paper).

- Le Navenec, Carole-Lynne & Laurel Bridges—**CREATING CONNECTIONS BETWEEN NURSING CARE AND CREATIVE ARTS THERAPIES: Expanding the Concept of Holistic Care.** '05, 358 pp. (7 x 10), 33 il., 8 tables.

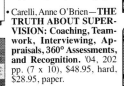

- Aasved, Mikal—**THE BIOLOGY OF GAMBLING. Volume III.** '04, 372 pp. (7 x 10) $86.95, hard, $57.95, paper.

- Brooke, Stephanie L.—**TOOLS OF THE TRADE: A Therapist's Guide to Art Therapy Assessments. (2nd Ed.)** '04, 256 pp. (7 x 10), 19 il., $53.95, hard, $35.95, paper.

- Carelli, Anne O'Brien—**THE TRUTH ABOUT SUPERVISION: Coaching, Teamwork, Interviewing, Appraisals, 360° Assessments, and Recognition.** '04, 202 pp. (7 x 10), $48.95, hard, $28.95, paper.

- Magniant, Rebecca C. Perry—**ART THERAPY WITH OLDER ADULTS: A Sourcebook.** '04, 256 pp. (7 x 10), 26 il., 2 tables, $56.95, hard, $36.95, paper.

- Marvasti, Jamshid A.—**PSYCHIATRIC TREATMENT OF SEXUAL OFFENDERS: Treating the Past Trauma in Traumatizers-A Bio-Psycho-Social Perspective.** '04, 220 pp. (7 x 10), $49.95, hard, $34.95, paper.

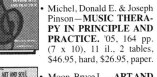

- Marvasti, Jamshid A.—**PSYCHIATRIC TREATMENT OF VICTIMS AND SURVIVORS OF SEXUAL TRAUMA: A Neuro-Bio-Psychological Approach.** '04, 234 pp. (7 x 10), $53.95, hard, $33.95, paper.

- Michel, Donald E. & Joseph Pinson—**MUSIC THERAPY IN PRINCIPLE AND PRACTICE.** '05, 164 pp. (7 x 10), 11 il., 2 tables, $46.95, hard, $26.95, paper.

- Moon, Bruce L.—**ART AND SOUL: Reflections on an Artistic Psychology. (2nd Ed.)** '04, 184 pp. (6 x 9), 15 il., $44.95, hard, $28.95, paper.

- Paton, Douglas, John M. Violanti, Christine Dunning, & Leigh M. Smith—**MANAGING TRAUMATIC STRESS RISK: A Proactive Approach.** '04, 258 pp. (7 x 10), 6 il., 17 tables, $61.95, hard, $41.95, paper.

- Transit, Roxanna P.—**DISCIPLINING THE CHILD VIA THE DISCOURSE OF THE PROFESSIONS.** '04, 212 pp. (7 x 10), 3 il., $47.95, hard, $29.95, paper.

- Aasved, Mikal—**THE SOCIOLOGY OF GAMBLING. Volume II.** '03, 458 pp. (7 x 10), 3 tables, $85.95, hard, $60.95, paper.

- Donahue, Brenda A.—**C. G. JUNG'S COMPLEX DYNAMICS AND THE CLINICAL RELATIONSHIP: One Map for Mystery.** '03, 302 pp. (7 x 10), 15 il., $64.95, hard, $44.95, paper.

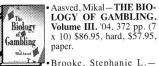

- Feldman, Saul—**MANAGED BEHAVIORAL HEALTH SERVICES: Perspectives and Practice.** '03, 460 pp. (7 x 10), 6 il., 10 tables, $77.95, hard, $57.95, paper.

- Heuscher, Julius E.—**PSYCHOLOGY, FOLKLORE, CREATIVITY AND THE HUMAN DILEMMA.** '03, 388 pp. (7 x 10), 1 table, $53.95, hard, $33.95, paper.

- Moser, Rosemarie Scolaro & Corinne E. Frantz—**SHOCKING VIOLENCE II: Violent Disaster, War, and Terrorism Affecting Our Youth.** '03, 240 pp. (7 x 10), 1 il., 4 tables, $49.95, hard, $32.95, paper.

- Nucho, Aina O.—**THE PSYCHOCYBERNETIC MODEL OF ART THERAPY. (2nd Ed.)** '03, 326 pp. (7 x 10), 62 il., 4 tables, $72.95, hard, $48.95, paper.

- Perline, Irvin H. & Jona Goldschmidt—**THE PSYCHOLOGY AND LAW OF WORKPLACE VIOLENCE: A Handbook for Mental Health Professionals and Employers.** '04, 528 pp. (8 x 10), 6 il., 17 tables, $99.95, hard, $69.95, paper.

- Radocy, Rudolph E. & J. David Boyle—**PSYCHOLOGICAL FOUNDATIONS OF MUSICAL BEHAVIOR. (4th Ed.)** '03, 464 pp. (7 x 10), 9 il., 3 tables, $75.95, hard, $55.95, paper.

- Wodarski, John S., Lois A. Wodarski & Catherine N. Dulmus—**ADOLESCENT DEPRESSION AND SUICIDE: A Comprehensive Empirical Intervention for Prevention and Treatment.** '03, 186 pp. (7 x 10), 23 il., $32.95, spiral (paper).

5 easy ways to order!

PHONE: 1-800-258-8980 or (217) 789-8980

FAX: (217) 789-9130

EMAIL: books@ccthomas.com
Web: www.ccthomas.com

MAIL: Charles C Thomas • Publisher, Ltd. P.O. Box 19265 Springfield, IL 62794-9265

Complete catalog available at ccthomas.com • books@ccthomas.com

Books sent on approval • Shipping charges: $6.95 min. U.S. / Outside U.S., actual shipping fees will be charged • Prices subject to change without notice